Areas formerly settled by Eskimos

Areas currently inhabited by Eskimos

Present tree line

Sioux Indians

Salisch Indians

Algo

Pacific Ocean

Northwest Coast Indians

Tsimshian Indians

Haida Indians

Tlingit Indians

Mackenzie River

Athabascan Indians

Copper Es

Pacific Eskimos

Beringsea Eskimos

Yukon River

Mackenzie Eskimos

North Alaskan Coast Eskimos

N. Alaskan Inland Eskimos

Asiatic Eskimos

Bering Strait

Wrangel I.

Arctic Ocean

Chuchki

Koryak

SIBERIA

ESKIMO PREHISTORY

ESKIMO PREHISTORY

Hans-Georg Bandi

Translated by Ann E. Keep

Published by the *UNIVERSITY OF ALASKA PRESS, College 99701*

Distributed by the *UNIVERSITY OF WASHINGTON PRESS, Seattle 98105*

First published by Gustav Fischer Verlag, Stuttgart, 1964,
as *Urgeschichte der Eskimo*

English translation copyright © 1969 by the University of Alaska Press

First printing, 1969; Third printing, 1972

Printed in the United States of America

STUDIES OF NORTHERN PEOPLES
Number Two

Studies of Northern Peoples is published by the Department of Anthropology and Geography of the University of Alaska. The series is devoted to the dissemination of original research on peoples of the north, ancient and contemporary. Publications are of monograph length and appear at irregular intervals.

Editor—Edward H. Hosley

In Memoriam
James Louis Giddings
1909-1964
and
Ivar Skarland
1899-1965

FOREWORD

Archeological studies carried out in the Arctic and Subarctic during the last few decades have provided more and more evidence that the Eskimos, too, can boast of a prehistory, a past which goes back for several millennia. An ever greater number of cultural groups and stages of development are being established, distributed over a vast area stretching from the eastern tip of Siberia through Alaska and Arctic Canada to Greenland. It has also become clear that traces of prehistoric Eskimos are to be found, not only in the coastal areas where with few exceptions they live today, but also in the interior of Alaska and Canada. In order to understand Eskimo prehistory it is necessary to include these regions, which must have served the ancestors of the modern Eskimos as hunting grounds. On the other hand, not all prehistoric finds made in the area formerly or presently inhabited by Eskimos are necessarily of Eskimo origin. Therefore, the correct title of this book would have been somewhere between 'The Area of Eskimo Prehistory' and 'Prehistory of the Eskimo Area'.

Although the ground in the Eskimo area is often frozen even in summer, an approximate idea of the way in which Eskimo culture originated, developed and spread can be gained from the work of archeologists — mainly Danes, Americans, Canadians and Russians — who have brought to light a good deal of material. These studies are, however, still far from complete: much remains uncertain or hypothetical; and further field work in the limitless Arctic tundra will no doubt provide further surprises. But we can already see matters fairly clearly, so that it is worthwhile outlining our present state of knowledge.

The survey given here was originally written for German-speaking readers by and large unfamiliar with the problems of Eskimo archeology. Later, however, at the suggestion of Dr. Frederick Hadleigh-West, the University of Alaska became interested in an English edition. Thanks to Dr. Sylvia Ciernick, who undertook the necessary negotiations, it was possible to commission Dr. Ann E. Keep, London, with the task of translation. Dr. Edward H. Hosley did some supplementary editing of the translation. This volume, which appears as a result of their efforts, will, I hope, also be of interest to English-speaking readers. It differs in several points from the German editions, as I have tried to take account as far as possible of suggestions and objections from my colleagues and to incorporate the results of the latest research. I am particularly grateful for the advice I have received from Dr. Charles E. Borden of Vancouver, Eigil Knuth, Dr. Helge Larsen and Mag. Jørgen Meldgaard of Copenhagen. Dr. Yvette Mottier and my wife were most helpful to me by reading the proofs.

I began to study Eskimo prehistory at first hand in the summer of 1948, when Dr. Kaj Birket-Smith of the Danish National Museum, Copenhagen, and the Museum of Ethnology, Basel, made it possible for me to travel to northeast Greenland as a member of Eigil Knuth's Danish Pearyland Expedition. Jørgen Meldgaard and I were able to continue the studies of a large settlement at Dødemandsbugten which Helge Larsen had begun in the 1930's. This memorable stay in the Arctic wilderness finally cemented my interest in Eskimo archeology. Unfortunately, owing to other commitments, for many years I could give only part of my time to this field of study. I received a fresh impetus in 1958, when I attended a 'Circumpolar Conference' in Copenhagen at which Scandinavian, American, Canadian and Russian scholars discussed the most pressing issues of Arctic archeology, ethnology and physical anthropology. The following year, thanks to an invitation from Brown University at Providence, Rhode Island, and to a grant kindly provided by the Wenner-Gren Foundation for Anthropological Research, New York, I was able to take part in the late James Louis Giddings' excavations on Cape Krusenstern in Northwestern Alaska. In response to an invitation by the late Dr. Ivar Skarland and Dr. Frederick Hadleigh-West, I joined the staff of the Department of Anthropology at the University of Alaska, as a visiting professor in 1962-63. The winter I spent at College, near Fairbanks, gave me the opportunity to fulfill the plan which I had had in mind for a long time, namely to write the present volume. In the summer of 1964, together with Dr. Hadleigh-West, I carried out field work in the interior of Alaska, and in the summer of 1965 I had the chance to visit St. Lawrence Island to plan the resumption of former excavations in this area; this plan was realized with a mixed Swiss-American group in the summer of 1967.

Some of the illustrations were obtained through the kindness of Dr. Kaj Birket-Smith, Copenhagen; Dr. Henry B. Collins, Washington; Dr. J. Louis Giddings, Bristol, R.I.; Dr. Elmer Harp, Hanover, N.H.; Count Eigil Knuth, Copenhagen; Dr. Frederica de Laguna, Bryn Mawr, Pa.; Dr. Helge Larsen, Copenhagen; Mag. Jørgen Meldgaard, Copenhagen; and the US Coast and Geodetic Survey. I am also very much indebted to Dr. H. Müller-Beck, Bern, who provided me with the charts explaining the early infiltrations from Siberia to the New World. For most of the drawings my thanks are due to Mrs. Barbara Stucky-Böhrs, Miss Winifred Mumford, and Mr. Harry Zaugg, Bern. I am very much indebted to all the colleagues, authorities and foundations who in one way or another have contributed to the appearance of this book. My thanks are also due to all those scholars who, by laborious and often dangerous field work or by skillful critical analysis, have provided the material on which it is based. I extend my esteem to the Eskimo pioneers who after a long struggle lasting thousands of years succeeded in conquering the Arctic.

Hans-Georg Bandi

Bern, Switzerland and College, Alaska, 1967.

x

CONTENTS

INTRODUCTION

In 1866, an article in the London *Saturday Review,* by the British archeologist W. Boyd Dawkins, expressed the opinion that the Eskimos were descendants of late Ice Age reindeer-hunters of Western Europe. This hypothesis had been put forward shortly before by the French scholar Ed. Lartet, but had aroused little interest. In his later works Dawkins endeavored to substantiate his theory more fully by showing that the Eskimo culture and way of life had much in common with that of the Magdalenian population of the late Upper Paleolithic, between about 17,000 and 10,000 years ago. As the climate became warmer, this population must have gradually migrated north and east with the most important game animals, the musk-ox and the reindeer. In this way, the Ice Age hunters were said to have gradually reached the area where the modern Eskimos live. This 'following-the-reindeer' theory shortly afterwards found support from physical anthropologists: in 1899 the Frenchman L. Testut examined a Magdalenian skeleton from Raymond Cave near Chancelade in the Dordogne, and came to the conclusion that distinct affinities could be established with the Eskimos. Dawkins' hypothesis thereby gained additional weight and was accepted by many scholars. Among others the Englishman W.J. Sollas expressed his support as late as 1911 in his work *Ancient Hunters and their Modern Representatives.*

More recently archeologists and physical anthropologists have re-examined the question whether there is a relationship between the Magdalenian and Eskimo cultures. In the early 1930's Frederica de Laguna made a thorough comparison of late Ice Age art with that of the Eskimos, and obtained results which suggested that there were certainly no close connections between them. Eskimo sculptures in and engravings on ivory, reindeer-antlers, and bone bear no greater affinity to mobiliary art objects of the late Ice Age than they do to the art of other primitive peoples, apart from the fact that in general the Eskimos use the same raw material as was worked by the Upper Paleolithic people. On the other hand, Sir A. Keith and Henri V. Vallois showed that the Chancelade skeleton cannot be considered Mongoloid but is close to other Upper Paleolithic skeletons in Europe.

In the meantime, much has been learned since Boyd Dawkins' day about prehistoric cultures in the vast region between western Europe and the Arctic areas that are inhabited by the Eskimos. Today scholars no longer accept this theory of far-reaching and close links. But Dawkins was not entirely wrong: at the close of the Ice Age some Magdalenian hunters must have migrated from western to northern and central Europe in pursuit of wild reindeer herds; but they can hardly have got much further. Nor can the possibility be ruled out that, before Magdalenian culture became extinct, some cultural influences found their way via the Mesolithic Maglemosian culture into the circumpolar area, and may even have reached the Eskimo area.

This brings us to another problem, that of circumpolar cultural connections. Kaj Birket-Smith, the Danish ethnologist, and his compatriot G. Hatt pointed out some time ago that various cultural elements such as shamans' drums, hanging or carrying cradles, needle-cases etc., are disseminated over an area extending from northern Eurasia as far as North America. This idea was taken up again in the 1940's by the Norwegian ethnologist and archeologist Guttorm Gjessing, who in his work *The Circumpolar Stone Age*, sought to show that the roots of these far-reaching links go back to the Stone Age. His distribution charts suggest that in the case of the large skin boat of the Eskimo umiak type, of toggle harpoon heads, and of slate used as raw material for stone implements he assumes the existence of early links over an area from northern Scandinavia to Greenland. He sought to trace other contacts further south in the Subarctic forest zone, where the main role was

played by stone implements and ceramic ware. Similar conclusions were reached by A.C. Spaulding. Gjessing finally
points to some cultural elements which occur at various places
in the circumpolar zone but do not reveal any continuous dissemination: for example, settlements with semi-subterranean
houses or animal figures with a so-called life line, a line running from mouth to heart or some other important organ.

There is no doubt as to the existence of cultural links in the
circumpolar zone, some of which may be of a very early date.
But this does not suffice to explain the origin of Eskimo culture, all the more so as some of Gjessing's conclusions are ob-
solete. Recently objections were raised in this respect, based in
particular on findings since published by Soviet scholars. Both
the Russian A.M. Zolotarev and the American Chester S.
Chard reject Gjessing's distribution charts. According to
Chard, skin boats bearing some resemblance to Eskimo
umiaks occur in Siberia only among the Chukchi and Koryak
in the extreme east; information about similar boats among the
Samoyed he regards as insufficiently reliable. Toggle harpoon heads are absent in northern Siberia west of the Kolyma.
Slate implements are to be found, apart from the Pacific coast
only in western Siberia, where they must be traced back to
European influences. Thus both scholars are firmly opposed
to the theory that Eskimo culture originated on the basis of a
circumpolar cultural diffusion.

In the following pages we shall deal briefly with the present-day Eskimos and their culture — so far as it retains its original character, for they are at the end of a process of development that, as we shall see, lasted for thousands of years.

The Eskimos are the only native population living in both
the Old and New Worlds. As can be seen from the accompanying distribution chart (inside cover), the Eskimo area begins in
the easternmost part of the Chukchi Peninsula. Elsewhere in
the Soviet Union, on the Commander Islands to the east of
Kamchatka, there are some Aleuts who, however, were trans-
ported there as recently as the nineteenth century. There is
disagreement about the position of the Aleuts on the Aleutian
Islands, the chain of islands belonging to the United States,
and on the Alaskan Peninsula: for the most part they are re-

garded as genuine Eskimos, but some see them as Eskimoized remains of an earlier population. On the North American continent the Eskimos are disseminated over an area extending from the Copper River or Prince William Sound northwards along the coast of Alaska; in some places they are also to be encountered further inland, for example along such major Alaskan rivers as the Kuskokwim, Yukon, Kobuk, Noatak and Colville. Across the Canadian border in the Mackenzie River area they are again to be found in the coastal area and on islands of the Arctic Archipelago. West of Hudson Bay the Eskimo area extends up to 500 kilometers inland; but the lands south of Churchill River are Indian territory. Eskimos also inhabit the areas on either side of Hudson Strait, Baffin Land and the northern coast of the Labrador Peninsula. On Southampton Island they died out as late as the turn of the century. The easternmost Eskimo area is Greenland, the largest island in the world, which belongs to Denmark. Large parts of the coast are still inhabited by Eskimos today, but most of them have an admixture of European blood and therefore call themselves Greenlanders rather than Eskimos. They are to be found in Thule district in the northwest, then mainly along the west coast, and finally in two areas of the east coast, Angmagssalik and Scoresby Sound. Altogether there are probably about 55,000 Eskimos and 1500 Aleuts; if the calculation is based upon language, the ratio inclines slightly in favor of the Aleutian element. The Eskimos are increasing in number, since they are among those native populations who, although temporarily in jeopardy, are strong enough to survive the influence of modern civilization.

The Eskimos are thus distributed over a vast area and are separated by immense distances: from Bering Strait to the Atlantic coast of Labrador and Greenland it is 10,000 kilometers as the crow flies. Moreover, we must bear in mind that here, 'at the edge of not only the inhabited, but also the habitable world', as Kaj Birket-Smith says, the distribution map may repeatedly alter as a consequence of changes in the climate and in the stock of game. In any case it is certain that at times the Eskimo inhabited an area somewhat larger than that in which they live today. This can be substantiated by archeological finds. On the other hand it is noteworthy that the area of habitation is always restricted to the coastal zone, except for the Barren Grounds west of Hudson Bay and several places in Arctic Alaska. The interior is Indian territory.

Birket-Smith, whose excellent summary of the Eskimo problem I am chiefly following here, distinguishes within this area of distribution the following regional groups: Asiatic Eskimos; Aleuts; Pacific Eskimos in Southern Alaska; Bering Sea Eskimos; Coastal and Inland Eskimos of Northern Alaska; Copper, Netsilik, and Igloolik Eskimos of the Arctic Archipelago; Caribou Eskimos in the interior of Arctic Canada; Baffin Land Eskimos; Labrador Eskimos; Polar Eskimos in northwest Greenland; western and eastern Greenlanders. Most of these are divided into a number of sub-groups of varying size. One cannot, however, speak of tribes as these are geographical, not political units. On the other hand, they may be classified into three main groups: Western Eskimos in Alaska, Central Eskimos in Arctic Canada, and Eastern Eskimos in Greenland.

From the point of view of physical anthropology, the Eskimos are remarkably uniform. We may mention the following common features: they are relatively small in stature, powerfully built but not fat, and brown-skinned; the face is 'pentagonal' in form and gives the impression of being flat; the so-called Mongolian fold is not very marked and occurs irregularly; the iris is light or dark brown in color; the coarse black hair is usually straight and less often slightly curly. Differences exist in that some bear more marked resemblance to the Asiatic-Mongoloid type, and others have Indian features, especially those encountered among such northern tribes as the Chipewyan. It is, however, certain that the Eskimos occupy a special position and cannot be classified as belonging to either the Indian or the Asiatic-Mongoloid race, although they are linked with them in various ways. Soviet scholars at present incline to the view that the Eskimos together with the Paleo-Siberian Chukchi, Koryak, Yukagir and Itelmen (Kamchadal) form a particular ethnic group which is said to have originated from the Bering Sea area and is termed Arctic-Mongoloid.

As Birket-Smith points out, the following differences exist in regard to the shape of the Eskimo skull: whereas in other parts of the Eskimo area long or dolichocephalic skulls occur, in Alaska by contrast a larger percentage of brachycephaly, i.e., relatively broad skulls, has been established; among the Aleuts this element is in fact preponderant. But from prehistoric skulls we know that the dolichocephalic type originally played a leading role in this zone as well. Since an increase of brachycephaly among other Eskimo groups can also be observed today, the special position of Alaska and of the Aleutians may be due to the fact that this tendency of development had already advanced further here.

The linguistic connections within the Eskimo area are also of interest. The dialects spoken between Arctic Alaska and Labrador and Greenland, collectively known as 'Inupik' (or Inyupik), are very closely related to one another. According to Birket-Smith the difference between the language spoken in Greenland and in the Bering Strait area is not much greater than that between the Danish used in Copenhagen and the Swedish in Malmø, thirty kilometers away, so that it is very easy for people from these two regions to understand each other. Dialects are less developed in Alaska than they are further east. On the other hand the Yukon, which divides Alaska into two halves, northern and southern, forms a very pronounced linguistic barrier; the natives on either side of this fortuitous dividing-line, which represents no obstacle to communication especially in winter, cannot understand each other any more readily than Germans and Englishmen. The 'Yupik' of Southern Alaska, which also includes the 'Yuit' spoken by the Eskimos in Siberia and on St. Lawrence Island, comprises in addition three dialects which differ from it considerably: the 'Yuk' south of Norton Sound and in the Kuskokwim area, the 'Čuk' on Nunivak Island, and the 'Suk' of the Pacific Eskimo. The differences become more marked in the case of an Aleutian dialect; the vocabulary in particular, and to a lesser extent the grammar, have such obvious peculiarities that some philologists have even doubted whether the Eskimo and Aleut languages are related. Modern linguistic scholarship, however, inclines to the view that the Eskimo and Aleut dialects originally formed a unit but have since grown apart. The following diagram (Fig. 1) represents this process of linguistic differentiation:

Using the lexicostatistical method of glottochronology, (based on the assumption that isolated linguistic groups, after splitting off from the common stock, lose approximately 19% of the morphemes of the 'mother tongue' every one thousand years), Morris Swadesh claims to have shown that the separation of Eskimo dialects and Aleut began some three thousand years ago; K. Bergsland thinks that it may have been

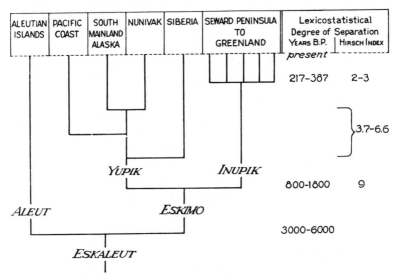

Fig. 1 - Schematic diagram of some internal Eskaleutian linguistic relationships. After D.E. Dumond (1965).

as much as six thousand years ago. In any case, Eskimo and Aleut together constitute an individual group of languages which cannot as yet be linked with any other group. Yet mention may be made of early attempts by C.C. Uhlenbeck and A. Sauvageot to relate Eskimo to Uralic languages (Finno-Ugric and Samoyed). K. Bergsland has recently continued work along these lines, and it is interesting that B. Collinder, the Swedish linguist, should expound the hypothesis that the Uralic languages are related to the idiom of the Yukagir, who live in the area between the mouths of the Indigirka and the Kolyma in Northeastern Siberia. In this connection we may recall that Russian physical anthropologists consider both the Yukagir and the Eskimos to be part of an Asiatic-Mongoloid ethnic group.

Turning now to the culture of the present-day Eskimos — or rather of the Eskimos of yesterday, since unfortunately genuine and original Eskimo culture hardly exists any longer—we have to point out that in this respect, too, Eskimos and Aleuts form a unit. But as Birket-Smith has said in the Swiss edition of his summary of Eskimo culture, 'one of the most characteristic features of Eskimo culture is the difference that exists in some basic points between the Aleuts and Pacific Eskimos on one hand and all remaining tribes on the other, although the inhabitants of Bristol Bay and the Yukon and Kuskokwim delta occupy an intermediate position.' The contrast was expressed *inter alia* in clothing, the shape of the blubber lamp, the preference for the spear instead of the harpoon for whaling, and furthermore in a kind of primitive mummification of bodies, which were interred in caves in a crouched position. We thus see that the Yukon once again forms a dividing-line.

Apart from this dualism in Eskimo culture, which has still not been explained satisfactorily, there are other differences. It has long been evident that the Central Eskimo culture in Arctic Canada has a special position vis-à-vis that of the Western and Eastern Eskimos in Alaska and Greenland respectively. In the Central regions (the coastal area and the Arctic Archipelago between Alaska and Greenland) certain cultural elements are lacking which are present in the western and eastern parts of the Eskimo area—for example, the large skin boat known as an umiak, the seal net, and gut-skin frocks—or at least they occur rarely or in a modified form. Other elements are disseminated particularly widely in the Central area, such as special implements for so-called breathing-hole hunting, i.e. the harpooning of seals through a hole in the ice. A long and detailed discussion has been going on in an effort to explain this difference between the central and peripheral areas, and to draw some conclusion in regard to the origin and dissemination of Eskimo culture.

A further cultural difference exists in so far as the Eskimo mode of life from Alaska to Greenland is in general closely bound up with the coast, with the hunting of large sea-mammals such as the whale, walrus and seal; this at least has been the case up to recent times. There are, nevertheless, some small groups whose mode of life has a markedly inland character, with caribou hunting providing them with their means of existence. These groups comprise in particular the Caribou

Eskimo in the Barren Grounds west of Hudson Bay, and smaller groups in the area of the Colville and Noatak Rivers in Northern Alaska and in the Yukon-Kuskokwim delta.

Finally, it must not be overlooked that certain cultural features are due to influences exerted, with varying degrees of intensity, by Indian and Siberian peoples. Incidentally, Eskimo culture also radiated influences upon other groups.

Despite these differences, recent Eskimo culture is surprisingly uniform in character. But we shall see that this has not always been the case. It was only at a relatively late date, some one thousand years ago, that the dissemination of the Thule culture, which spread from Alaska as far as Greenland, led to this unification. A few centuries ago the Thule culture, since somewhat modified, began to retreat into Alaska from the central areas, which further accentuated this leveling process.

In view of the heritage of prehistoric Eskimos, the main aspects of modern Eskimo culture, relying on ethnographical studies, should be summarized. It goes without saying that in the lives of a typical Arctic people two problems predominate, indeed practically govern their whole existence: the struggle for food and for protection from the cold. These are of such importance that almost all elements of their material culture — and it is almost exclusively such elements that can be discovered from examining sites in the Eskimo area — are in some way associated with them.

We shall not attempt to discuss in detail here the differences which according to Birket-Smith exist between the High Arctic, Arctic and Subarctic forms of Eskimo culture, but shall confine ourselves to a few general remarks. The methods and implements employed in the struggle for food are in principle the same everywhere; the differences are only of degree. Some contrasts exist, as hunting at sea differs from that on land and the requirements are not the same in winter as they are in summer. The main emphasis is on hunting at sea and in winter. The whole process is repeated in annual cycles. The methods differ according to the area (open water, ice or mainland), the season and the kind of animal hunted.

The raw materials used to make implements, weapons and other objects are or were limited. The most important are parts of animals killed in hunting: skin, gut, sinew, bone, teeth, ivory, claws, antler, horn and baleen, occasionally also shell. In addition one may mention wood, mostly driftwood, grasses and other pliable plants for weaving, clay and stone (varieties of flint that can easily be polished; soapstone, used to make pots and lamps). Metals such as solid copper or meteoritic iron played at most a minor part. Not all these materials are of course equally well-suited for preservation. Frequently the excavator finds no more than a stone inventory, everything else having disintegrated. The Arctic has nevertheless the advantage that it is not unusual for wooden or even leather objects to be preserved in the frozen ground, and thus in the Eskimo area one can draw a more complete and colorful picture of prehistoric cultures than is possible elsewhere.

Among objects of archeological importance we may next mention the means of transport used to approach the game. The kayak consists of a wooden frame covered with skin and several components of bone and ivory employed to attach weapons and implements – an ideal means of hunting seal, usually designed for one paddler, in South Alaska and on the Aleutian Islands occasionally also for two. The umiak, today also referred to as the 'woman's boat', likewise consists of a wooden frame covered with skin; in contrast to the kayak however, it is open on top and with its length of approximately nine meters has room for several persons; it is thus suited for the dangerous pursuit of whale-hunting. Of sledges, an important type is that with runners and drawn by dogs. Here too the frame is of wood, with components of ivory, baleen or bone; these parts, and especially the runners and the swivels (trace buckles) of the dogs' harness often provide the only evidence available to the archeologist. There are also smaller hand-drawn and toboggan-like sleds, of the Indian type without runners, the only difference being that the Eskimos tie on for this purpose strips of baleen.

The most important hunting weapon is (or rather was, for nowadays the rifle is used almost exclusively) the harpoon, which has been developed by the Eskimos in a most ingenious way (Fig. 2). It consists of an ivory or bone toggle harpoon head, with a line of seal thong fastened to it, which, depending on the method of hunting, either is attached to an inflated

float made of sealskin with a bone mouthpiece, or is held in
the hand. The harpoon rests loosely in a bone or ivory foreshaft which in turn is attached, either fixed or movable, to a
wooden shaft. The harpoon was used in summer, in hunting
seal from the kayak; in autumn, in smooth-ice hunting, when
the hunter noiselessly approaches the spot where a seal is
breathing; in winter, when tedious waiting at breathing-holes
is necessary; in hunting walrus from the edge of the ice or from
an umiak; and in whaling from an umiak. Some details, which
the archeologist can often also identify, show the kind of hunting for which a harpoon was used: for example, the kayak harpoon is lighter and has a movable foreshaft fastened to the
shaft; harpoons for breathing-hole hunting have at the butt
end a bone or ivory pick for cutting holes in the ice; harpoons
used for hunting walrus and whale are correspondingly larger.
In Greenland alone kayak harpoons were thrown with the
aid of throwing-boards. Otherwise use was made of a similar
but lighter type of weapon, called a 'harpoon dart' or 'bladder
dart'. Also in connection with harpoon hunting, mention may
be made of the lance, which was used to stab wounded animals
to death; furthermore of wound plugs, mostly of wood, designed to prevent the game sinking into the water when attached to the side of the kayak; finally of the especially ingenious equipment used in the Central regions in breathing-
hole hunting, the 'indicator'. The lance, however, also plays a
part in hunting the polar bear and musk-ox, in the first instance when the game had to be encircled and brought to bay
by dogs; it was also used to kill caribou from kayaks when the
animals were suddenly attacked while crossing a fjord or river.

Otherwise the main weapon in hunting caribou was the bow
and arrow. Wood, antler or baleen was used to make bow-
shafts; arrows mostly have a head of antler, with or without a
stone point. Darts with three prongs or a central point with
three side-prongs were used in hunting birds, as were the
bow, various kinds of nets, the bola, consisting of several
round weights each fastened to a cord, and hook-like implements.

For fishing, too, there are of course a considerable number
of implements: leisters, which often have two or three pointed

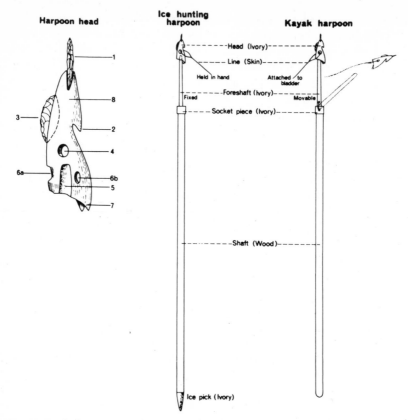

Fig. 2 - Toggle harpoon heads are of special importance in dating archeological remains in the Eskimo area and assigning them to particular cultures. The characteristic features are as follows:

1.) front end with or without end-blade (parallel or vertical to the line hole);
2.) barb (on one side, both sides or absent);
3.) inserted side-blade (on one side, both sides, parallel or vertical to the line hole, or absent);
4.) line hole;
5.) socket (closed or open);
6.) device for winding around an open socket; a notch (6a) or slit (6b) which in some pieces are not combined, as in this example, but exist on either side;
7.) spurs (single, multiple or absent);
8.) ornaments (present or absent).

In ice-hunting, harpoon shafts with a fixed foreshaft are used, but in kayak-hunting, where the weapon is thrown, mostly a movable foreshaft is used, so that the head comes off easily.

prongs, various kinds of hooks and fishing accessories, nets with floats and sinkers, weirs etc.

We may go on to consider briefly the clothing which the Eskimos have ingeniously developed in their struggle against the cold. Skin dress, for which various kinds of leathery skins, furs or occasionally the skins of birds are used – depending on the purpose they are to serve – is based on the same principle as the double window, i.e. of an inner and an outer layer; the air between the two layers is a poor conductor of heat, so that the warmth of the body cannot escape. The outer clothing consists of an overcoat with a hood, trousers, mittens, skin stockings and boots. But not much of this is to be found in excavations. On the other hand, one can identify such objects as carved toggles, ornaments, labrets, combs, brow-bands, helmet-like head-coverings or visors and snow goggles, used to protect the eyes and made of less perishable materials; and also 'snow beaters' for cleaning garments before entering houses.

Also noteworthy in this connection is armor made of plates of bone, which in the Bering Strait area was worn for fighting.

Let us return to the matter of protection against the cold. As important as clothing is housing. When one thinks of Eskimo dwellings, one's first idea is generally the snow hut. But we should not overlook the fact that such 'igloos' are used as permanent winter dwellings only in the Central areas and partly also in Labrador. Elsewhere, particularly in Arctic Alaska and North Greenland, they are used only by travelers and hunters. Only indirect archeological evidence of these snow shelters is available, namely the typical snow knife used to cut blocks of snow when building them.

The situation is not much better in regard to the skin tents which afford shelter against inclement weather during the warmer seasons. The wooden tent poles and the skin coverings are of course removed when the inhabitants move to another place. On the other hand – even after thousands of years – it is often possible to identify tent rings by stones arranged in a circular, oval or rectangular pattern which were employed as weights to hold down a tent.

Of greater importance to the archeologist, however, are the semi-subterranean houses with walls of stone or sod and roofs of driftwood beams or whale bones and covered by skins or sod, and in winter, of course, by snow as well. A tunnel-like entrance passage, which affords protection against snow, wind and cold, leads into the rectangular, round or pear-shaped interior — which by our standards is in most cases a rather small, or occasionally incredibly tiny area, in which whole families were accommodated. Exceptions are only found in some places where there are larger community houses for several families, men's houses or meeting houses. Another means of entering a house was through an opening in the roof, which at the same time was used to permit smoke to escape and daylight to penetrate. Almost everywhere inside the houses, along the side walls or rear wall, there were raised benches covered with dried plants and skins, for sitting or sleeping. In some places, especially Alaska, there were open hearths. Elsewhere the blubber lamp, made of clay or carved in soapstone, was the sole source of warmth and light. Food was cooked in clay or soapstone pots over this lamp; nearby, clothing was dried on racks suspended from the ceiling. But these are not the only objects that archeologists find in the interior of winter houses which, after the roof has caved in, appear as depressions in the ground and can be identified fairly easily. Apart from weapons and hunting implements, ornaments and parts of clothing, all sorts of other possessions of the former owners lie about, mixed with refuse, especially animal bones. The most typical tools are axes, adzes, drills (mouthpiece, drill-shaft with drill and bow), whetstones, skin-scrapers, scrapers with stone blades for working wood and bone, men's long-bladed knives, women's crescentic knives known as ulus, tools for twisting bowstring, flakers for flint, chisels, shovels, and mattocks, and women's sewing equipment including needle-cases and thimble holders. Other household goods, in addition to those already discussed are: wooden dishes, baskets, ladles and smaller spoons, boxes made of wood or baleen, hooks, blubber-mashers, and fire drills. The presence of children is documented above all by finds of toys, either everyday objects of reduced size or else human and animal figures.

In places that were settled for a long time there are heaps of refuse or 'kitchen middens', since houses were erected at the same spot time and again. Assemblages of this kind of course afford particularly rich yields for the archeologist, as he finds there layers arranged in a chronological sequence from top to bottom, and the stratigraphy provides crucial information about the relative age of individual objects.

The daily struggle for food and protection against cold in winter also left its mark upon the social life of the Eskimos, their outlook on the world and their religious practices. But of this, very little or nothing can be ascertained by the methods of the archeologist. Noteworthy are, for example, amulets of various kinds such as animal skulls, teeth or claws; also the drum, which was used in dances and in the singing of satirical songs between quarreling parties, or by the shaman in exorcising ghosts. Masks had particular significance in Alaska at major dance festivals, when the shamans related their experiences in the spirit world. Also of interest are a variety of small carvings and other objects which the shamans fastened to their clothing, especially to their belts.

Finally, burial places likewise provide the archeologist with valuable information. These vary fairly considerably according to the area: in Alaska one finds Indian platform burial practiced, the body being wrapped in a skin and placed on a wooden frame, as well as interment in a crouched position or a primitive kind of mummification. In the Central areas, the dead were frequently exposed on the tundra, while further east interment took place in a kind of stone cyst, sometimes almost of megalithic dimensions. The deceased were always accompanied by their wordly goods.

This is a very brief survey of what was important to the existence of the Eskimos and what is identifiable by the archeologist. It is far from exhaustive, since a full description would take much more space than is available here. The reader is referred to E.W. Nelson's work on the peoples of the Bering Strait or to K. Birket-Smith's and E. Weyer's comprehensive descriptions of the Eskimos.

The ethnologists have developed many theories concerning the origin of Eskimo culture. As early as 1767, D. Cranz stated in his *History of Greenland* that the Eskimos had migrated from Asia to America at a late date and did not reach Greenland until the fourteenth century A.D. In the 1870's the Dane

Heinrich J. Rink came to the conclusion that they must have originated in Alaska, since there the transitions from Indian to Eskimo culture seemed to indicate that the coastal culture had developed from that of the interior; he proceeded from the assumption that the cradle of Eskimo culture would have to be sought in the area where adaptation to coastal life had taken place. However, as Birket-Smith declares, 'the transition is due to the fact that the Eskimos have exercised a very strong influence upon the Ingalik Indians of the lower Yukon, while both peoples have at the same time been under the strong influence of the Tlingit, who are representatives of that remarkably developed culture on the northern Pacific coast—the peak of American non-agricultural cultures.'

In the 1880's John Murdoch held that the homeland of the Eskimos must be sought south of Hudson Bay, since the tribes in this area were the most primitive. Simultaneously Franz Boas designated the 'Central area' in Arctic Canada as the place of origin, since this zone coincided more than any other with the data given in Eskimo legends. Subsequently this hypothesis was supported by H.P. Steensby, who carried out a systematic study of the age of numerous cultural elements in various parts of the Eskimo area. In his comprehensive work, *An Anthropological Study of the Origin of Eskimo Culture* , published in 1916, he expressed the view that Eskimo culture developed in the area between Coronation Gulf, in the north of the Canadian Arctic, and Hudson Bay, i.e. in the Central regions. The term 'Central' has already been applied to the region between Alaska and Greenland that consists of the coastal area and the Arctic Archipelago, and not the interior of Arctic Canada. Steensby considered the large number of seals and vast herds of caribou, the smooth ice sheet that covers the sea for several months of the year, and the lack of timber as the proper conditions for the development of the earliest forms of Eskimo culture, which he terms Paleo-Eskimo. It was said to have spread to the Bering Strait area, where Neo-Eskimo culture developed under more favorable environmental conditions and influences from Siberia. The new form of Eskimo culture was stated to have then spread eastward as far as Greenland without, however, gaining a foothold in the Central areas, where the Arctic climate was extreme. As Birket-

Smith points out, Steensby's theory is based largely on the assumption that the absence of Neo-Eskimo cultural elements in the Central regions is due to environmental conditions. G. Hatt has, however, shown that this is most unlikely in many instances (for example, the absence of umiaks, seal nets, gut clothing, urine tanning). He states that this is due to impoverishment, so that the culture of the Central Eskimos would on the contrary be of earlier date.

Birket-Smith gives a different explanation of the special position occupied by the Central regions. In his view it is based upon the fact that in Arctic Canada the inland Eskimos with a more primitive culture made a late advance in the direction of the Central coastal areas. He believes that Eskimo culture first developed as an inland hunting culture, which spread from Siberia into the zone north of the timber line in Alaska as far as Hudson Bay; he called this stage Proto-Eskimo. A final remnant of this would be the Caribou Eskimos in Arctic Canada. Then, especially in response to influences from Siberia, a gradual adaptation to coastal life took place, although still without whaling; this stage, which is said to be authenticated by archeological finds from Alaska to Greenland, Birket-Smith calls Paleo-Eskimo. Finally from this a third stage, the Neo-Eskimo culture, is said to have developed with the knowledge of whaling and it likewise spread from west to east, and survived into historic times. This sequence developed by an eminent ethnologist is a mosaic of innumerable details. Many small increments have been supplied by archeological research, and it is time now to deal with the problems raised by the archeological investigations.

Bibliography: Bandi, 1949; Bergsland, 1959; Birket-Smith, 1929, 1948, 1959; Boas, 1888; Chard, 1959a; Collins, 1959; Dawkins, 1874; Gjessing, 1944, 1948; Hatt, 1916; de Laguna, 1932-33a; MacNeish, 1960; Meldgaard, 1960; Moberg, 1960; Murdoch, 1888; Nelson, 1899; Rink, 1887; Sollas, 1911; Spaulding, 1946; Steensby, 1916; Swadesh, 1954, 1962; Thalbitzer, 1912, 1952; Weyer, 1962.

THE FIRST DISCOVERERS OF AMERICA

Before dealing with Eskimo archeology, let us examine briefly what is known about the earliest movements of population to the New World. These took place long before Vikings from Greenland reached 'Vinland' and before America was finally made accessible to Europeans by Columbus. For a long time it has been agreed that the route from Asia to America must have been by way of the Bering Strait. The idea that it ran along the Aleutian island chain is ruled out by most scholars since it would first have been necessary to reach the Commander Islands, which are situated approximately 150 kilometers from Kamchatka, and these islands are in turn situated almost 300 kilometers from Attu, the westernmost point of the Aleutians; moreover, the Commander Islands do not seem to have been inhabited before the Russians arrived there. There is of course no question of trans-Pacific journeys taking place in early times. Other theories, for example, that immigrants came from Europe across the North Atlantic or from Australia by way of the South Pole, belong to the realm of fantasy. Views have differed, and still do, as to the date when the first men arrived on the American mainland; but there are probably few who still support the hypothesis that this did not happen until after the end of the Ice Age. The discussion is, rather, concerned with the problem of whether infiltration had begun toward the end of the last glaciation or even somewhat earlier.

Like Eurasia, the American continent went through a cycle of at least four major glacial stages, with intervening warmer periods, during the Ice Age, or Pleistocene. The glaciations proceeded on the one hand from the great mountains in the west, the coastal ranges and Rocky Mountains, and on the other hand from an area comprising eastern Quebec, the coastal ranges of Labrador, Baffin Land and Ellesmere Land. Glacial deposits from the northeast reached the foot of the Rocky Mountains, where they came up against the local glaciers of this area. At its greatest extent the ice sheet came close to the 38th parallel of latitude, roughly that of St. Louis. On the other hand, some parts of Alaska that were cut off by the ice barrier remained ice-free (Fig. 3). The last glacial age, called the Wisconsin, seems to be more or less contemporaneous with the Würm glacial in Europe and may thus be dated broadly between 90,000 and 10,000 years ago. Both in Europe and in the New World the latest glacial age may be subdivided into several phases of cold climate, or stadials, and warmer interstadials. The stadials are known by the names Iowan, Tazewell, Cary and Valders. Between Cary and Valders lies the Two Creeks oscillation, which by radiocarbon dating can be shown to correspond with the Alleröd oscillation in Europe, i.e. it occurred about 12,000 to 11,000 years ago. The maximum of the Valders stadial has been put at 10,700 years ago, which corresponds to the beginning of the later Dryas period in Europe. A little later there seem to have been two more cold periods, Pembroke and Cochrane, but their significance is in dispute. Sufficient data are not yet available to show the extent of ice cover during individual phases of the Wisconsin glacial. But it seems that links between Alaska and ice-free areas further south were interrupted during the period from 23,000 to 13,000 years ago, while the ice barrier was at its maximum extent approximately 20,000 years ago. After 13,000 years ago there gradually developed once again an ice-free corridor between Alaska and the south, which according to E. Antevs ran east of the Rocky Mountains.

It is also necessary to indicate another problem of great importance for our theme, which has been thoroughly studied by the geologist David M. Hopkins. This is the distribution of water and land during the Neopleistocene and early Holocene in the area of what is now Bering Strait. With the aid of marine charts it can be established that a lowering of the sea level by 35 meters would produce a land bridge between Siberia and

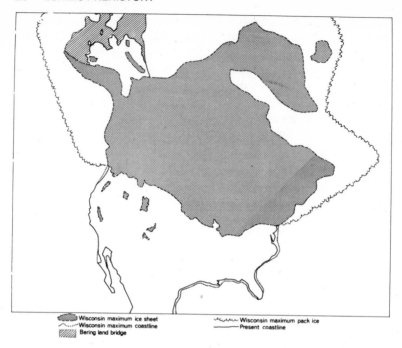

Wisconsin maximum ice sheet
Wisconsin maximum coastline
Bering land bridge

Wisconsin maximum pack ice
Present coastline

Fig. 3 - North America during the maximum of the last glaciation (Wisconsin). The ice sheets, radiating in particular from eastern Canada and the Rocky Mountains, completely separated Alaska from the ice-free southern parts of the continent during the period approximately 23,000 – 13,000 years ago.

Alaska, linking the two continents. During the last phase of the Neopleistocene, when the Wisconsin glaciation had reached its peak and vast quantities of water were removed from the sea and stored in the form of continental ice, the sea level may have sunk by some 90 to 100 meters, which must have resulted in a corresponding broadening of the Bering land bridge. This 'drainage' of water seems to have taken place repeatedly during the middle and late phases of the Neopleistocene, i.e., from approximately 90,000 to 10,000 years ago. According to H. Müller-Beck, the first occasion was more than 40/35,000 years ago, and cannot yet be ascertained exactly; subsequently, as a result of warmer temperatures, the area was again flooded, i.e., the two continents were separated by the Bering Strait. A further lowering of the temperature around 28/25,000 years ago caused the sea level to sink once again and formed another land bridge. This was particularly extensive when the Wisconsin glaciation reached its maximum, between 20,000 and 18,000 years ago (Fig. 4). Subsequently it became increasingly narrow. Leaving aside the possibility that it may have also been temporarily broken during the Two Creeks oscillation, i.e., between approximately 12,000 and 11,000 years ago, its complete separation can be assigned to the period about 10,000 years ago. Since that time, i.e., from the beginning of the Holocene, Alaska and Siberia have remained parts of two different continents. Hopkins has emphasized that the land bridge was exposed to an Arctic climate with severe winters and cool summers, so that one must imagine it as a treeless tundra. Nevertheless, it may be assumed that conditions of life were relatively favorable on the southern shore, which was probably not exposed to cold currents.

Combining the data relating to the land bridge and the ice barrier, it follows that during the late Neopleistocene a continuous connection between Asia and America as a whole existed only from 28/25,000 to 23,000 years ago and again from approximately 13,000 to 10,000 years ago. Before 28/25,000 years ago and after 10,000 years ago Siberia was separated from Alaska by Bering Strait, and between 23,000 and 13,000 years ago the ice barrier represented an insurmountable obstacle which cut off Alaska from other parts of the American continent.

Theoretically it is of course quite possible that infiltrations also took place when the land connection was broken by the rise in sea level. The distance between Siberia and Alaska is even today no more than approximately 80 kilometers and may temporarily have measured less. Moreover, the Diomede Islands are situated midway between the two continents, so that land is practically always visible. Nevertheless, one should bear in mind that the current must have been stronger when the Strait was narrower, which naturally made it harder to cross in a simple boat. The same is true in regard to the possibility of crossing on the ice in winter. This is almost impossible at the narrowest part of the Bering Strait, as the ice is moving practically all the time, but conditions are more favorable a little further to the north.

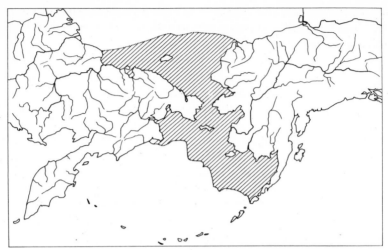

Fig. 4 - The Bering land bridge during the last or Wisconsin glaciation. The hatched area indicates its maximum extent, when Siberia and Alaska were joined by land and the sea level was 90-100 meters lower than it is today.

We have to consider, however, that Stone Age hunters – and only a population of this kind can be considered as the first settlers in the New World – were probably more likely to cross over in pursuit of game. Thus it may be presumed that such entirely unconscious infiltrations, which were no more than expansions of the Siberian hunting area, most probably took place when a land bridge existed.

Turning now to the archeological evidence, it must first be mentioned that experts do not agree whether America has any evidence which can be assigned to a period earlier than the end of the Ice Age and the early post-glacial period. This is understandable, since most of the objects discussed in this connection were surface finds at various places in the United States, Mexico, and even South America, and have been ascribed to an early period merely on account of their primitive form and method of production. The presence of man at an early date in the New World has been based, together with other evidence, on objects excavated in 1933 near Tule Springs, southern Nevada. These consist of broken and charred bones of extinct animals such as the camel, bison and horse, as well as some stone tools which are more or less clearly associated with them. Radiocarbon dating was first thought to indicate an age of 28,000 or even 33,000 years, but this has recently been seriously questioned, as the samples examined consisted of carbonized material and not of charcoal as had previously been presumed. Also in dispute is the age of the site of Lewisville near Dallas, Texas, which several scholars regard as a settlement from the period some 38,000 years ago. Nevertheless it is certain that there are in North, Central, and South America a series of sites with primitive stone industries of early date, which have been tentatively classified by A.D. Krieger as a 'pre-projectile point stage'. He estimates them to be between 40,000 and 25,000 years old.

So far, however, as mentioned above, no finds are known in America which can clearly be dated so far back either stratigraphically or by radiocarbon dating. On the other hand, there are a number of artifact complexes which from a typological standpoint are evidently ancient, raising the possibility that influences may have been exerted at an early date from the Chopper cultures rooted in southeast Asia. In this connection great importance attaches to the discoveries made by Charles E. Borden in Lower Fraser Canyon near Vancouver in southern British Columbia. From 1959 onwards three sites on the terraces on the left bank have been studied; one site has yielded one of the longest, if not the longest, sequence of cultures yet known in the Western Hemisphere. With the aid of archeological observations, geological data and radiocarbon dating, Borden was able to show that the settlement of Fraser Canyon began some 12,000 years ago with the Pasika complex; it is distinguished by crude pebble tools, and appears to have existed until some 9,000 years ago. Borden presumes that this culture originated further to the south, for it was only from this direction that British Columbia was accessible about 12,000 years ago. Thus here we would already have a 'retrograde movement', indicating that the original advance from north to south must have taken place much earlier.

Other sites that can be classified here, according to Müller-Beck, are Manix Lake, east of Los Angeles in California, the importance of which is however strongly disputed, and Ventana Cave in Arizona, where the age of a corresponding stratum has been estimated at more than 10,000 years.

Should it in fact be possible to prove, on the basis of these and further finds, that infiltrations of the Chopper horizon reached as far as America by way of secondary centers either in northern China or on the Pacific coast of Siberia (Fig. 5), it

40/35,000 B.P.

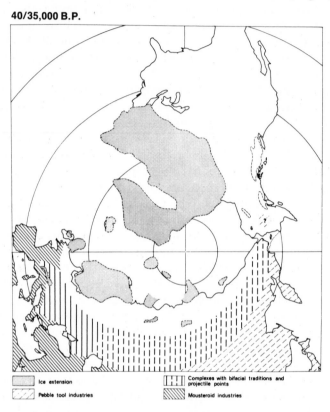

Fig. 5 - Archeological complex areas at the end of the middle Neopleistocene. The possibility of a land bridge existing in the Bering Sea area during this period has been indicated by a dotted line. After H. Müller-Beck (1966), with alterations.

would indeed also be necessary to determine whether this had already taken place at the time of the land bridge before 40/35,000 years ago or only during the period between 28/25,000 and 23,000 years ago. In this connection it must finally be noted that the so-called Desert culture, which appeared in the western United States about 9,000 years ago, could be an offshoot of this early infiltration. It is as yet impossible to say whether and to what extent this infiltration, which would form the basis of the 'pre-projectile point stage' and thus in the last instance also of the Desert culture, can be designated as originally 'Indian'. In view of the dating one may even have to consider the possibility of an immigration by Neandertaloid elements. But this hypothesis is very unlikely and has so far not been borne out by the slightest evidence. Borden correlates the Pasika complex in Fraser Canyon with an Indian ethnic group.

We may use the term Indian, or rather 'Paleo-Indian', with certainty when dealing with a further infiltration from Asia to America, of which at least the starting and terminal points can be distinguished more clearly than they can in the case of the movement we have just discussed. To understand this problem properly, we must first of all make a digression to Eurasia. Müller-Beck has pointed out that the second infiltration presumably derives from a complex that spread over wide areas of the Eurasian plain from the early Neopleistocene onwards, and especially during the middle Neopleistocene. It is characterized by the so-called leaf-shaped points, which supplement an inventory of flakes fashioned by the Mousterian technique; no tendencies have as yet been established to suggest the evolution of an Upper Paleolithic blade technique. Although hitherto we have only been able to follow the traces of this leaf-shaped point complex as far as western Siberia, Müller-Beck believes it possible that offshoots reached the Bering Strait area toward the end of the middle Neopleistocene, i.e., some 30,000 years ago. As we have noted, another land bridge appeared in this area shortly afterwards, at the latest time 25,000 years ago, and it is therefore quite obvious that representatives of this leaf-shaped point Paleolithic crossed to America in pursuit of the game they were accustomed to hunt. Since they apparently made a relatively rapid advance southwards, in any case before Alaska was cut off from the south by ice, this can only have taken place in the period between 28/25,000 and 23,000 years ago (Fig. 6). The trail of these immigrants can, however, only be picked up in the southern United States, in the so-called Llano complex. This is characterized by projectile points with bifacial retouch, a

28/25,000 B.P.

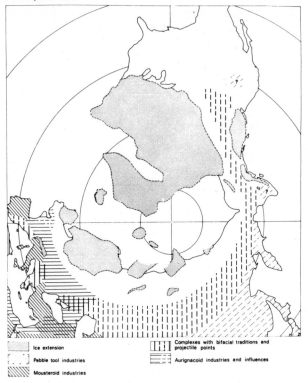

Ice extension		Complexes with bifacial traditions and projectile points
Pebble tool industries		Aurignacoid industries and influences
Mousteroid industries		

Fig. 6 - Archeological complex areas at the beginning of the late Neopleistocene, when a land bridge was formed in the Bering Sea for the last
time. After H. Müller-Beck (1966), with alterations.

technique that Müller-Beck derives from Eurasian leaf-shaped points. He stresses the fact that the material found in level
5 at the Ukrainian site of Kostienki I is particularly akin to the
American Llano complex. Characteristic forms are projectile
points of a very special type (Fig. 7), which were usually bifacially retouched. Some types went through a second process,
whereby flakes were skillfully detached from each surface
dorsally and ventrally to produce fluting; points of this type
are called 'fluted points'.

The earliest culture of the Llano complex may be the Sandia, named for Sandia Cave in Las Huertas Canyon, situated in
the Sandia Mountains of New Mexico. In general, these points

have no fluting, but on the other hand they frequently taper on one side of the lower part, recalling the shouldered points of some Upper Paleolithic cultures in Europe. These are only to be found in some areas of the west and especially the Southwest of the United States. Various dates are ascribed to the Sandia culture owing to uncertain stratigraphic conditions at the type site, but it may have existed before the Valders stadial, i.e., some 13,000 years ago or even earlier.

Approximately contemporaneous is the Clovis culture, which has been studied much more thoroughly. The name comes from a site near the border between Texas and Mexico, where excavations have been carried out since 1932. In 1936-7

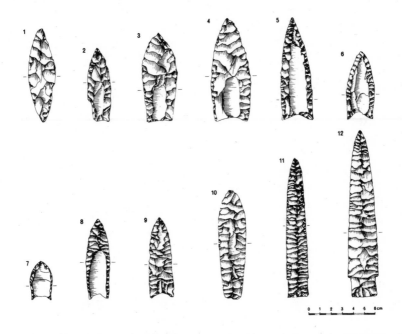

Fig. 7 - Projectile points of the American Llano complex: 1, 2 Sandia points (Sandia Cave, New Mexico); 3-6 Clovis points (3 Lewisville, Texas - 4 Dent site, Colorado - 5, 6 Bull Brook, Massachusetts); 7, 8 Folsom points (Lindenmeier site, Colorado); 9 Plainview point (Plainview, Texas); 10 Agate Basin point (Agate Basin, Wyoming); 11 Eden/ Scottsbluff point (Horner site, Wyoming); 12 Scottsbluff point (Horner site, Wyoming). By courtesy of H. Müller-Beck.

the first evidence was found of fluted points in association with mammoth bones. Clovis points are disseminated throughout the United States, but more rarely west of the Rockies, and sporadically also in Canada and Alaska, as well as in Mexico. The Clovis culture is, with some reservations, assigned to the period between 13,000 and 9000 years ago. No doubt the representatives of this culture followed the ice as it gradually receded northward.

Next is the Folsom culture, named after a locality in New Mexico. In 1926 projectile points were discovered here which were clearly associated with bones of an extinct species of bison. The fluting is more pronounced than in the Clovis points. The Folsom culture encompassed an area from Texas to the Canadian prairies, and from the Rocky Mountains to the western basin of the Mississippi. Radiocarbon dating indicates an age of 11,000 to 9500 years. It should be emphasized that the Folsom culture also yields occasional points of a somewhat different type. These are worked by a new technique in which the artifact is bifacially retouched with carefully executed parallel retouch.

At the end of the Folsom culture the 'fluted points' soon disappear and the predominant type of points are those mentioned above whose surfaces are covered with parallel retouch running either horizontally or diagonally. They belong to various types collectively termed Plano tradition (previously Yuma complex). In spite of certain differences the projectile points of this complex bear a close resemblance to one another and may be dated at from 9500 to 6500 years ago.

Another area to examine is the eastern United States and southeastern Canada, from the Atlantic coast to the area west of the Mississippi. First, in this region there is evidence of the Llano complex which R.J. Mason ascribes to the late Neopleistocene or early postglacial period. He assumes that this indicated a rapid spread of the western Clovis culture. At about 11,000 years ago it began to split up into a considerable number of specifically local groups that were not distinguished primarily by fluted or unfluted points.

In many areas of North America the stone industries with characteristic projectile points which are referred to as 'Paleo-Indian' or — if the fluting is lacking — as 'Proto-Archaic' and later as 'Archaic', represent a level of specialized or advanced hunting cultures. It is a noteworthy fact that the American Llano complex, which for the time being can be identified as far back as approximately 13,000 years ago, originally had no Upper Paleolithic, i.e. Gravettoid or Aurignacoid elements. It must have acquired its particular character after contact with Siberia had been broken off, probably in the southwestern United States (Fig. 8). In theory this infiltration could again be the work of a Neandertaloid element; but also in this case there is not a single clue to support such a hypothesis. The population which, as we have said, immigrated by way of the Bering land bridge during the period from 28/25,000 to 23,000 years ago, and then advanced fairly rapidly southward, is rather to be termed proto- or semi-Mongoloid. Toward the end of the late Neopleistocene it spread over wide areas of North and South America, and at the beginning of the Holocene some groups returned north to the regions that were now becoming ice-free.

In order to assess subsequent developments it is necessary once again to deal briefly with conditions in Eurasia. Here, according to Müller-Beck, it can be ascertained that inventories distinguished by leaf-shaped projectile points and flake tools of Mousteroid technique showed increasing Gravettoid tendencies from the end of the middle Neopleistocene, or were replaced by Upper Paleolithic industries. In northeast Asia, too, this development is clearly apparent from 20,000 years ago at the earliest and with certainty from 15,000 years ago; for example, in the Lake Baikal area, at the most important site at Mal'ta and on Hokkaido, which at that time was still linked to the mainland. The stone industries concerned bear an evident Upper Paleolithic stamp. This likewise seems to indicate that the representatives of the American Llano complex must have become separated from those of the Eurasian complex of leaf-shaped points before this became modified or was ousted by the appearance of Gravettoid elements. We have already shown that this development must have taken place in the southwestern United States without any signs of Upper Paleolithic influences. On the other hand, the Upper Paleolithic infiltration, which can be authenticated in northeast Asia from 15,000 years ago at the latest, may have gradual-

20,000 B.P.

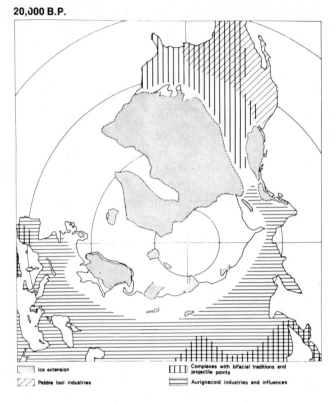

Fig. 8 - Archeological complex areas at the time of the maximum ice extension in the late Neopleistocene. After H. Müller-Beck (1966), with alterations.

ly advanced into the area of the Bering land bridge, which was
still in existence at that time (Fig. 9). This can be proved by
recent finds on Kamchatka. Gravettoid elements found their
way to America relatively quickly, as may be inferred from the
fact that genuine burins have been identified in the Levy
rock-shelter in Texas together with an industry known as
'Epi-Clovis' and dated to the period about 9000 years ago. It
is unlikely that this type of tool could have developed locally
along independent lines with the Clovis, and its appearance
in the Llano complex must presumably be linked with the infiltration of Upper Paleolithic elements in the late Neopleistocene.

11/10,000 B.P.

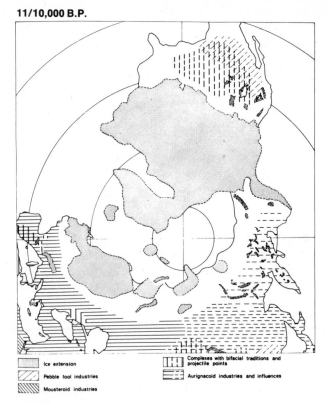

Ice extension

Pebble tool industries

Mousteroid industries

Complexes with bifacial traditions and projectile points

Aurignacoid industries and influences

Fig. 9 - Archeological complex areas at the end of the late Neopleistocene. After H. Müller-Beck (1966), with alterations.

On the other hand, it may be noted that this Gravettoid infiltration, in contrast to the two earlier ones, left clearly identifiable traces in Alaska, whereas it reached the south only to a limited extent.

As a matter of fact, Alaska has hitherto yielded no finds which could be plausibly associated with the two earliest immigrations from Asia to America. The information obtained hitherto is much too vague. Consider, for example, the finds of the Palisades I complex on Cape Krusenstern in northwestern Alaska, thus named by J. Louis Giddings after a rock formation; these were surface finds and were, moreover, on account of their disintegration, separated from other finds assembled at the same location and ascribed to a more recent date, so that their age is uncertain. A similar situation occurs in the case of the British Mountain complex discovered by R.S. MacNeish in the Engigstciak area on Firth River, some 25 kilometers south of the Arctic Ocean and 60 kilometers east of the Alaskan-Canadian border, which has been thought very ancient. Further atypical material was found by J.M. Campbell in the Anaktuvuk Pass area in the Brooks Range, northern Alaska (Kogruk complex) and by R. Solecki on the Katakturuk River, which flows into Camden Bay in Arctic Alaska. It would no doubt be a mistake to assign without further study a great age to such apparently primitive artifacts.

Very recently some discoveries were made which may help to fill in this gap. One of them concerns a stratigraphy at Healy Lake near Indian Village, about 125 kilometers southeast of Fairbanks. John Cook from the University of Wisconsin located there in 1967 an industry characterized by well-worked scrapers below a layer with rather old archeological remains and separated from it by a sterile layer. It certainly has some resemblance to industries of the late Lower Paleolithic of the Old World. As there are some samples for radiocarbon analysis, we may soon learn more about the absolute age of this industry.

The other discovery was made at Onion Portage in Northwest Alaska on the Kobuk, about 160 kilometers inland from the mouth of this river. Also in 1967, Douglas Anderson and Ruth Giddings succeeded in identifying an industry called 'Akmak culture' under clear stratigraphic conditions. It looks like a mixture of elements of the leaf-shaped point complex of the late Lower Paleolithic of northern Eurasia and others of Upper Paleolithic character. This later was called 'very old' by geologists, but a final judgement is not possible before this find has been published in detail.

As has been mentioned, a number of finds suggest that offshoots of the Llano complex coming from the southern United States found their way into Canada and Alaska at the end of the Ice Age. This is indicated in particular by projectile points which correspond to Paleo-Indian types. Points with parallel retouching occur, as do those with fluting, and it seems that they survived longer in the north than in the areas further south whence they originated. In the northern part of North

America these retrograde movements, which may have taken place in successive stages, exerted some influence upon the third infiltration mentioned above, which appeared in Alaska from Siberia at the time when the last phase of the late Neopleistocene was giving way to the Holocene. But in this respect much still remains unclear and for this reason in the following pages we shall deliberately content ourselves with referring to the appearance of Paleo-Indian projectile points by the very general term 'Northern Point tradition'. Nor shall we broach the subject whether in the north miscegenation occurred between representatives of the Northern Point tradition, who had returned from southern North America, and the Epi-Gravettian people who arrived there simultaneously from Siberia; in this respect we are still groping entirely in the dark, partly due to a lack of skeletons from this period which can be easily identified and classified.

It has already been mentioned that traces of the third infiltration, in contrast to the two preceding ones, have been clearly identified in Alaska as well as in other parts of the Arctic and Subarctic zones of North America. An ever-increasing number of clues suggest that an ethnic group, thought to be of Arctic-Mongoloid stock, crossed the land bridge, infiltrated Alaska, and then advanced fairly rapidly further eastward through the Canadian Arctic as far as Greenland. We can hardly go wrong in associating this 'American Epi-Gravettian', which has a tendency in favor of small implements, with the origins of Eskimo culture and in surmising that its representatives were the ancestors of the Eskimos. Thus we have finally reached the prehistory of the Eskimo area, the subject of our discussion in the following pages.

Bibliography: Anderson, 1968; Borden, 1965; Bosch-Gimpera, 1962; Bushnell and MacBurney, 1959; Butler, 1961; Byers, 1957; Campbell, 1963; Chard, 1956, 1958a, 1958b, 1958c, 1959a, 1959b, 1960, 1963; Colinvaux, 1964; Collins, 1943, 1963; Griffin, 1960, 1962; Haag, 1962; Hadleigh-West, 1963a; Hopkins, 1959, 1965, 1967a, 1967b; Irving, 1963; Jenness, 1940; Jennings and Norbeck, 1964; Krieger, 1962; Leroi-Gourhan, 1946; MacNeish, 1959a, 1963; Mason, 1962; Michael, 1958; Mitchell, 1965; Movius, 1953; Müller-Beck, 1966, 1967;

Narr, 1964; Nelson, 1937; Okladnikov, 1960; Okladnikov and Nekrasov, 1959; Rudenko, 1961; Wormington, 1957, 1963.

MILESTONES IN RESEARCH

The early Arctic explorers encountered sporadic traces of the prehistoric Eskimos. But most finds of this kind were difficult to distinguish from contemporary native objects, so that it was not possible at first to grasp their proper historical significance.

In the eighteenth century, and to a greater extent in the late nineteenth and early twentieth centuries, a good deal of material was collected, especially in Greenland, and some of it has been discussed in the professional literature. At that time, however, scholars were mainly concerned with the natives of the day and made only incidental references to the Eskimo past. Around the turn of the century interest in archeological finds gradually began to crystallize. An example is the extensive collection which M. Porsild brought to Denmark from the west coast of Greenland, and the attempt by O. Solberg, the Norwegian ethnologist, to substantiate a Stone Age phase in the culture of West Greenland on the basis of materials from Disko Bay. The beginning of archeological exploration in East Greenland is associated with such names as C. Ryder, L. Mylius-Erichsen, G. Amdrup and C. Bendix Thostrup. In North Greenland the first prehistoric finds were recovered near Umanaq, near Thule, by R.E. Peary's expeditions and the Crocker Land expedition of Captain Comer, who had already collected archeological remains in the Hudson Bay region. Comer's material from North Greenland was published by Clark Wissler.

In this connection the work of Danish archeologists on the

legacy of medieval European settlers in southwest Greenland should be mentioned. Actually this started when Hans Egede came to Greenland in 1721 in search of the supposed descendants of the Norsemen.

But scholarly Eskimo archeology did not begin until the second or third decade of this century. It is associated with several famous expeditions.

In 1912 Knud Rasmussen inaugurated the important series of Thule Expeditions with the initial purpose of exploring North Greenland. Some archeological discoveries were made on the first expedition, but to a greater extent on the second, when in 1916 Lauge Koch and Peter Freuchen thoroughly examined a site near Umánaq in Thule district, which had been discovered by Captain Comer and was for this reason termed 'Comer's midden'.

But the most important for modern Eskimo archeology was the Fifth Thule Expedition, once more led by Knud Rasmussen. It lasted from 1921 to 1924. A group of Danish scholars set out from Copenhagen and, after stopping at Thule in North Greenland, with some Greenlander assistants went on to explore various aspects of the Hudson Bay region from a base camp on the little Danish island south of the Melville Peninsula.

Their archeological studies were mainly conducted by Therkel Mathiassen, but Knud Rasmussen also participated in the work as did other members of the expedition including Kaj Birket-Smith, Peter Freuchen and Helge Bangsted. Important excavations were carried out at many places in the northern part of the Hudson Bay area. The extensive archeological collections from the Central Eskimo regions which were assembled found their way into the Danish National Museum. In addition to this Knud Rasmussen subsequently undertook a journey along the coast of the Arctic Ocean, as far as Alaska and the Siberian coast of the Bering Strait, and returned with a large number of specimens mostly obtained from the natives. This material enabled Therkel Mathiassen to establish clearly for the first time the existence of a widely disseminated prehistoric Eskimo culture, the Thule culture.

Almost simultaneously two other Arctic expeditions took place under the leadership of Vilhjálmur Stefánsson, an American of Icelandic origin, which also had archeological research as one of its tasks. In 1912 the Stefánsson-Anderson expedition discovered an early Eskimo culture at Point Barrow in Arctic Alaska; it was called Birnirk culture. During the Canadian Arctic Expedition of 1913-18 the archeological work was done primarily by Diamond Jenness. After a very difficult start in 1913 — the expedition's biggest ship, the *Karluk,* was lost in the ice and some of its members, among them the French ethnologist Beuchat, lost their lives — Jenness reached the area of the Copper Eskimos on Victoria Island in the Arctic Archipelago in the summer of 1914. During his two-year stay in this region he assembled two important collections, one ethnographical, and the other, a comprehensive archeological one. Both are now housed in the National Museum of Canada at Ottawa.

These remarkable enterprises were the basis for all the archeological research done later in the Eskimo area. Under most difficult conditions, material was recovered which pointed very clearly to the fact that Eskimo culture was of considerable antiquity.

It would take us too far from our theme to enumerate all the archeological exploration that has since been carried out in the Eskimo area. We can only indicate a few of the milestones, and shall deal separately with the different parts of this vast zone. Afterwards we shall familiarize ourselves with the various prehistoric Eskimo cultures in geographical order; but here more emphasis will be placed on the chronological order of the discoveries.

Let us begin with the Bering Strait area. Here an early Eskimo culture was noted by Diamond Jenness during his stay on Little Diomede Island in 1926. He called it the Old Bering Sea culture. This was later fully substantiated through excavations carried out by Henry B. Collins, Otto Geist and others on St. Lawrence Island. In 1928 Collins was able to establish on the northernmost of the three Punuk islets, off the east coast of St. Lawrence Island, a somewhat more recent cultural phase, which he called the Punuk culture. In 1930 the same explorer carried out an excavation near Gambell on the northwestern cape of St. Lawrence Island, which as well as more recent finds yielded extensive collections of objects from the Punuk and Old Bering Sea cultures. Otto Geist, who had worked in the Gambell area, between 1929 and 1936 examined a huge mound at Kukulik, near Savoonga, on the north coast of St. Lawrence Island. This mound, comparable to the tells of the Near East, likewise yielded several finds of the Punuk and Old Bering Sea cultures. In 1931, he discovered on the northernmost Punuk islet a copious site which he excavated in collaboration with Ivar Skarland in 1934, and in the process identified the Okvik culture. This was the earliest phase of Eskimo culture hitherto known on the Asiatic side of the Bering Strait, a forerunner of the Old Bering Sea culture and of the still more recent Punuk culture. Further finds of the Okvik culture were made by Louis Giddings, who in 1939 examined another settlement near Gambell.

More recently, archeological work was carried on by Russian scholars in the westernmost parts of the Eskimo area, on the Siberian coast of the Bering Strait. In 1945 S.J. Rudenko carried out excavations near Uelen on Cape Dezhnev (East Cape), on the eastern tip of Chukchi Peninsula, where he found a sequence of cultures similar to that on St. Lawrence Island. Between 1955 and 1959, M. Levin and R.V. Chubarova carried out further excavations of a cemetery near Uelen.

On the American coast of the Bering Strait Giddings unearthed important material in 1948 at Iyatayet, on Cape Denbigh in Norton Sound: unexpectedly he encountered a stone industry consisting of small tools to which he gave the name of Denbigh Flint complex. The first indications of small-tool cultures had already appeared in 1933, when small tools were discovered at College, near Fairbanks in Alaska, on the very site where the University of Alaska presently stands. Likewise in 1948 Giddings discovered at Iyatayet and nearby at Nukleet two more recent cultures which he called Norton and Nukleet.

In 1949 and 1950 Danish and American scholars studied the Bering Strait area. Among their most important achievements was the examination, by Helge Larsen and his team, of Trail Creek Caves, some 50 kilometers south of Deering on Seward Peninsula; they also succeeded in localizing other sites, especially that of a huge community house or *qalgi* of the Ipiutak culture near Deering, in the north of Seward Peninsula.

In 1951 Wendell Oswalt carried out excavations in the Hooper Bay area, southwest of the Yukon delta, and in the process came across remains of the period between about 1600 and the present day. Further south, in the Kuskokwim Bay and Bristol Bay areas, Helge Larsen and his collaborators discovered some interesting sites in 1948. L.S. Cressman and D.E. Dumond, who have worked in the same area since 1960-61, have also been successful, and R.E. Ackerman discovered some new sites in 1962 as well.

On the Aleutian Islands, W.H. Dall dug as early as 1871-4. He was followed in the Aleutian Archipelago by Waldemar Jochelson in 1909-10 and by A. Hrdlička in 1936-8. From 1949 onwards an extensive program has been in progress, directed by William S. Laughlin, under the title 'University of Wisconsin Aleut-Konyag Prehistory and Ecology Project'. The center of archeological work is situated near Nikolski on Umnak Island. A.C. Spaulding's research on Agattu Island, in the extreme west, occurred in 1949. A relatively late phase of settlement was examined by Oswalt in 1954-5, near Kaflia in the Katmai National Monument, in the eastern part of the Alaskan Peninsula.

On Kodiak Island—the home of the largest species of bear extant today—work was done by A. Hrdlička from 1931 to 1936, mostly at Uyak Bay in the north of this big island. His collection was later studied and published by R.F. Heizer. Recently, new discoveries have been made by the field project of the University of Wisconsin mentioned above.

In the central part of southern Alaska our attention is drawn to Kachemak Bay, in the south of the Kenai Peninsula, where Frederica de Laguna carried out extensive archeological work between 1930 and 1932, on behalf of the US National Museum, Washington. She was able to identify three stages of a culture which she called Kachemak I-III. In 1933 she continued her studies in collaboration with Kaj Birket-Smith on the coast of Prince William Sound, east of the Kenai Peninsula.

In Arctic Alaska the excavations begun by Stefánsson at Birnirk on Point Barrow were taken up again on a larger scale in 1932 by James A. Ford, whose work was sponsored by the US National Museum, Washington. In 1951 and 1952 Wilbert Carter of Harvard University worked at the same site; the results of his excavations have not yet been published. Other sites are located in the neighborhood of Barrow and were extensively exploited by W.B. van Valin and A.H. Hopson as well as by natives.

Particularly surprising was the discovery by Helge Larsen, Froelich G. Rainey and J. Louis Giddings in 1939 of a large settlement, with its cemetery, at Point Hope, the northwestern corner of the American continent. Excavations brought to light numerous remains of a peculiar culture which its discoverers introduced into the literature as the Ipiutak culture. At the same time they also found traces of a related culture referred to as Near Ipiutak and more recent remains.

In 1956 Giddings succeeded in identifying on the Choris Peninsula southwest of Kotzebue another hitherto unknown group of objects which he called Choris culture. It appears to be older than Ipiutak and has features common to those of the Near Ipiutak culture.

These studies convinced Giddings that archeologists could obtain chronological clues from certain well-known formations (along the coasts of the Chukchi Sea) most properly called 'beach ridges'. Approximately from the end of the post-glacial climatic optimum, some 6000 years ago, the sea graddually deposited, at certain places along the shore, ridges whose age is greater the further inland they lie. Since the Eskimos, being hunters of sea-mammals, always settled near the coast, these conditions have produced a kind of 'horizontal stratigraphy': near the shore the archeologist encounters finds of recent date, and as he goes inland he comes across successively older periods – provided that the area concerned was more or less regularly frequented by Eskimos.

One such a place was discovered by Giddings on Cape Krusenstern, north of Kotzebue. Since he began work there in 1958 he had been able to show that on the beach ridges, which stretch for about two kilometers from the sea to a large lagoon, there are traces of several different cultures dating back over five or six thousand years. The earliest of all are the remains of the Denbigh Flint complex, which was found quite close to the lagoon. Other sites were also discovered on the hills across the lagoon, which may have been settled before the first ridges were formed; we have already encountered them under the name 'Palisades' (Fig. 10).

In the hinterland between 1940 and 1947 Louis Giddings

carried out work along the Kobuk in connection with dendro-chronological studies in the area of this vast river system east of Kotzebue. Various relatively recent cultural phases he grouped together under the name of 'Arctic Woodland culture'. Of greatest significance is his discovery at Onion Portage, where an important stratigraphy exists.

In the Brooks Range in Arctic Alaska, Ralph S. Solecki, William N. Irving, John M. Campbell and others encountered stone industries which may be classified under the name American Epi-Gravettian mentioned earlier, as well as more recent Eskimo cultures.

Moving from Alaska to the Canadian Arctic we enter territory, both in the western and eastern Arctic, where the Canadian National Museum in Ottawa is carrying out, with Amer-

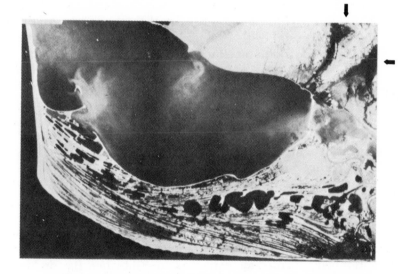

Fig. 10 - Cape Krusenstern, a strip of land about two kilometers wide between the Chukchi Sea and a large lagoon. This aerial photograph shows that the cape consists of a considerable number of beach ridges, which were formed during the last five or six thousand years. Scattered over them are numerous settlements and other sites belonging to Eskimos of different periods. The closer the ridges are situated to the present shoreline, the more recent they are, and the more recent are the cultural remains upon them. Top right (at the point where the arrows intersect): the hill with the site known as 'Palisades'. Photo by courtesy of US Coast and Geodetic Survey.

ican and Danish support, a tremendous effort to clarify the prehistory of the Eskimo area. In the western parts of this vast region Richard S. MacNeish is the scholar who has been chiefly involved. His work includes the Firth River in Yukon Territory — we have already come across his findings in the British Mountain complex, about which much remains obscure; in the vast region between Great Bear Lake and Athabaska Lake; and finally, much further south near Fort Liard, in the extreme southwest of the Northwest Territories.

Elmer Harp has carried out most valuable studies, with minute attention to detail and thorough analysis, in the Dismal Lake area between Great Bear Lake and Coronation Gulf. He has also investigated the Keewatin district west of Hudson Bay and the area of Belle Isle Strait, which separates northern Newfoundland from Labrador.

This brings us to the eastern part of the Canadian Arctic. After the successful Fifth Thule Expedition, no further excavations took place in this area for a long time.

On the other hand, the natives were now aware of the white man's interest in the antiquities of their area, and thus gradually an increasing number of objects came into the hands of missionaries and traders, and eventually found their way into Canadian museums. On the basis of this material Diamond Jenness recognized as early as 1925 that in the Hudson Bay area an earlier culture must have existed before that of Thule. This he named Cape Dorset culture, or simply Dorset culture, after a cape on the southwestern corner of Baffin Land.

Between 1948 and 1955 Henry B. Collins of the Smithsonian Institution in Washington, who is already familiar to us from his studies in Alaska, made seven expeditions in collaboration with Canadian explorers to Frobisher Bay in the south of Baffin Land, to Cornwallis Island in the northern part of the Arctic Archipelago, and also to Southampton, Coats and Walrus islands in the north of Hudson Bay. Of the Canadians who participated in this archeological work in the eastern part of their Eskimo territory, we may single out for mention: W.E. Taylor, who discovered many sites south of Hudson Strait as well as far to the north in the Arctic Archipelago; G.R. Lowther, who in 1960 found small tools near Cape Sparbo on Devon Island, also situated in the far north; and M.S. Maxwell who in 1958, in connection with the Canadian Defence Research Board Expedition, identified traces of Dorset and more recent cultures, though as yet no inventory of small tools, in eastern Grant Land in the north of Ellesmere Island, at a crossing to Greenland.

Returning to Hudson Bay, we may note the small-tool industry which Giddings collected in 1953 on North Knife River,

Fig. 11 - Excavations near Alarnerk in the north of Melville Peninsula (Igloo-lik area). Photo by courtesy of J. Meldgaard.

northeast of Churchill. Also of importance are the investigations carried out by Jørgen Meldgaard in the northwest of Melville Peninsula between 1954 and 1957. He discovered not only five different stages of the Dorset culture, but also earlier traces, referred to as Pre-Dorset and forming part of the American Epi-Gravettian (Fig. 11).

This brings us back to the starting-point of this chapter: Greenland. After the archeological discoveries of the Fifth Thule Expedition were studied and published, intense systematic research began. For this reason Greenland is today the best studied part of the Eskimo area from an archeological point of view. In 1926 some objects were recovered and published by D. Johnson, a member of the British Cambridge East Greenland Expedition, which explored the area between 72° and 75° N. Of particular note are the 1929 excavations of Therkel Mathiassen, in Upernivik district in West Greenland, which led to the identification of the Inugsuk culture, an off-shoot of the Thule culture; in 1930 near Kangamiut in the southern part of the west coast; in 1931-2 at Angmagssalik and near Skjoldungen in the southern part of the east coast; in 1933 in the Disko Bay area on the west coast; and in 1934 further south near Julianehaab. This pioneer of Eskimo

Fig. 12 - Dødemandsbugten: a site of the northeast Greenland mixed culture on Clavering Island, 74° 30' N. Photo by the author.

archeology was soon joined by other Danish scholars. In 1931 Erik Holtved worked in the Lindenows Fjord area on the southern tip of Greenland. In 1931-2 Helge Larsen started to investigate a large settlement near Dødemandsbugten on Clavering Island in northeast Greenland (Fig. 12). M. Degerbøl carried out research at Kangerdlugssuaq in East Greenland in 1932, P.V. Glob further north in the Ella Island area in 1932-33, and Helge Larsen once again at Kangerdlugssuaq in 1935. Between 1935 and 1937 Erik Holtved investigated the Thule culture in the Inglefield Land area of the Thule district, North Greenland. In 1939 Eigil Knuth began his archeological exploration of Peary Land in North Greenland, which he resumed shortly after World War II and is still continuing to the present day; we owe to him the discovery of several early sites which he groups together under the term

Fig. 13 - Sermermiut on Jakobshavn Isfjord on Disko Bay, West Greenland.
Photo by courtesy of J. Meldgaard.

'Independence culture'. Also noteworthy are the excavations near Jakobshavn on Disko Bay in West Greenland (Fig. 13), which were begun by Helge Larsen and Jørgen Meldgaard in 1953 and continued by Therkel Mathiassen in 1955. They found an interesting sequence of strata which shows that, long before the medieval Inugsuk culture, the Dorset culture penetrated this area, and before that the small-tool Sarqaq culture, named after a site on the north of Disko Bay. Similar material was discovered by Meldgaard in 1960 further south, near Godthaab.

Parallel with their study of Eskimo archeology, Danish scholars also continued their exploration of Norse ruins. Noteworthy are the work of Poul Nørlund, Ch. Leif Vebaek and more recently also Jørgen Meldgaard.

We have been able to give only a few indications of the course of archeological research in the Eskimo area; a proper history has yet to be written. When it does appear it will be able to tell of many a heroic endeavour, of hard-fought successes and costly setbacks.

Bibliography: Amdrup, 1913; Birket-Smith, 1948, 1959; Crantz, 1767; Holm, 1883; Larsen, 1961; Porsild, 1915; Rudenko, 1961; Solberg, 1907; Thostrup, 1911.

SITES, FINDS AND PREHISTORIC CULTURES IN THE ESKIMO AREA

In this principal section we shall endeavor to investigate in detail the results of the archeological explorations listed earlier. The most lucid arrangement would seem to be one whereby the various zones are dealt with separately and developments in each traced chronologically from the earliest times onwards. We may begin with the western parts of this vast area, whence the prehistoric Eskimo culture spread eastward, and end with Greenland, which forms a kind of *cul de sac* in the Eskimo advance.

Alaska

The importance of Alaska in Eskimo prehistory is so great that this vast territory should be discussed in the greatest detail, taking each area separately (Fig. 14).

BERING STRAIT AREA

1. The Land Bridge

It may seem somewhat strange that we should take as our starting point an area which is no longer accessible, for the Bering land bridge disappeared beneath the sea about 10,000 years ago, when, according to geologists, the sea level became the same as it is today. And yet we have to consider this zone, as both theoretical and practical evidence exists that the land bridge was still used as a migration route by groups of hunters

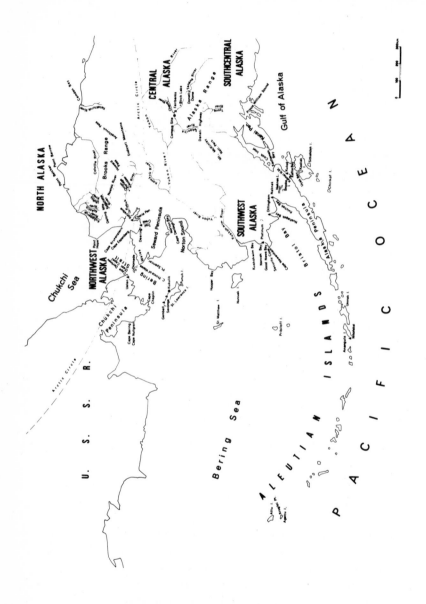

Fig. 14 - Map of Alaska, showing places and sites mentioned in the text.

whom we may associate with the beginnings of Eskimo prehistory.

In the first place it should be borne in mind that, when the
sea level dropped by 90 to 100 meters, a broad strip of land appeared, the southern shore of which ran from the coast of Siberia near Cape Navarin to the tip of the Alaskan Peninsula,
then turned toward the southwest, and enclosed the eastern
Aleutians as far as Umnak Island. This extensive area was apparently accessible to human beings until the end of the late
glacial period or thereabouts. Since then the situation has
greatly changed, as the entire land bridge has disappeared and
there remain only a few islands such as the Diomedes, St.
Lawrence, St. Matthew, Nunivak and the Pribilofs, which formerly stood out as elevations above the plain. There is some
possibility that traces of early migrants may be found on these
islands, but so far nothing has been discovered.

On the other hand, a short while ago an interesting discovery
was made on the shore of the former land bridge in the Aleutian area. In the early 1950's, W.S. Laughlin carried out investigations on Umnak Island, to be discussed below, in the
course of which finds were assembled from nearby Anangula
Island; these pieces are undoubtedly of great importance with
reference to the problem of the American Epi-Gravettian. In
1962 examination of the site was resumed, and it was found to
be far more extensive than had originally been assumed and
led to clear stratigraphic placement of the specimens. Radiocarbon dating of a charcoal sample from this site suggests an
age of 8425 ± 275 years. The specimens belong to a clearly
marked blade industry: cores of a wide range of size and shape
(apparently including some of the 'boat-shaped' type to be discussed in detail below), a wide range of unretouched and retouched blades (including 'microblades'), burins and scrapers,
platform flakes, and irregular waste flakes. Since Umnak and
Anangula were probably still accessible by land some 10,000
years ago, it seems likely that this material must be associated
with groups of hunters who entered the area shortly before a
land connection ceased to exist. Laughlin thinks it feasible
that the southern shore of the Bering land bridge and the Pacific coast of Siberia as far south as Hokkaido were frequented
as early as 15,000 to 10,000 years ago by people whose culture

formed part of what I call Epi-Gravettian. In this connection
he also points to common anthropological and linguistic features between Eskimos and Aleuts on the one hand and Paleo-
Siberians on the other.

A glance at the map will show that the hunters who crossed
from Siberia to Alaska by way of the land bridge can hardly
have first set foot in the New World at the place where the gap
between the two continents is narrowest today, for the Seward
Peninsula is mountainous on the side facing the Bering Strait
and does not offer a very inviting route into the interior. On
the other hand southwestern Alaska, with its vast river systems
—the Yukon-Tanana and Kuskokwim in particular—affords
natural routes for immigrants. In fact it appears that at least
some groups of the American Epi-Gravettian people came by
this route. An indication of this can be found on the site of the
University of Alaska campus at College, near Fairbanks in the
interior of Alaska, although this lies far removed from the Bering land bridge.

In 1933 a campsite of Stone Age hunters was discovered on a
hill with a commanding view of the Chena River area, which
must have abounded in game. Excavations carried out between 1934 and 1936 and subsequent prospecting operations
have yielded interesting material which is still awaiting detailed publication (Fig. 15). It includes, as well as waste material, a relatively large number of scrapers, some pieces recalling
Mousterian scrapers, and a series of projectile points sugges-
tive of Paleo-Indian influences, so that one may speak of a
Northern Point tradition; finally—and this is the most important thing—the Campus site at College also yielded microblades and a rather large number of curious artifacts generally
called cores, although some of them may also have been used
as keel-shaped scrapers or burins; burins proper are lacking—
i.e., there are only some atypical examples of this type of tool.
Shortly after their discovery the characteristic cores, which
were called 'boat-shaped' or 'keel-shaped' and recently also
'elongated prismatic', were compared by N.C. Nelson with
similar artifacts in small-tool complexes from the Gobi desert
in Mongolia. They are rather carefully prepared nuclei of small
dimensions which have at one end traces of the flaked-off
microblades. Since Nelson's publication it became evident

that in Asia the same type occurs not only in the Gobi desert but also in the Harbin area of northern China, near Irkutsk and Minusinsk in Siberia, on Hokkaido in northern Japan, and on Kamchatka. It thus appears that these curious cores are among the characteristic features of an Upper Paleolithic-Mesolithic horizon which is widely disseminated in northeast Asia. As

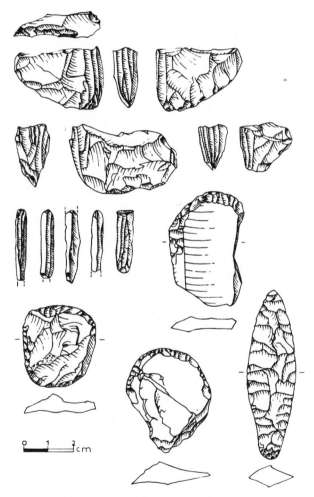

Fig. 15 - Stone implements from the Campus site at College, near Fairbanks. Top and second row: cores. Center: microblades and scrapers. Below: scrapers and projectile point or knife.

has been mentioned, this seems to be an offshoot of the late eastern Gravettian, an Epi-Gravettian in which small tools tend to occur. It is highly interesting and hardly fortuitous that this group should bear a distinct resemblance to the pieces found in the Campus site. By measuring the hydration layer of some obsidian flakes Y. Katsui obtained a date of 8400 B.P. for the Campus site industry. It may, however, be observed that this group also shows influences of the Northern Point tradition; this suggests that some time had already passed since the Epi-Gravettian tradition made its appearance in Alaska. More material was gathered at the Campus site in 1966 and 1967 by excavations directed by Morris Morgan and Edward Hosley respectively.

It may be that a slightly earlier date than that of the College Campus site must be ascribed to a complex from Teklanika River, in the eastern part of Mount McKinley National Park, on the northern slopes of the Alaska Range. Fred Hadleigh-West worked on this complex, which comprises larger blades and cores pertaining to them as well as microblades and tiny boat-shaped cores. Affinities with the Campus site are unmistakable, but the material gives the impression of being a more primitive intrusion; this may, however, be due in part to the raw material used. Further material of this kind was discovered by Hadleigh-West in the summer of 1964 in the Donnelly Dome area on the Richardson Highway south of Delta Junction, also in Central Alaska. He uses the general term of 'Denali complex' for early core and blade industries in Central Alaska, the age of which he estimates at about 10,000 B.P. In any case this is a relatively early phase of the American Epi-Gravettian, which has been designated by MacNeish and Irving as the Northwest Microblade tradition. The further course of development was no doubt considerably influenced by the fact that almost simultaneously reflections of the Paleo-Indian, i.e., Llano and Proto-Archaic, cultures further south, which we have referred to as the Northern Point tradition, became noticeable as far away as Alaska. This finds expression in the material from the College Campus site, as we have seen.

Another noteworthy point in this connection is the fact that toward the south, in other words up the Yukon, there are a number of sites with material which seems to represent a mix-

ture of Epi-Gravettian elements of small tools and those of the
Northern Point tradition. In the case of one site on Birch Lake,
some 90 kilometers south of Fairbanks, described by Ivar
Skarland and Louis Giddings, it is striking to find an almost
conical type of nucleus used in the production of microblades.
Further observations were made in adjacent Canadian areas,
for example by F. Johnson and D. Leechman at Kluane Lake
in southwestern Yukon province, or by R.S. MacNeish in the
zone between Fort Liard, in the southwesternmost part of the
Northwest Territories, and Fort Simpson, the point where the
Liard discharges into the Mackenzie. He distinguishes in that
area four groups of objects, of which the Sandy Lake complex
seems to be a component of the Northern Point tradition,
whereas the Pointed Mountain complex and the Fisherman's
Lake complex are connected with the American Epi-Gravettian. Here we have of course left the Eskimo area far behind
and have entered Indian territory settled – today at least – by
the Athapaskans.

Bibliography: Befu and Chard, 1960; Hadleigh-West, 1965b;
Johnson, 1946; Laughlin, 1963b; Laughlin and Aigner, 1966;
Laughlin and Marsh, 1954-55; Laughlin, Marsh and Leach,
1952-53; Leechman, 1943; MacNeish, 1954; McCartney and
Turner II, 1966; Morlan, 1967; Nelson, 1937; Péwé, Hop-
kins and Giddings, 1964; Rainey, 1939, 1940; Skarland and
Giddings, 1948; Sugihara and Tozawa, 1960; Turner (MS.).

2. The American Side

Returning now to the coastal area and examining what clues
exist on the American side of Bering Strait, we shall deal first,
not with the further development of the Epi-Gravettian tradition, but with a completely different group of objects. In this
connection, too, a short trip will have to be made into the interior, but our observations can begin with the coastal area.
Near Cape Krusenstern, north of Kotzebue, on a hill on the
landward shore of the lagoon – the same site whence the
material originates that has been called Palisades I – J.L. Giddings discovered in 1959 an inventory which he introduced

into the literature as Palisades II (Fig. 10). These too, are surface finds, but he distinguishes them from those of the Palisades I complex because the chert and chalcedony artifacts have not undergone any chemical change but are only patinated on the exterior. Scrapers, in addition to broad bifacially retouched projectile points or knives, deserve mention, as do the particularly characteristic arrowheads with basal side-notching (Fig. 16). Giddings estimates the age of this culture at around 6000 years. We may add in this connection that a little earlier I. Skarland and C.J. Keim, who investigated the Ratekin site on Denali Highway in the south of the Alaskan interior, published a similar inventory comprising scrapers and other artifacts reminiscent of the Mousterian technique, as well as notched points. Further to the south, on Tyone River, W.N. Irving likewise encountered notched points. Another find, made by R.E. Ackerman near Cape Newenham, will be discussed in connection with southwestern Alaska. Also evident are common features with the Tuktu complex which J.M. Campbell localized in the area of Anaktuvuk Pass in the Brooks Range and assigned to the period between 4000 and 3000 years ago. Here, too, notched points occur, but in addition there are microblades and small polyhedral cores, with resemblances to the American Epi-Gravettian tradition.

This appearance of generally rather small points with notches at the base may also be linked with a retrograde movement from the south; in other words, with the Northern Point tradition. This is in any case more probable than a derivation from Asia, where there seem to be no parallels that fit.

According to J.L. Giddings it is possible that the tradition of notched points at Palisades II recurs in the 'Old Whaling culture' which he also discovered on Cape Krusenstern in the summer of 1959. It was observed that whale bones were to be found under the sod on the fifty-third beach ridge, situated 1.5 kilometers from the sea, as well as on neighboring ridges. In the end it was possible to localize a combined summer and winter settlement which when excavated yielded some surprises. In the first place it became apparent that the people who had once settled here had subsisted by hunting small species of whale and seal. The large spearheads and smaller arrowheads, all with notched basal parts, are of unusual shape,

Fig. 16 - Finds from Palisades, Cape Krusenstern, northwestern Alaska. The pieces in the top row and the large one in the center are designated Palisades I, and all the others as Palisades II. After J.L. Giddings and H.-G. Bandi (1962).

but in general are more regular in shape and larger than the points from Palisades II; on the other hand, it is striking that they are relatively thick compared with other prehistoric specimens from Alaska. The latter also holds true for other flint implements, such as scrapers, which likewise have notch-

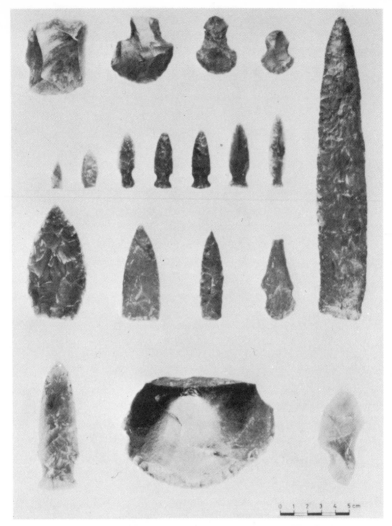

Fig. 17 - Stone implements of the Old Whaling culture. After J.L. Giddings
         and H.-G. Bandi (1962).

ed bases (Fig. 17). There is nothing to suggest that links existed with the American Epi-Gravettian tradition. On the other
hand, one may note the large broad pieces, thought to have
served as inset points for harpoon heads used in whaling; these
are retouched bifacially. Grinding of stone seems to have been

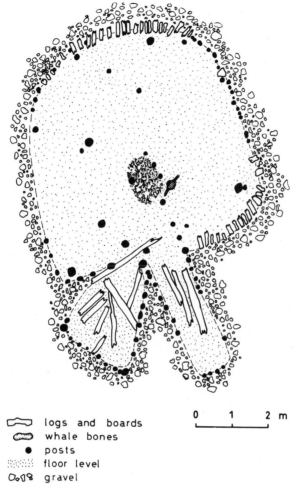

☐ logs and boards
◐ whale bones
● posts
░ floor level
○₀○⊗ gravel

0   1   2 m

Fig. 18 - Ground plan of a house from the Old Whaling culture on Cape Kru-
    senstern, northwestern Alaska. On the left, next to the narrow en-
    trance passage, a trapezoidal annex; the open hearth was in the cen-
    ter of the main room, the rear wall of which bulges out like an apse.
    After J. L. Giddings and H.-G. Bandi (1962).

unfamiliar, pottery is likewise absent. Hitherto only a few objects have been found where the substance is organic, including a piece which Giddings describes as a toggle harpoon head
used in seal-hunting.

The ruins of winter dwellings from the Old Whaling culture have a more or less round ground plan, an entrance passage about 3.5 meters long, and from one to three 'annexes'. In the center of the main room, which on the average measured 5 x 6 meters, was a hearth (Fig. 18). The summer dwellings, which were probably tent-like and rather large, had an oval ground plan. The animal bones found show that the inhabitants kept dogs. Radiocarbon measurements which have been begun in Philadelphia suggest that the Old Whaling culture may be assigned to the period between 4000 and 3500 years ago, and most probably is some 3800 years old.

It would be rather difficult to correlate this newly discovered culture with any other groups in the Eskimo area unless it were possible to establish a connection with Palisades II, and thus indirectly with the Northern Point tradition which was regarded as a 'feedback' from the south.

After this digression we may return to the development of the small-tool cultures in the Bering Strait area. As has been noted, J.L. Giddings came across three different cultural strata in 1948 when he carried out excavations at Iyatayet, at Cape Denbigh on Norton Sound. The lowest layer contained graceful implements of chert, jasper, chalcedony and obsidian, but unfortunately not a single object of organic matter. Radiocarbon dating together with paleoclimatic and geological data made it probable that this very thin layer of artifacts must be ascribed to the period between 5000 and 4500 years ago.

As already mentioned, this inventory of stone implements was termed by Giddings the Denbigh Flint complex. He divides it into several categories: first, forms well known from the Old World Paleolithic and Mesolithic; secondly, implements which can be correlated with characteristic projectile points of the Paleo-Indian and Archaic cultures of the New World, in other words with the Northern Point tradition; thirdly, carefully prepared cores and microblades, the latter often reworked by retouching; finally, types of which most are either found universally or else occur only sporadically, thus affording no evidence for the cultural classification of the complex (Fig. 21).

Prominent in the first group are burins. In my view three categories can be distinguished: first, true burins, not distinguishable from the Mesolithic types of the Old World; then those produced from pieces already retouched on one or both surfaces, which can be called 'retouched burins'; finally, a form which I should like to term 'pseudo-burin', for, although it apparently was made by striking off typical burin spalls, close observation shows that this did not produce the cutting edge of a true burin, but instead a triangular point. J.L. Giddings succeeded in establishing that the spalls, which I proposed to call pseudo-burin spalls, are different from the usual burin spalls, because they frequently bear at the lower end traces of fine secondary reworking, or at least of retouching caused by use. They seem to have served as tools, so that they may be called spall burins once employment of this kind is identifiable. In contrast to other types of burins, the pseudo- and the spall burin seem to be absent in the Old World and may thus be a phenomenon which appeared in Alaska in the context of the American Epi-Gravettian tradition, though it is still possible that in the future these types will be found in northeastern Asia.

The second group of Giddings' classification of the Denbigh material includes a fluted point and a few other points with carefully worked parallel retouching. This leads to the obvious assumption that the Northern Point tradition exerted an influence here.

The third group is distinguished mainly by small blades detached from cores of a fairly regular shape, most of them polyhedral. Microblades of this kind were used to make small narrow artifacts, which take on a very thin shape because of the extremely careful parallel and diagonal retouching, mostly on both surfaces. As regards the small double points, these were probably attached to the front of arrowheads of antler or bone; on the other hand, those that are crescent-shaped or scalenes probably were fixed in slots or grooves along the sides of such weapons.

Of the fourth group we may single out only some small broad and isosceles points with concave bases and parallel flaking. These bear so great a resemblance to corresponding pieces which were discovered in the Ipiutak culture in association with harpoon heads, to be discussed later, that Giddings thinks it very likely that they served a similar purpose.

In the Denbigh Flint complex we are thus dealing with an industry which on one hand fits into the framework of the American Epi-Gravettian tradition but at the same time seems to have a considerable intermixture of other elements. Although we do not know what organic matter went with it, it is very likely that the population concerned hunted small sea-mammals, especially seal.

In this connection an account may be given of the results which Helge Larsen and his collaborators obtained in 1949-50 when they investigated two caves on Trail Creek, some fifty kilometers south of Deering in the interior of Seward Peninsula (Figs. 19, 20). In Cave 2, measuring approximately 21 meters in length and not quite 2 meters in width at the entrance, the lowest part of the sediment, consisting of clay, yielded slender arrowheads made of antler with grooves along the sides with inset blades of flint. Some of these are decorated with simple geometric designs, and according to Larsen recall types of the Mesolithic Maglemosian culture in northern Europe. Above these were specimens which Larsen

2 ↓   ↓ 9

9
←

←
2

Fig. 19 - Limestone rocks with the Trail Creek Caves, Seward Peninsula. (Caves 2 and 9 are situated at the point of intersection of the numbered arrows). Photo by courtesy of Helge Larsen.

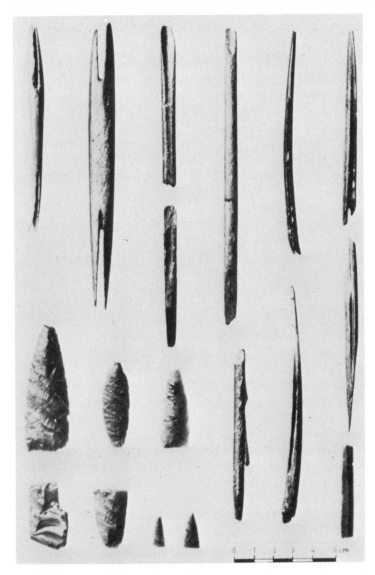

Fig. 20 - Artifacts from the Trail Creek Caves. According to H. Larsen, the
three pieces on the extreme right may be a little earlier than Denbigh; the four arrowheads made of antler depicted next to them, as
well as some of the flint points, he correlates with the Denbigh Flint
complex; the other finds (left half of the illustration) are of a later
date (Choris and Near Ipiutak). Photo by courtesy of H. Larsen.

ascribes to the Denbigh Flint complex, the Choris culture, Near Ipiutak, the Western Thule culture, and to even more recent phases.

Similar discoveries were made in Cave 9, in which Ipiutak arrowpoints lay on the surface of the sediment. Remains of willow roots unearthed from a depth of approximately 80 cm were dated by radiocarbon analysis to 5993 ± 280 years ago; among them was a fragment of a retouched blade. It thus appears that the Trail Creek Caves have yielded on the one hand objects earlier in date than the Denbigh Flint complex but on the other some which bridge the gap between Denbigh and Ipiutak.

Also noteworthy is the fact that traces of the Denbigh Flint complex were discovered north of Kotzebue at Cape Krusenstern as well: in one instance a little below the Palisades site, on the landward shore of the great lagoon, approximately 60 meters above the present sea level; in the other instance on the innermost of the 100 beach ridges that lie between the lagoon and the sea shore, and which must have been formed after the end of the climatic optimum, i.e. after 6000 years ago, as has been mentioned above (Fig. 21).

On the other hand the Denbigh Flint complex has not yet been authenticated on the Siberian shore of the Bering Strait. It is also rather unlikely that offshoots of this relatively late phase of the American Epi-Gravettian tradition will ever be discovered in that region.

There are other groups which can as yet only be authenticated on the American shore of the Bering Strait. First there is the Battle Rock phase, which J.L. Giddings has established on the basis of a rich find in a large stone-lined multiple burial north of Cape Krusenstern, and has interpreted as a link between the Denbigh Flint complex and Ipiutak; he says that 'the styles of projectile points show a close relationship to Norton culture, but the large size of all the Battle Rock pieces and a new engraving style indicate that the dating will prove to be earlier than Near Ipiutak at Point Hope.' But we know too little about this to be able to venture a firm opinion.

Not very much is as yet known either about the Choris culture, which J.L. Giddings discovered in 1956 and 1958 when examining ruins of huge oval houses situated on relatively

Fig. 21 - Stone implements of the Denbigh Flint complex, from the innermost beach ridges on Cape Krusenstern, northwestern Alaska. After J.L. Giddings and H.-G. Bandi (1962).

early beach ridges on Choris Peninsula on Kotzebue Sound. He ascribes them to the period about 2650 years ago or earlier. The stone implements seem to have certain features in

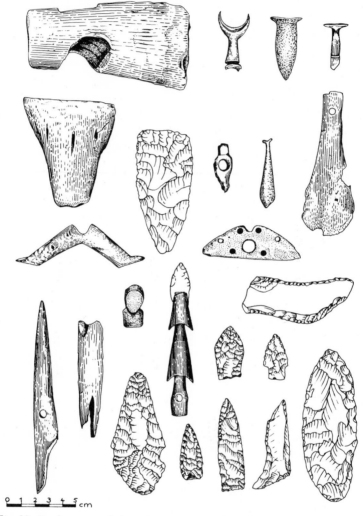

0 1 2 3 4 5 cm

Fig. 22 - Implements of the Choris culture. Redrawn after J.L. Giddings (1961).

common with the forms of the Denbigh Flint complex, especially the projectile points with carefully worked diagonal and parallel flaking; on the other hand, there is an absence of the microblade technique, burins and inset blades for arrowheads. There is a rather large number of flint tools, such as knives, scrapers, drills, and adzes, frequently roundish in shape. Slate was only rarely used and then not particularly well ground. Among artifacts of organic matter one may note simple toggle harpoon heads, needles and a few small human figures. Ivory is occasionally incised with fine lines. There is also evidence that labrets were worn (Fig. 22).

There is also some pottery, the clay being tempered with fibers or feathers and well-fired; the outside was decorated with a linear pattern stamped by means of paddle-shaped instruments. The Choris people also used stone lamps.

From the animal bones excavated it may be assumed that caribou-hunting played the foremost part, whereas seal do not seem to have been of such great importance. There is no evidence of dogs.

Giddings thinks it possible that the Choris culture forms a stage in the development of the Denbigh Flint complex toward more recent culture forms. He has authenticated the Choris culture also on Cape Krusenstern, on the 50th beach ridge and also on some more recent ones. The adjacent ridges 39-35 yielded remains of the somewhat different Norton culture, which as its name shows, is mainly centered a little further to the south. This facies was established by Giddings for the first time when excavations were carried out at Iyatayet on Cape Denbigh, between the layer containing Denbigh material and a more recent culture named Nukleet after another site close by. On the basis of several radiocarbon analyses he estimates it to a period between 400 B.C. and shortly after the beginning of the Christian era. The Norton settlements investigated on Cape Denbigh revealed rectangular houses with short entrance passages, which Giddings regards as permanent winter dwellings occupied each successive year by a population living on the coast, though it obtained some of its means of subsistence by hunting further inland. The stone implements, usually of basalt or silicified slate, take on the form appropriate to the function they fulfill, but are otherwise usually a little irregular; they include small inset blades and points with retouching on both surfaces, knives, scrapers and drills. Large crescentic slate knives are ground in a cursory fashion, whereas elongated labrets, some of them made of jade, and adze blades are sometimes elaborately polished. Such polished adzes were still absent in the Choris culture, as were stone net-sinkers and oil lamps which in Norton occur frequently, the sinkers probably designed for salmon-fishing. By comparison with slightly earlier or roughly contemporaneous cultures, such as Okvik or Ipiutak, one is also struck by the fact that all these objects are executed unevenly and less carefully. Statistics published by Giddings show that the weapons of the Norton people on Cape Denbigh were chiefly used for hunting small seals (68%) and large seals (18%), whereas only 6% of the bones assembled were from the white whale (beluga) and the walrus respectively, and the remaining 2% from the caribou. The Norton ceramics consist mainly of small and rather thin-walled vessels, with a bottom which may be convex, flat or concave. The clay is tempered with sand and well-fired. The outer sides have a good deal of decoration, in most cases check-stamped designs, but in rare instances linear ones. One single crudely-worked armless figure is an indication of ivory carving. Ornaments seem to have been of no great importance.

Giddings mentions a strong relationship between Choris and Norton, with the latter manifesting some new elements; but he also emphasizes links with southern Alaska and the Aleutians as well as with the Near Ipiutak culture centered further to the north. D.E. Dumond says that 'people of the Norton-like horizon were spread from the Alaska Peninsula to the Mackenzie River by the beginning of the Christian era, and were the linguistic and to an extent the cultural ancestors of all modern Eskimos.'

Before these questions are discussed, however, other happenings in the Bering Strait area must be considered. For this purpose, one must turn to the Asiatic shore, not only the Siberian mainland, but also St. Lawrence Island, which is much more easily accessible from the west than it is from Alaska.

Bibliography: Ackerman, 1962; Bandi, 1963; Chard, 1955; Giddings, 1949, 1950, 1951, 1952b, 1955, 1956a, 1960a, 1960b, 1962b, 1962c, 1963, 1964; Hopkins and Giddings, 1953; Jenness, 1928a; Larsen, 1951, 1953, 1962; Laughlin, 1967; Skarland and Keim, 1958.

3. The Asiatic Shore

The earliest group of specimens hitherto known on the Asiatic shore of the Bering Strait belongs to the Okvik culture. It is reported that the name originates from the St. Lawrence Eskimos who assisted Otto Geist in excavating a site he discovered in 1931, on the largest and most northerly of the three Punuk islets east of St. Lawrence Island; since large quantities of ivory were found the locality was referred to as 'Okvik', which means 'that place where many walrus came on land'; the word has to be pronounced as *Oochvik*. Later F.G. Rainey used the name to designate this cultural phase in the Siberian area of the Bering Strait. More recently S.J. Rudenko established the Okvik culture in what he believes to be a somewhat earlier form near Uelen on Cape Dezhnev (East Cape), and suggests the double term 'Uelen-Okvik'.

The dating of Okvik presents some difficulties since radiocarbon analyses have produced very divergent results and have even opened up the possibility that the Old Bering Sea culture, to be discussed below, might be earlier than Okvik. Contrary to findings which ascribe Okvik to a relatively late period, in any case to the Christian era, Giddings assumes that the most likely measurement is one suggesting an age of 2258 ± 230 years. This was taken from a sample originating from another Okvik site, Hillside, near Gambell in the northwest of St. Lawrence Island. Here excavations were first carried out in 1939 by H.B. Collins, and were taken up later by J.L. Giddings, who believes in an earlier Okvik stage which he puts at approximately 300 B.C. or earlier (Okvik I), and a more recent one between 300 B.C. and 100 A.D. (Okvik 2). From a chronological point of view, the latter seems to run roughly parallel to the earliest phase of the Old Bering Sea culture. In recent years the Russians seem to be more and more inclined to think that Okvik was synchronous with a developed form of the Old Bering Sea culture. This corresponds to the fact that an Okvik house excavated in the summer of 1967 at Hillside near Gambell gave me a C-14 date of 1370 ± 60 B.P. (B-892).

The area in which the Okvik culture spread, so far as is at present known, comprised the coastal areas of the Chukchi Peninsula from Nunligran in the east by way of Cape Chaplin in the south to Cape Dezhnev in the north, probably radiating as far as Cape Baranov some 70 kilometers east of the mouth of the Kolyma; also St. Lawrence Island with the Punuk islets. Its influence reached the Diomede Islands and even north-western Alaska, as we shall see when discussing the Ipiutak and Birnirk cultures; and probably also southwestern Alaska, the Aleutians, Kodiak Island and Central Southern Alaska in the Cook Inlet area.

Since the type site afforded no clues to the nature of Okvik dwellings, we have to depend mainly on the Hillside site mentioned above. It was here that Giddings discovered a house ruin with a round ground plan, at least partly subterranean, about six meters in diameter, with a paved floor and an open hearth in the center; this is all that could be established. Two other houses excavated by Collins may perhaps also be ascribed to the Okvik culture. Since they are rectangular in plan with an entrance passage, Giddings presumes that a change in the house type took place during the second Okvik stage.

For a description of the Okvik material (Fig. 23) we are indebted in the first place to F.G. Rainey and S.J. Rudenko. It is evident that it was a culture highly specialized in sea-mammal hunting. This can be authenticated chiefly by the presence of fully developed toggle harpoon heads used in hunting seals, walrus and whales, as well as other parts of harpoons and implements connected with this kind of hunting. In addition, polar bears were hunted, and on the mainland caribou and of course small mammals and birds as well; fishing has likewise been proved.

Sleds were known in the form of heavy and light hand-drawn vehicles for the transport of umiaks or loads across the ice, or for hunting expeditions. Sleds drawn by dogs do not seem to have been in use as yet, although bones of dogs have been found; it is possible that these dogs were raised mainly for their meat. Besides the hand-drawn sleds there were baleen toboggans. In connection with winter transportation there are the Okvik snow goggles, of which Rainey, however, found only one example. A striking feature of these are the curious round apertures for the eyes, which differ from the narrow slits in the goggles used in other Eskimo cultures; otherwise the shape is similar. Another interesting feature is the 'ice creep-

Fig. 23 - Typical finds from the Ikvik culture. Photo by courtesy of K. Birket-
   Smith.

er' used to prevent skidding on slippery ice, like the modern
crampon.

The umiak can be authenticated indirectly, from whaling harpoons, and the kayak directly by discovery of parts of equipment.

There are a large number of toggle harpoon heads, of various types. Rainey distinguishes five major and five minor types. The most common has an open socket, a multi-pronged spur, sharp edges (no inset side-blades), an inset point oriented in the same way as the line hole, or else the blade is inset laterally. Large harpoons suitable for whaling are clearly in the minority. In connection with harpoon heads and hunting with harpoons, the foreshafts, socket-pieces, finger-rests, ice picks, plugs for sealskin floats, harpoon supports for kayaks etc., must be considered. Lances, spears, throwing-boards and bows which seem to have been used for hunting birds with blunt arrows, as well as multi-pronged bird darts, fish-spears with leisters, and fishhooks were lines of hunting equipment. Arrowheads with long barbs were used for fighting.

Besides projectile points and implements such as knives, drills or scrapers of retouched flint-like material, we observe men's knives and ulus in ground slate, and polished axe blades mostly of basalt. Objects of bone, antler, walrus, ivory or wood include flaking tools, parts of drills, tools for skin work (i.e. fat and blubber-scrapers, awls, needles and needle-cases), picks and mattocks of ivory or bone to break up the ice and to obtain turf, shovels made of seal and walrus shoulder blades and such household utensils as fire drills and oval or round containers of wood. In the same category is the Okvik pottery, found in small fragments, which was crudely tempered and inadequately fired. A few pieces showed lineal decoration. Rainey concludes that they belong to simple cooking pots and lamps.

The ornaments consisted of pendants, beads and buttons of organic material. About the clothing of the Okvik people we have only indirect evidence, which we owe to the fact that small human figures, most of them carved of walrus ivory, are a rather frequent element in this culture. One figure has traces of a lavishly decorated parka such as was worn by the Alaska Eskimos and their Siberian kinsmen in historic times. The figures also show that facial tattooing already played an important part in Okvik culture, the marks being similar to those of Eskimo women until very recently or even today. In most cases the figures have a carefully worked elongated head, whereas the shaping of the body was indefinite, and legs are almost entirely lacking. Rainey interprets the Okvik figures as idols and mentions that until recently the crews of whaling boats from St. Lawrence Island still took with them carved wooden figurines, which also played a part in whale-hunting ceremonies, whereafter they were burnt or otherwise destroyed. For this reason he believes that most of these Okvik figures are probably to be regarded as auxiliary spirits, or had some similar significance in contrast to the small toy dolls of other Eskimos. This is comparable to the customs of the Chukchi and Koryak. In this context we may also recall that the female figurines widely disseminated in the Old World Upper Paleolithic probably originated in the eastern Gravettian area, where they were erected in dwellings and may have been venerated as the 'ruler of animals'. Particularly curious is a carving known as 'the Madonna of Okvik', representing a woman with a peculiar facial expression, holding a child or more probably a dog or a bear in her hands (Fig. 24). Rarer are animal figures such as whales, seals, walrus, polar bears, dogs or birds; they show a distinct predilection for fantastic forms. Most of these, too, are interpreted by Rudenko as ceremonial objects.

Very frequently the most varied objects of Okvik culture are lavishly decorated with engraved ornaments. The motifs used, such as spurred lines, Y-figures, nucleated circles, parallel lines and ladder-like patterns, are the same as those of the Old Bering Sea and Punuk cultures. But the way in which the single motifs were combined with one another must be regarded as a characteristic feature of Okvik; the whole impression seems more simple, less regular and less harmonious than examples in the Old Bering Sea culture. Parallel with the two Okvik stages, according to Giddings, a distinction must be made between two different styles of which the second is identical with the ornamentation from the beginning of the Old Bering Sea culture. Collins claims that he can identify two further distinctions, but relevant stratigraphic evidence has not as yet been discovered.

But let us return once more briefly to the religious concepts and customs of the Okvik people, which has already been mentioned in connection with their carved human figures. It is noteworthy that two small mask-like carvings and also some of

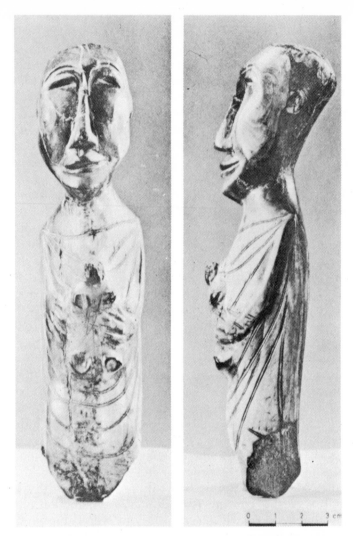

Fig. 24 - 'The Madonna of Okvik'. Ivory carving from the type site of the Okvik culture on the Punuk islets. Photo by courtesy of J. Meldgaard.

the animal figures seem to have been fastened on to something, so that one cannot help drawing a comparison with the
iron objects used by Siberian shamans; in a similar way chains
with several links carved from a single piece of ivory and other
curious objects can be correlated with regalia worn by Siber-

ian shamans. Rainey mentions that one piece identified as an Eskimo tambourine may indicate the long cultural history of the drum in Eskimo culture. Rudenko, on the other hand, is of the opinion that drums did not come into use in the Bering Strait area until the Punuk culture.

Finally, there are a number of peculiar ivory carvings, termed 'winged objects'; the central part, which has a socket, tapers off on either side to form wing-like extensions. The purpose of these objects, which are often lavishly decorated with engraved ornaments, is still in dispute. In the Okvik culture they are relatively small and simple, but they undergo a process of development during the Old Bering Sea and Punuk cultures (Figs. 26, 27). It has been assumed that they may have played a part in magical ceremonies in connection with whale or caribou hunting; the latter is less likely, since caribou never existed on St. Lawrence Island, where a considerable number of 'winged objects' have been found. Rudenko assumes that they had a head and a tail attached to them to form birds or butterflies, and were suspended in whaling ceremonies. But the careful details of these pieces lead me to believe that they had some more practical use. The most convincing hypothesis of all seems to be the one, mentioned by several authors, that they are weights fastened to the rear end of harpoon shafts in order to stabilize them. This assumption is reinforced by the fact that the Kwakiutl Indians on the northwest coast of America had harpoons with a shaft ending in a very similar shape, the object of which was to make the weapon glide along the surface of the water in the direction of the animal when it had been sighted. Finally, it must be borne in mind that there is a certain resemblance to the shape of the bannerstones found in the eastern part of the United States, which have likewise not been explained satisfactorily.

This brief description of Okvik shows that it is a fully developed culture of sea-mammal hunters with a considerable degree of specialization. Whaling did not yet play a vital part, but was no doubt known. In other respects, too, all the essential features of a culture adapted to sea-mammal hunting are found, and it is quite feasible that from an ethnic point of view its representatives were Eskimos speaking an Eskimo language.

But this raises the question of the origin of this group, which is clearly identifiable during the latter half of the last millennium B.C. There is no doubt that it must have resulted from a long process of development. Where this development took place, in Alaska or on the Asiatic shore of the Bering Strait, is a question we shall discuss later.

Stratigraphic data from St. Lawrence Island and in Siberia have shown that the Okvik culture was succeeded by the Old Bering Sea culture. It is astonishing that in 1926 Diamond Jenness could identify its existence on the basis of a handful of ivory artifacts which he had obtained from natives of the Diomede Islands. The Old Bering Sea culture has very strong links with Okvik. Specimens related to it are known from St. Lawrence Island, including the Punuk islets, from the two Diomede Islands and from the coast of Chukchi Peninsula, i.e. from Cape Bering in the south to Cape Dezhnev in the north. In Siberia its influence also penetrated as far as Cape Baranov, some 70 kilometers east of the mouth of the Kolyma River, and in Alaska it reached the Seward Peninsula, Kotzebue Sound and the northwest.

The radiocarbon datings so far given are not entirely uniform, but seem to point to the fact that the Old Bering Sea culture originated about the beginning of the Christian era. Giddings reckons with an earlier phase contemporaneous with his second Okvik phase, i.e. 300 B.C. to 100 A.D., a middle one from 100 to 300 A.D., and a more recent one from 300 to 500 A.D. Rudenko also assumes that the origins of the Old Bering Sea culture go back to the last centuries B.C., thus giving a certain chronological overlap with Okvik. He does not exclude the possibility of a purely local continuation of development based on Okvik, but in his view it was more likely that new influences from the south acted as a stimulating factor.

By and large the differences between the Okvik and Old Bering Sea cultures are not very great. The basis of subsistence was the same; whaling continued to remain relatively insignificant. The small rectangular houses which now predominated, some of them semi-subterranean, with paved floors and walls of horizontal timbers and whale bones, may possibly derive from a type which appeared during the late Okvik culture; they have a long narrow entrance passage, the floor of which is lower than that of the house, thus producing a kind of 'cold trap'.

From excavations on the Chukchi Peninsula we know that the Old Bering Sea people buried their dead in graves constructed of large bones, timbers and stones.

A new type of harpoon head appears, regarded as particularly characteristic of the Old Bering Sea culture (Fig. 25). Its features include an open socket, symmetrical three-pronged spur,

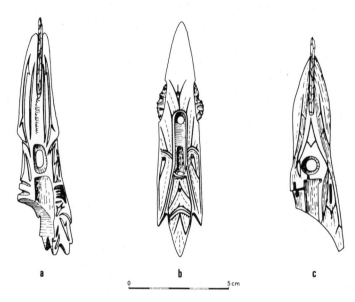

Fig. 25 - Toggle harpoon heads from the Okvik culture (a), from the Old Bering Sea culture (b), and from the Punuk culture (c). Redrawn after Rainey (1941).

two line holes and two inset side-blades set at a right angle or parallel to the line hole, no inset point at the fore end, and in most cases ample ornamentation. Toward the end of the Old Bering Sea culture or at the beginning of the subsequent Punuk culture this type of harpoon head was modified in such a way that the spur was moved toward the side and the second line hole disappeared. But the types of harpoon heads which were already well-known at the time of the Okvik culture also still occurred during the Old Bering Sea culture, sometimes with slight modifications.

In regard to stone implements it may be observed that, as usual, retouched flint artifacts are far more frequent than those of ground slate or other stone. The number of polished axe-blades and knives increase considerably however.

At the same time lamps and deep cooking-pots with thin walls and a convex bottom were made of crudely tempered and poorly fired clay. Most vessels were undecorated but in some cases were ornamented with a paddle stamp.

Also noteworthy is the fact that 'winged objects' of the Old Bering Sea culture were of a different shape than those of Okvik, in that their lateral extensions became larger and more rounded. They are often referred to as butterfly-shaped (Figs. 26, 27).

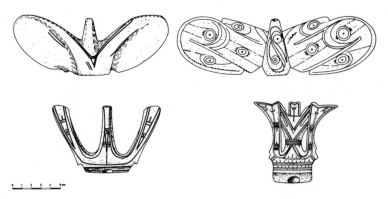

Fig. 26 - Above: 'Winged objects' decorated in Okvik and Old Bering Sea style; below: 'Tridents' and other objects of the Punuk culture.

It is of interest, too, that the use of iron has been established by the discovery of an engraving tool with an iron point in a grave at the cemetery at Uelen on Cape Dezhnev (East Cape). This find is not only of importance in regard to the ornamental style of the Old Bering Sea culture, to be discussed below, but also shows that metal became known relatively early in the extreme northeast of Siberia. This tallies with the reference in Chinese sources to the working of iron on the northern Pacific coast as early as the third century B.C. It is thus possible that smaller quantities may have reached the Bering Strait area at the time of the Old Bering Sea culture, or possibly even during the Okvik culture.

The most characteristic feature of the Old Bering Sea culture is, however, the ornamental decorations. They are in a fully-fledged and variegated 'curvilinear' style, in which three stages may be identified. According to Collins, style 1 (parallel to Okvik 2) is still relatively simple and primarily linear. Rudenko mentions an abundance of radial lines, long and short spurs and broken lines, concentric circles and slightly curved lines. This means that all the basic elements of Old Bering Sea decoration are present, but not all their possibilities are yet realized. Style 2 is highly curvilinear and differs to a certain degree from style 1 though it uses the same design elements: straight, curved and broken lines, short spurs, and hand-drawn circles between diverging lines. It often concentrates on the decoration of rounded ivory surfaces. Style 3 is distinguished

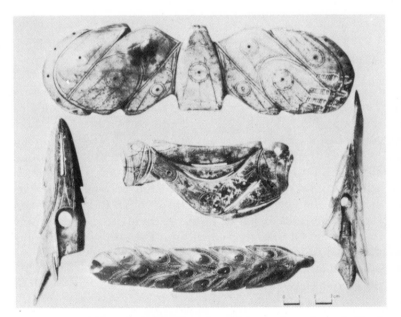

Fig. 27 - Decorated ivory carvings from the Old Bering Sea culture. Left and center: style 2; above, right and below: style 3. Photo by courtesy of the Smithsonian Institution.

mainly by the incorporation of numerous raised bosses, framed by relatively large concentric circles or ellipses. Frequently the bosses are arranged in pairs with inlays of jade in the center, giving the impression of eyes. Between stages 1 and 2 and also between 2 and 3, there are gradual transitions.

Although after the end of the Old Bering Sea culture there is some continuity of development on the Siberian side of the Bering Strait, the subsequent Punuk culture changes in some respects. Giddings believes that during the sixth century A.D., an influence was exerted by the Birnirk culture, which had developed in the meantime in northwestern Alaska, thus creating a transitional phase, influenced by Birnirk, between the Old Bering Sea culture and that of Punuk. Rudenko associates the development of the Punuk culture with the interruption of relations with the areas south of the Bering Strait while at the same time strong influences from northeastern Asia made themselves felt during the third or fourth century A.D. Basing his theory on some radiocarbon datings from St. Lawrence Island, Giddings assigns early Punuk to 600 - 900 A.D., and the fully developed Punuk to 900 - 1100 A.D. Then from 1100 - 1500 A.D. there was a late phase influenced by Western Thule culture.

The Punuk culture, as we know, was discovered by H.B. Collins in 1928 on the northernmost and largest of the three Punuk islets east of St. Lawrence Island. The chronological position of Punuk culture was identified by finds on St. Lawrence Island at the three sites of Miyowagh, Ievoghiyoq and Seklowaghyaget, near Gambell, and also at Kukulik mound, situated a little further to the east near Savoonga. The area in which Punuk culture was disseminated is roughly the same as that of the Old Bering Sea culture. On St. Lawrence Island the number and extent of Punuk settlements is greater than those of the Old Bering Sea culture. From this one may draw the conclusion that an increase of population occurred. On the Asiatic mainland traces of Punuk settlements have been identified from Cape Bering in the southeast of the Chukchi Peninsula to Cape Dezhnev (East Cape) in the north. Its influence also extended in Alaska from Cape Prince of Wales in the extreme west of Seward Peninsula as far north as Point Hope and Point Barrow.

The way of life of the Punuk people was by and large the same as that of the Old Bering Sea people; but whaling may have increased in importance. Dwellings were constructed similarly, the only difference being that they were larger; whale bones, especially skulls, were frequently employed as building material. Large bones from whales and walrus were also used for the construction of burials. Such graves, which remind one of those of the Siberian Old Bering Sea culture, have recently been found near Gambell on St. Lawrence Island. During the late Punuk culture the dog-drawn sled appears as well as types formerly familiar. Most of the equipment is either the same as in the preceding stage or evolved from it. In the case of toggle harpoon heads we note the appearance of a new type which is somewhat simpler in form than the earlier ones. Among its characteristic features, in addition to open and closed sockets, are a more or less clearly marked lateral spur, no lateral inset blades, but an inset point at the front which could be placed parallel with or vertical to the line hole, and finally decorations in typically Punuk style (Fig. 25). Ground implements now occur much more frequently than flaked ones.

Another peculiar feature is that 'winged objects' do not occur any longer, but are succeeded by the so-called 'tridents', which may have had a similar function. They may be associated with another category of elaborately worked carvings, collectively known as 'wedge-shaped objects'. In my view one can detect here influences of the Scytho-Siberian animal style, a phenomenon which shall be discussed in connection with Ipiutak culture.

Punuk ornaments have associations with those of the Old Bering Sea culture, and like these appear to have been executed, in some cases at least, with the aid of engraving tools with a metal point. But new decorative elements also appear which are probably derived from external influences.

The Punuk sites have yielded only isolated naturalistic whale and seal figures or stylized human sculptures. All the more striking, therefore, is the torso of an ivory figurine found at the type site on the northernmost Punuk islet; it not only represents a pregnant woman in a realistic manner but also is strongly reminiscent of Upper Paleolithic sculptures in Siberia

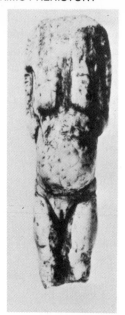

Fig. 28 - Female torso. Ivory carving of the Punuk culture, from the northernmost of the three Punuk islets. Photo by courtesy of the Smithsonian
Institution.

and further west (Fig. 28). And finally it must be pointed out
that stimuli from Siberia were responsible for the introduction
into the Punuk culture of a whole series of new elements which
were absent from the preceding stages: for example, plate-armor made of bone. The origin of this equipment may be traced
back to Japan, whereas its sporadic appearance in Alaska is
doubtless due to influences from Siberia. Other novel features
are the reinforced bow, some hitherto unknown types of ivory
arrowheads and wrist guards, the appearance of which, together with the plate-armor, is explained by Rudenko as the
result of an advance by hostile groups of people into northeastern Siberia or of a gradual spread of such weapons and
equipment, probably together with more advanced techniques
of warfare, in the direction of the Bering Strait. Also noteworthy are the bola used for catching birds, a claw-like scratcher
employed in sealing, heavy ivory net-sinkers, long knives and
daggers of the same material, long-handled spoons of bone or

antler, and the shaman's drum; the latter had hitherto played only an insignificant role, if indeed any role at all, in the Eskimo cultures of the Bering Strait area.

From approximately the beginning or middle of the last millennium B.C. there appeared in the Bering Strait area, including St. Lawrence Island, several closely related cultures — Okvik, Old Bering Sea, and Punuk — which followed in direct sequence, partly overlapping one another. They may be considered highly specialized Eskimo cultures. The means of subsistence was derived mainly from the hunting of sea-mammals, including the whale. The large supply of this kind of game, as well as of land-mammals, birds and fish, in the Bering Strait area enabled the natives to develop and improve their hunting methods, weapons and implements. It also gave them the leisure in which to decorate innumerable objects with engraved ornaments or carved figures. Hunting may well have been concentrated in the first place upon the walrus, of which large numbers were in existence; this provided meat and fat for food, blubber for lamps, skins for roofing houses, boat coverings and thongs, as well as bone for implements and ivory particularly well-suited for carved utensils and figures. In addition foreign influences were continually making themselves felt from different directions, introducing new cultural elements, social and religious as well as material.

It has been suggested that the late Punuk culture on the Asiatic shore of the Bering Strait may have been influenced by the Western Thule culture, which had in the meantime also appeared in the Point Barrow area in the context of the Birnirk culture. Although the Arctic coast of Siberia between Cape Dezhnev (East Cape) and the mouth of the Kolyma has not yet been adequately explored, Rudenko thinks it possible that the Western Thule culture found its way also into this zone. Thus it appears as if there evolved from the late Punuk culture, which was to some extent influenced by that of Thule, a late prehistoric cultural form which survived into historic times.

Bibliography: Ackerman, 1961, 1967; Arutyunov, Levin and Sergeyev, 1964; Arutyunov and Sergeyev, 1964; Beregovaia, 1957; Collins, 1935, 1937a, 1937b, 1940; Geist and Rainey,

1936; Giddings, 1960a, 1960b; Jenness, 1928a; Larsen (in press); Levin, 1959, 1960, 1964; Levin and Sergeyev, 1964; Michael, 1964; Rainey, 1941; Rudenko, 1961, 1964.

4. Later Development On The American Side

On the American side of Bering Strait, where Norton culture existed from 400 B.C. to the beginning of the Christian era, subsequent developments were different in spite of the fact that connections certainly existed with other Eskimo cultures across the Strait. There is still a period of about one thousand years for which no evidence has yet been found, although the gap will probably be filled in the future, chiefly by Norton derivatives. Giddings, however, is doubtful whether the Nukleet culture, which appeared between approximately 1100/1200 and 1600/1700 A.D. is derived directly from Norton. This culture, as has been mentioned, is named after a site on Cape Denbigh on Norton Sound. During the relatively long period for which it existed the Nukleet culture does not appear to have undergone any important modifications; nevertheless Giddings believes that he can distinguish three successive phases of development, of which the earliest (approximately eleventh and twelfth centuries A.D.) is reminiscent of the early Punuk, whereas the middle one (approximately thirteenth and fourteenth centuries A.D.) has firmer links with northwestern Alaska, and the more recent one has a predominantly local character. The means of livelihood seem to have been much the same throughout: hunting sea-mammals (without any, or with only slight importance being attached to whaling), fishing and, in the interior, caribou hunting. The population of the first stage lived in semi-subterranean dwellings with long, deep entrance passages. Characteristic features of the middle phase of the Nukleet culture include ground slate implements, carving with beaver teeth, the working of birch bark, and thick-walled pottery inferior to that of the preceding Norton culture in regard to tempering and firing. The associations with the Punuk culture finds expression chiefly in toggle harpoon heads and ivory carvings.

During the second Nukleet stage harpoon heads and arrowheads show influences of the Western Thule culture of north-western Alaska, as well as strong local traditions.

Nukleet III is distinguished by a new type of pottery: clay tempered with sand and fragments of shell was used to make large vessels with fine decoration. According to Giddings this may be due to influences from Kamchatka and the Kuriles. He states 'that we are dealing with a pottery complex that derives little out of the older base of north Alaskan pottery form and methods, and it indicates the time of arrival in rather definite relative terms. However, the ways in which this transmission may have taken place across the lower Bering Sea, or the North Pacific Ocean, are still obscure.' The final stage of the Nukleet culture forms a bridge to a late prehistoric phase and to historic times.

Bibliography: Giddings, 1949, 1964; Griffin, 1953; Hopkins and Giddings, 1953.

SOUTHWESTERN ALASKA

Further southward between Norton Sound and Bristol Bay, there lies a vast *terra incognita*. Information from this region is from the work carried out by a group of scholars under the direction of Helge Larsen in Bristol Bay and Kuskokwim Bay in 1948. Near Platinum, at the entrance to Goodnews Bay, and to the north and south of it in Nanvak Bay and Chagvan Bay, near Cape Newenham, relatively early cultural remains could be established which, according to Larsen, show associations on the one hand with cultures such as Norton, Near Ipiutak and Ipiutak further north, and on the other hand with prehistoric cultures on the Aleutian Islands and in Central Southern Alaska. In the excavation at Platinum it was possible to identify particularly distinct links with Ipiutak on the basis of a large number of retouched stone implements and the absence of pottery; but its individuality is emphasized by stone lamps, drills and notched net-sinkers. At Nanvak Bay and Chagvan Bay pottery was found resembling that of the Norton culture; it was made of finely tempered clay, thin-walled, well-fired, and featured stamped or linear decorations. In addition, Larsen's explorations in the Bristol Bay area led to the discovery of further earlier complexes near Pavik, near Naknek on Kvichak Bay, near Dillingham in the interior of the Nushagak Bay area and at Platinum.

In the meantime, L.S. Cressman and D.E. Dumond have published the results of field work which they carried out in 1960-61 in the region drained by the Naknek River on the northern Alaska Peninsula. They were particularly active in the area of Brooks River, which connects Brooks Lake with Naknek Lake. Traces of earliest frequentation are assigned to the 'Brooks River Gravels phase', which dates from the first half of the second millennium B.C. and is associated with the Arctic Small-Tool tradition, i.e. with the American Epi-Gravettian. In the subsequent 'Brooks River Hilltop phase', which is assigned to the latter half of the second millennium, it is possible also to identify links with cultures in which there is a tendency toward small tools. No objects are yet available from the first millennium B.C. At the beginning of the first millennium A.D. a culture appeared whose 'check-stamped' ceramic ware and stone implements were reminiscent of the Norton culture. This 'Smelt Creek phase' led to the 'Brooks River Weir phase' and toward the end of the first millennium A.D. to the 'Brooks River Knoll phase'. A characteristic feature of the latter is the presence of ground slate implements. These diminish in importance during the following 'Brooks River Falls phase' about 1000 A.D., and become more important in the 'Brooks River Camp phase' around 1200 or 1300 A.D. After that development proceeded continuously, flowing into a late prehistoric Eskimo occupation (Brooks River Bluff phase) and a post-contact phase (Pavik).

In 1964 D.E. Dumond extended his work to the Pacific coast of the Alaska Peninsula where he seems to have come across some interesting discoveries. Among them are said to be parallels with two Ocean Bay phases on Kodiak Island, which will be discussed later.

Helge Larsen's studies were also carried on in 1962 by R.E. Ackerman, who worked mainly at Chagvan Bay and also visited Platinum, Nanvak Bay and Security Cove near Cape Newenham. In the Security Cove area he was able to assemble on the

surface an inventory of stone implements characterized princi-
pally by side- and corner-notched projectile points or knife
blades as well as scrapers, sections of bifacially flaked knives
or large points, large bifaces, choppers and net-sinkers. Ackerman correlates this 'Security Cove phase' with the material
from Cape Krusenstern which Giddings termed Palisades II,
and points to other similar groups of objects in the interior of
Alaska which have already been mentioned. Ackerman also
describes the 'Chagvan Bay Bluff and Beach phases', which he
regards as a continuation of the Denbigh-Norton development.
Both of them are distinguished by the addition of hair temper
to pottery, as is also the case in Dumond's Smelt Creek phase,
which begins at approximately the same time.

Finally, relatively recent settlements have been investigated
by W. Oswalt in the Hooper Bay area, roughly halfway between the mouths of the Yukon and the Kuskokwim, and on
Kaflia Bay in the Katmai National Monument, opposite Kodiak
Island; and separately by W.A. Davis near Kukak, a little north
of Kaflia.

This review may show that there is reason to regard southwestern Alaska as a promising area for archeological research.
In the few places where excavations have been carried out,
vital discoveries have been made. Whether it will be necessary
to retain all the terms introduced for the various cultures, only
the future can tell; some simplification and coordination ought
to be possible. Of particular importance seems to me the discovery that stone industries from the American Epi-Gravettian area appeared at a relatively early date in southwestern
Alaska and that also the later cultural development in this region should have left distinct traces behind.

Bibliography: Ackerman, 1964; Cressman and Dumond, 1962;
Davis, 1954; Dumond, 1963, 1964, 1965; Larsen, 1950, 1953;
Oswalt, 1952, 1955; Workman, 1966.

ALEUTIAN ISLANDS, KODIAK ISLAND
AND CENTRAL SOUTHERN ALASKA

1. Aleutian Islands

Our next step takes us from the Alaska Peninsula to the Aleutians. This chain of islands, extending far into the northern Pacific, was explored by W. Jochelson and A. Hrdlička—the former very carefully, the latter rather superficially. After World War II, W.S. Laughlin set about an extensive program of investigation on the Aleutians, comprising not only archeology but also physical anthropology, linguistics and biology. The center of his excavations is situated on Umnak Island, at the eastern end of the chain, where the chief work had been carried out at the site of Chaluka, near Nikolski, which was settled for a long time. In connection with this, evidence of early infiltrations across the land bridge, already mentioned, was discovered on the small island of Anangula, off Umnak.

Some fairly well-defined radiocarbon datings show that Paleo-Aleutian culture must have reached this area no later than 4000 years ago. The representatives of this culture were already identified by A. Hrdlička as men with long and narrow skulls, whom he called 'Pre-Aleuts'. Laughlin, who regards them as a variant of the Eskimo-Aleut ethnic group, renamed them 'Paleo-Aleuts'. He describes them as distinctly Mongoloid and also points to common features with skeletons from Ipiutak on Point Hope in northwestern Alaska. On the other hand it is uncertain whether and to what extent the Paleo-Aleuts were related to the Indians of the day who inhabited the Alaskan mainland. The two races may possibly have been more closely connected than the present-day Eskimos and Aleuts are with the Indians. The Paleo-Aleut culture seems to have spread from the east along the entire island chain. It is regarded as unlikely that it originated from the west, especially since the Commander Islands, which are situated equally far from Attu, the westernmost Aleutian island, and from Kamchatka, were apparently settled as late as 1826 at the behest of the Russians, and according to Hrdlička did not yield any traces of earlier habitation. But the last word on this matter may not yet have been said. It is also uncertain whether the Paleo-

Aleuts on their arrival encountered any descendants of the pre-
vious Epi-Gravettian population, traces of which have been
discovered on Anangula Island. Laughlin mentions that the inventory of stone implements seems to point in this direction;
in the Chaluka stratigraphy blades corresponding to those from
Anangula decrease in frequency from the bottom toward the
top.

The Paleo-Aleut culture was based upon sea-mammal hunting. From the outset the whale seems to have been hunted as
well as the seal, sea otter and walrus. Accordingly we encounter an equipment comprising, *inter alia,* various types of rather

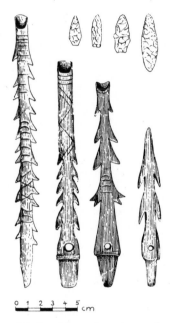

Fig. 29 - Prong harpoon heads of the Paleo-Aleut culture and corresponding
    stone points.

simple harpoon heads. Usually these have relatively long bone
prongs with barbs on both sides and a line hole on the base.
The unusual way in which a stone point was set in the front of
these weapons, which we should like to call 'prong harpoons',
distinguishes them from the typical Eskimo 'toggle harpoon'.

The Paleo-Aleut prong harpoon has a depression to receive the stone point, which is lashed to it (Fig. 29). The same technique is found in only one type of toggle harpoon in the Paleo-Aleut culture. This unusual way of fastening also occurs, as A. Leroi-Gourhan has shown, on the other side of the North Pacific, on the small island of Repum, northwest of Hokkaido. The

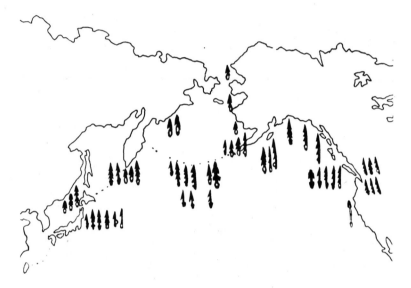

Fig. 30 - Map showing distribution of prong harpoon heads in the Bering Sea area. After A. Leroi-Gourhan (1946).

same author points out that the dissemination of prong harpoons in the North Pacific is quite peculiar. They are most frequently found on the one hand in Japan and Kamchatka and on the other on the Aleutians, on Kodiak Island and in Central Southern Alaska. In the intervening Bering Strait area prong harpoons occur much more rarely than toggle harpoons. This of course may also be due to a fortuitous absence of relevant finds. But in any case one should not exclude entirely the possibility that cultural connections were maintained by sea between the Asiatic mainland and the Aleutians (Fig. 30).

As other typical elements of Paleo-Aleut culture Laughlin mentions fishing-spears, bird darts, fishhooks, bolas, ulu blades of retouched stone, men's knives with a handle, and labrets. There is indirect evidence of the use of throwing-boards. Stone lamps provided warmth and light, but there were no ceramic vessels of any kind.

Paleo-Aleut man was thus well-equipped culturally to utilize for his subsistence all the natural possibilities that the chain of islands offered. All the animals extant—'from whales to sea otters, from albatross to hummingbirds, from halibut to trout and from octopus to limpets' as Laughlin states—could be caught or snared by means of the implements and techniques available. Within the area on which Paleo-Aleut culture spread, measuring some 2000 kilometers from one extremity to the other, there seem to have been no great distinctions in regard to the mode of life. The changes that took place over the course of time are likewise rather insignificant.

The Paleo-Aleuts also doubtless had skin-covered boats at their disposal—presumably the umiak as well as the kayak. Without these settlement of the island chain would not have been possible. On the other hand they had no need of sleds, which may have been the reason why they did not keep dogs.

It is not yet certain what type of habitations the Paleo-Aleuts had. Laughlin believes that they may have been entirely different from the semi-subterranean houses known from later periods in the same area. He mentions oval arrangements of stones which may have outlined the ground covered.

It is also uncertain whether the Paleo-Aleut people were already familiar with the custom of mummifying the bodies of the deceased and interring them in caves in a crouched position—a custom prevalent until very recently.

Finally, it should be noted that Paleo-Aleut implements were occasionally decorated with simple linear designs or with carved human faces. This may possibly have been done in part with the aid of copper tools.

An interesting insight into conditions on the westernmost Aleutian islands is afforded by diggings which A.C. Spaulding carried out near Krugloi Point on Agattu for a brief period in 1949. Excavations were made in four different places which produced a paucity of types, particularly in the use of bone artifacts. There are, for example, no toggle harpoon heads, fore-shaft-sockets or composite fishhooks. On the other hand there is the occurrence of a considerable number of rather long narrow projectile points of stone, some of them with diagonal parallel flaking, a tang at the base and in some cases serrated edges. Also remarkable are Mousterian-like scrapers. Radiocarbon analyses carried out on a sample of driftwood from the bottom of one section excavated gave an age of 2630 ± 300 years. Spaulding regards this as the earliest visit to the island and assumes that the settlement of Agattu began about 500 B.C. He points out the great difficulties involved in identifying the strange composition of this complex and concludes that the frugality of this culture can be explained only by the fact that it reached the western Aleutians at an early date and hardly developed any further because these islands were so isolated. This would account for the different nature of the finds on Umnak Island.

Once again one must turn to the eastern Aleutians. It was here that the dolichocephalic Paleo-Aleut type was superseded at a relatively late stage — about one thousand years ago — by men with short round heads whom Hrdlička referred to as Aleuts and whom Laughlin has recently termed 'Neo-Aleuts'. It is not yet possible to say to what extent this was due to local evolution or to the arrival of new ethnic groups. All the same it is noteworthy that Neo-Aleut culture has features very similar to those of Paleo-Aleut, so that there may have been a considerable degree of continuous growth. Generally speaking, the implements are somewhat more simple; some new elements occur, such as plaited objects of dried grass and the use of vegetable poison in whaling. These might, however, have already been known in the Paleo-Aleut culture, even though they could not be traced by the archeologist. In this context it is worth noting that the use of poison in whaling has also been authenticated in Kamchatka.

It is therefore very probable that Neo-Aleut culture by and large evolved out of the Paleo-Aleut stage. Laughlin thinks it possible that the relatively late appearance of round-headed man on the Aleutians and in other parts of southwestern Alaska could be the beginning of a development which has been observed recently in other parts of the Eskimo area as well.

2. Kodiak Island

Our knowledge of the archeology of Kodiak Island, to the southeast of the Alaska Peninsula, depends largely on excavations carried out by Hrdlička at Uyak Bay, in the north of the island, between 1931 and 1936. He was mainly interested in skeletal remains and treated the archeological material superficially. He soon came to the view that in this area, too, a distinction could be made between an earlier population, the Pre-Koniag, and the more recent Koniag. Although Hrdlička's methods have been sharply criticized, there is no doubt that the island was first settled by dolichocephalic people, who were superseded by a round-headed type some one thousand years ago.

We are indebted to Robert F. Heizer for having re-worked in detail Hrdlička's finds at the Uyak site. In contrast to Hrdlička, who distinguished one earlier and one more recent Pre-Koniag stage, succeeded by the Koniag culture, Heizer combines the first two, giving only two stages: Pre-Koniag and Koniag. In general the finds have features in common with the Paleo- and Neo-Aleut material. Again prong harpoon heads are of greater importance than toggle harpoon heads. There is also no doubt that the population hunted sea-mammals, including the whale, as early as the Pre-Koniag stage. On the other hand, Pre-Koniag and Koniag culture possess certain singular features in common, and they also have associations with the Kachemak culture on the neighboring Kenai Peninsula.

But first let us give some account of the results achieved by the 'University of Wisconsin Aleut-Konyag Prehistory and Ecology Project' on Kodiak Island between 1961 and 1963. According to D.W. Clark, the Ocean Bay I phase is the earliest hitherto identified. It is named after a site on Sitkalidak Island, southeast of Kodiak. It is distinguished in particular by the fact that the implements found there are mostly flaked from chert and other cryptocrystalline rock whereas ground slate implements occur only exceptionally. Noteworthy is the find of a small stone lamp, triangular in shape. In southwestern Alaska and on the Aleutians no close parallels with this industry have yet been found; as mentioned above, only the researches of D.E. Dumond on the opposite coast of the Alaska

Peninsula seem to have yielded the first clues to support the hypothesis that such links existed. Radiocarbon analysis suggested an age of 5518 ± 78 years for a sample taken from the base of Ocean Bay I, which makes it a little older than had originally been thought; Clark is therefore cautious on this point. This phase is succeeded by 'Ocean Bay II', which could be authenticated at the same site. It is distinguished by a preponderance of ground slate implements. It may possibly be related to the Kachemak I culture in Central Southern Alaska, but in that case it would have to be somewhat older to judge by the stage of evolution reached; this assumption corresponds to a radiocarbon dating of 3944 ± 65 years. After a certain hiatus there followed the 'Old Kiavak phase', which is said to show links with Kachemak II culture, as well as with Heizer's Pre-Koniag culture from Uyak Bay on the north coast of Kodiak Island. Whereas it had formerly been assumed that it originated approximately from the beginning of the Christian era, a radiocarbon dating of 3278 ± 61 years suggests that it was probably of greater antiquity. The line of development apparent here is continued in the Three Saints Bay phase, which likewise gives evidence of close links with Heizer's Pre-Koniag culture or with Hrdlička's earlier Pre-Koniag stage. In Clark's view both of them could belong to the Kachemak III culture. But radiocarbon analyses suggest that the Three Saints Bay phase falls in the period between 100 B.C. and 900 A.D. Although this phase is not represented in ceramic ware, the latter plays an important role in the 'Koniag phase', which followed it after a hiatus. This corresponds to the Koniag culture at the Uyak site. Radiocarbon datings indicate that this last phase began during the sixteenth century A.D.

D.W. Clark emphasizes that Kodiak Island, which had presumably been densely settled for a long time, was the chief Pacific Eskimo population center, and for this reason may have had an important function to fulfill in spreading successive cultures. Unfortunately the sites which he located were badly affected by the tidal wave on Good Friday 1964, and in a number of other places the sinking of the coastline led to the destruction of archeological sites.

In 1962-3 W. Workman and D.W. Clark also made archeological discoveries on the small Chirikof Island, situated southwest of Kodiak. These show that at times there were distinct cultural features in common with Kodiak, whereas at other times there were equally distinct differences.

Finally, we may mention that engravings were made on granite bluffs and rocky boulders along the coast of Kodiak Island. Frequently the motifs are stylized human faces and geometric designs, occasionally also figures of human beings and whales executed in a more or less naturalistic style.

3. Central Southern Alaska

Since the early 1930's, when Frederica de Laguna began to explore Central Southern Alaska, we have known of the Kachemak culture, located in the area of Kachemak Bay in the southern Kenai Peninsula. Her excavations near Cottonwood Creek and on Yukon Island lead her to distinguish three stages. Kachemak I has somewhat archaic Eskimo features and its first appearance in Central Southern Alaska was originally ascribed to the beginning of the Christian era. But subsequent radiocarbon analyses suggest that it was somewhat earlier and may go back to the eighth century B.C. The sample examined was, however, not quite reliable, since it consisted of antler steeped in shellac. Kachemak II represents a continuation and was originally assigned by de Laguna to the period between 500 and 1000 A.D.; recently she has decided that it might be contemporary with the Choris and Norton cultures. The subsequent Kachemak III appears to have maintained itself until historical times, which would make it surprisingly long-lived.

Since only scanty skeletal remains are so far available, it has not yet been possible to ascertain whether the Kachemak Bay population was at first dolichocephalic, and later brachycephalic, as was the case in the Aleutians and on Kodiak Island.

The prehistoric Kachemak population lived in coastal settlements, but little is known about the nature and form of their habitations during the early phase. With reference to the second stage of Kachemak culture de Laguna mentions housebuilding of stones and the vertebrae of whales. This is remarkable in an area where there is an abundance of timber. For this reason de Laguna suggests that the population concerned may have originated from a treeless region. Later, on the other hand, logs were used for building houses, which were partly subterranean.

From the beginning they obtained their subsistence from

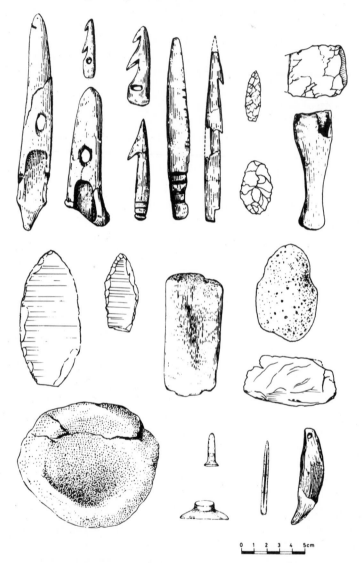

Fig. 31 - Implements from the Kachemak I culture. Redrawn after F. de Laguna (1934).

everything that could be hunted, collected or caught: caribou, moose, bear, as well as seal and other sea-mammals. There is apparently no evidence so far that whaling was carried on at the beginning of the early phase, but the slightly later use of whale bones in construction may indicate this, since this material can hardly have been obtained exclusively from the remains of animals that had perished and been washed ashore. In addition fish, birds and mollusks were also used.

In general the inventory of the earliest stage of the Kachemak culture contains the same elements and types as one finds in the two subsequent layers. But the first stage is somewhat simpler and according to de Laguna more distinctly rooted in the 'Eskimo culture'. The subsequent stages are more varied, and in them one can identify a process of development toward a particular cultural form of local character in which Eskimo elements recede into the background, possibly under Indian influence.

We cannot go into detail here about individual stages of the Kachemak culture, and a few remarks based on de Laguna's data will have to suffice (Fig. 31). Stone implements, including those of slate, were at the beginning usually retouched, rarely ground. Later ground slate became increasingly important. During the third stage stone saws were also found. A remarkable feature are the stones with grooves running completely round them, and from the second stage onwards also several stones with notched sides. De Laguna assumes that some of these were used as bola weights, and points to parallels in Kamchatka and Japan; they might, however, be net-sinkers. Beginning at the first stage realistic human figures carved of stone, as well as round or oval stone lamps are found. Characteristic features of the final stage include awls of slate, mirrors of the same material and stone lamps decorated in relief with figures of human beings or whales (Fig. 32). Moreover, a new type of axe is encountered, for chopping wood, a function formerly carried out with huge wedges made of bone.

Among implements of organic material, toggle harpoon heads appear in the first stage. They conform to harpoon type I of the Thule culture, which was much later spread from northern Alaska to Greenland. Besides these we also find here a number of prong harpoon heads of various types, which become even more important during the subsequent stages. The socket-pieces were originally short and had two parts, whereas later a longer and more slender type prevailed. Labrets are encountered in all stages, whereas other ornaments such as perforated beads are still absent at first. Linear decorations become more frequent as development proceeds. During the

Fig. 32 - Decorated blubber lamp of the Kachemak III culture, from Kenai Lake in the interior of the Kenai Peninsula. After F. de Laguna (1934).

Fig. 33 - Paintings in red from Sadie Cove in the south of Kachemak Bay. Above and below: highly stylized land animals (below, left: a dog?). Between them: whales. After F. de Laguna (1934).

third stage they seem to have been produced throughout with the aid of metal (copper?) tools, although copper cannot be authenticated until the end of this period. The same is true of pottery.

Burials with the body in a crouched position and associated with grave goods have been found, especially during the second stage. Noteworthy during the final stage is the strange custom whereby artificial eyes of bone or ivory were placed over those of the deceased. This affords a striking parallel with the Ipiutak culture on Point Hope in northwestern Alaska, to be described later. In one Kachemak grave equipped in this way two skull trophies appear to have been buried alongside two whole bodies.

Finally, it should be stressed that from the beginning the Kachemak people kept dogs, although they seem to have decreased somewhat in importance. Their rock paintings, for the most part highly stylized and representing human beings, whales etc., cannot be ascribed to any particular stage of the Kachemak Bay culture (Fig. 33).

In connection with the Kachemak culture de Laguna was the first to point to the probability of connections existing between Central Southern Alaska and adjacent areas on one hand and eastern Asia on the other. It is in any case a fact that not only the Kachemak culture but also the related Kodiak culture, as well as the Aleut culture, which to some extent fits into this context, have basically Eskimo features but in addition contain a number of elements which are lacking in the intervening Eskimo culture of Bering Strait and are not encountered again until one reaches the region between Kamchatka and northern Japan.

In this connection it is worthwhile to include some of the results of research in language. As we know, Swadesh sets the separation of the Eskimo and Aleut languages at about 3000 years ago while Bergsland goes back to 4000 B.C. which agrees more generally with archeological dating. Swadesh believes that the Inupik dialect spoken by the Eskimos north and east of the Yukon before 1500 - 2000 years ago separated from the Yupik dialect of the Siberian Eskimos and those of southwest Alaska. Furthermore, it is believed certain that the Siberian Yuit split off before the development of the three southwest Alaskan dialects in the Kuskokwim region around Nunivak Island and in Norton Sound.

One final point: de Laguna's studies in Prince William Sound enabled her to reconstruct a good deal of Chugach material culture as it must have been within the five hundred or so years preceding the discovery of Alaska. In this case we are dealing with another part of the fabric of the prehistory of Central Southern Alaska, Kodiak Island and the Aleutians – one that must be ascribed to a later period. Further studies by de Laguna in the Yakutat Bay area, halfway between Cordova and Sitka in southeastern Alaska, have demonstrated that in the prehistoric remains extant there, which are probably linked with the Eyak Indians who used to inhabit this area and were later driven out by the Tlingit, there is evidence of a considerable influence having been exerted by both the Eskimos and the Athapaskans. As de Laguna says, this may possibly be 'a very old-fashioned form of northern Northwest Coast culture, the basic elements of which appear to be ancient, since they are widely shared by the Eskimo and the Indians of Northwestern America.'

This leads to the assumption that during a considerable period of time successive waves of immigrants came to the Aleutians, Kodiak Island and Central Southern Alaska. Future research will show whether this assumption is correct. Another less urgent question that will have to be clarified is why some one thousand years ago the earlier dolichocephalic type was superseded by brachycephalic people, and why the cultures of the various zones underwent slight modification.

Bibliography: Aigner, 1966; Bank, 1954; Clark, 1966; Dall, 1877; Denniston, 1966; Heizer, 1956; Hrdlička, 1944, 1945; Jochelson, 1925, 1933; de Laguna, 1933b, 1934, 1940, 1956; de Laguna and others, 1964; Laughlin, 1951, 1952, 1958, 1962a, 1962b, 1963a, 1963b; Laughlin and Marsh, 1951; Laughlin and Reeder, 1966; Quimby, 1945a, 1945b, 1948; Spaulding, 1962; Weyer, 1929, 1930; Workman, 1966.

NORTHWESTERN AND NORTHERN ALASKA

This survey of the archeological situation in Alaska now comes to the coastal area in the northwest and north. The sensational discoveries made here center upon Point Hope, the northwestern tip of the North American continent. This narrow cape, situated between the Chukchi Sea and some lagoons, has been settled for a long time with a village existing there even today. The reason for this is probably that conditions were always favorable there for hunting sea-mammals and other animals.

During the extensive excavations carried out by Helge Larsen, Froelich G. Rainey and J. Louis Giddings between 1939 and 1941 the so-called Near Ipiutak culture was discovered. This name was chosen to suggest a cultural form which in some aspects is reminiscent of the better documented Ipiutak culture, yet differs from it in various ways. In the meantime a solution has been found to the question of the relative dating of Ipiutak and Near Ipiutak, which was originally still uncertain. Giddings' investigations on Cape Krusenstern have shown that the Near Ipiutak finds are located on older beach ridges than those of the Ipiutak culture. No definite date can yet be assigned to Near Ipiutak, but it may have begun simultaneously with the Norton culture some time between 500 and 300 B.C. It is not yet certain whether it lasted until the beginning of the Ipiutak culture around 100 B.C. or a little longer. It is also not definite whether any direct connections existed at all between Near Ipiutak and Ipiutak. In any case more evidence is available to suggest a relationship between the former and the Norton culture.

Knowledge of Near Ipiutak is based largely upon the investigation of a single house ruin, some refuse heaps and several burials on Point Hope. The house plan was square (4 x 4 meters) with a hearth in the center; the type of entrance could not be ascertained. The burials were visible on the surface in the form of slight elevations.

The favorite weapon seems to have been the bow and arrow. Antler arrowheads occur frequently, most of them with lateral grooves to receive inset pieces and points. Such terminal points were likewise fastened to harpoon heads—including those used in whaling. On the whole retouched implements played an important part, as in the Ipiutak and Norton cultures. Some artifacts differ from those of Ipiutak, namely arrowheads, fish-spears, leister prongs, adze haftings, hammers for stonework and two-handed scrapers. In addition some elements occur which are absent in Ipiutak: the blubber lamp, ground slate implements and pottery. The engraved decorations, which are relatively rare and simple, also differ from those of the Ipiutak culture.

But for the rest relatively little is as yet known about the Near Ipiutak culture, which Giddings refers to as a 'poorly defined phase'. The predominant impression, as has been noted, is that there were close links with the Norton culture. This may also explain why Helge Larsen discovered Near Ipiutak traces as far to the south as the Platinum area in southwestern Alaska.

The matter is quite different in the case of the Ipiutak culture itself. There is information about it, thanks to a splendid find and a detailed publication by Helge Larsen and Froelich G. Rainey. Additional material was salvaged by excavations in the summer of 1967 directed by Edward Hosley. Only the origin of this most singular culture is for the time being still lost in the obscurity of the past.

Ipiutak is the Eskimo name for a narrow strip of land which separates two lagoons in the north of Point Hope Peninsula, and it was applied to the large prehistoric settlement which extends across the strip of land formed by beach ridges. A very large number of house ruins can be identified with some difficulty by their external characteristics. Of these 575 could be measured, but Larsen and Rainey think that there were more and that some may have been washed away by the sea. Thus originally there may have been between 600 and 800 house ruins (Fig. 34).

The ruins, which are located on beach ridges that are higher and drier, seem to be built in five barely recognizable rows. This immediately raises the question whether this enormous complex came into being all at once or in stages. The excavations have not revealed any conspicuous differences between the house ruins, but so far only about one in eight of those identified has been investigated.

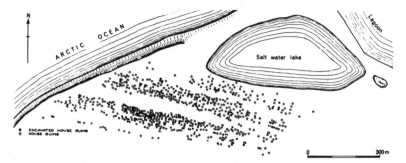

Fig. 34 - Sketch map of the Ipiutak settlement on Point Hope, northwestern
Alaska. Redrawn after H. Larsen and F.G. Rainey (1948).

On the assumption that each house was inhabited by six to
eight individuals, the population would have been between
3500 and 6500. It would have been quite impossible to supply
so many people with food, nor would there have been enough
driftwood to build such a large settlement so rapidly or to provide fuel for a population unfamiliar with the blubber lamp.
Finally, it must be borne in mind that the houses are often situated so close together that one blocked the entrance to another. All this shows that the Ipiutak settlement must have developed over a period of time, but how long that was is unknown.

The ground plan, shape and interior arrangement of Ipiutak
houses is so consistent that they can be considered as a uniform type (Fig. 43). They were rectangular and in most cases
measured 4 x 5 meters. Approximately in the middle of the
floor, which was covered with timbers, there was usually an
open space for the hearth. On three sides—i.e., on the north,
east and south—there were low benches of timbers and branches, which were originally covered with skins and must have
been used for sitting and sleeping upon. In some ruins, but not
in all of them, there were traces of an entrance on the western
side, on a level with the floor. But Larsen and Rainey think it
possible that some of the houses had roof-entrances. Little is
known about the construction of the walls and roofs. The walls
may have inclined inwards so that the roof, supported by strong
posts, was small and flat. In the center there may have been a
combination of smoke-hole and window, and this may also

have served as an entrance. The entire construction probably consisted of logs and possibly willow branches covered with sod and perhaps earth as well, to which in winter snow was added to provide insulation.

The Ipiutak population obtained their livelihood by hunting large land- and sea-mammals. The catching of birds and fishing only played a subordinate role. Unfortunately no thorough examination of animal bone deposits has as yet been made. But we do have information about animal remains from 14 houses, which yielded the following result: 76% seal (including bearded seal), 12% walrus, 10% caribou; the remaining 2% were from various kinds of birds, fox, squirrel, polar bear, whale, wolf and beluga (in order of diminishing importance). Larsen and Rainey emphasize the significance of caribou hunting to support their theory that the Ipiutak population spent only part of the year on the coast but at other times lived in the interior. Other evidence in favor of this view is the absence of the blubber lamp, the frequent working of caribou antler, the large number of arrowheads of varying shape made from this material, the use of birch bark to make receptacles and of willow to make benches for sitting or sleeping upon. On the other hand, Collins pointed out that so far there is nothing to suggest that the Ipiutak culture was disseminated in areas of Alaska far from the coast. In this connection one may also call in question Larsen's and Rainey's assumption that the Ipiutak population was unfamiliar with whaling. It is true that the harpoon heads are in most cases too small for this purpose, but one notes that in their report Larsen and Rainey depict as 'rare types' a few items which are large enough to be used in whaling (Fig. 35, below right). Let us bear in mind that large harpoon heads also occur fairly seldom in the Okvik and Old Bering Sea cultures, which we know engaged in whaling. Furthermore, the possibility must be considered that for some reason whales may have avoided the Point Hope area at the time when the Ipiutak people settled there. It is not justified to deny all knowledge of whaling in the Ipiutak culture and on this account to ascribe it to an earlier cultural level than that in the Bering Strait area discussed above.

Larsen and Rainey also assumed, despite the absence of relevant finds at Point Hope, that the Ipiutak people were

Fig. 35 - Ivory harpoon heads from the Ipiutak culture. The surfaces have been badly weathered. Photo by courtesy of H. Larsen.

familiar with both the kayak and umiak. In the meantime the use of kayaks or canoes has been found in the investigation of an Ipiutak community-house at Deering, on the Seward Peninsula. The same applies to the sled; at Deering one was discovered of the 'built-up' type, which is particularly interesting since dog bones were found in the Point Hope settlement.

Among Ipiutak artifacts of major importance belong those

associated with the bow and arrow. Of all Ipiutak artifacts 22% are made up of the following objects: 1172 arrowheads, 436 arrow points or end-blades, and 571 inset or side-blades of flint, 47 blunt bird arrows and some fragments of wooden bows. Most of the arrowheads are made of antler; they are elaborately worked and are often decorated. Eight different types may be distinguished, all of which have in common the smooth conical tang, or a tapering butt. A highly developed technique of workmanship is evident in the flint arrow points with a straight or concave base and in the lateral inset blades, most of which are made very thin by retouching on both surfaces (Figs. 37, 42).

In this connection it may be emphasized that the bow and arrow also served as a fighting weapon, for two human skeletons were found with arrow points in their chests, and in one case two arrow points were actually imbedded in the breastbone.

For hunting sea-mammals harpoon heads were used, as mentioned above, but these, together with other parts of harpoons, comprise no more than 3% of the total inventory of implements. Four principal and several secondary types may be identified. Type 1 is small with an open socket, multi-pronged spur and

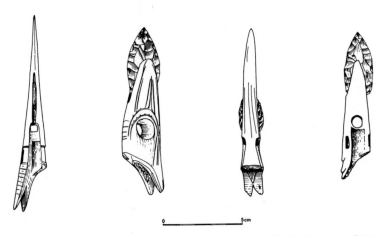

Fig. 36 - Ipiutak harpoon heads: Types 1-4. Redrawn after H. Larsen and F.G. Rainey (1948).

two side-blades parallel with the line hole but no inset point
at the end. Type 2 is broad with closed socket, multi-pronged
spur and an inset point at right angles to the line hole, and has
parallels in various Eskimo cultures. Type 3 again is small with
closed socket and two side-blades parallel with the line hole.
Type 4 is short, broad, with open socket and end-blade at right
angles to the line hole and is fairly rare and occurs relatively
few times. It was apparently not in general use. Whereas the
first three types of harpoon heads bear characteristic designs
the fourth only has simple linear ornaments (Figs. 35, 36, 42).

Other parts of the harpoon as well, such as foreshafts, socket-
pieces and ice picks, correspond completely with the types
familiar from other cultures, especially Okvik, Old Bering Sea
and Kachemak. Some other accessories, however, are missing,
such as finger-rests, and mouthpieces and plugs for floats. One
reason for this may be that they were made of wood and have
not survived.

Also noteworthy are bird darts and possibly fish-spears, as
well as the typical salmon spear with a center prong and two
side prongs each with two barbs turned inwards. Long spear
and lance heads made of antler with side-blades of flint are
usually difficult to distinguish from daggers of similar shape
(Fig. 42).

Among the tools found are the following: knives with han-
dles of organic material (antler, ivory or wood, the latter probably most common at first) and a flint blade inserted laterally;
engraving tools, usually elaborately decorated, slender ivory
or antler shafts with an inset point made of a sharpened inci-
sor, and in one case of iron, which was proven not to be of
meteoritic origin; adzes consisting of a ground blade (usually
silicified slate), mounted in a head of antler or bone lashed to
a wooden handle; chisel-like implements of ground slate;
grinding-stones; wedges of antler for splitting wood; strong
mattocks, probably used to cut sod when building houses and
pointed root-picks of walrus tusk; shovels, usually made of
whale ribs.

For skin- and leather-working, the tools found were: two-
handed scrapers either made from a metatarsal bone or else
having a wooden handle; marlinespikes, awls and cutting

boards, mostly made of ivory; and finally, thin bone needles with an eye, some only 1 mm in diameter. The needle-cases so popular elsewhere have not been definitely recognized.

The very important part which the flint technique played in Ipiutak culture also emerges from the presence of various typical tools used in stone-working; flint hammer-heads, usually made from the hard penis bone of the walrus, and flint-flakers

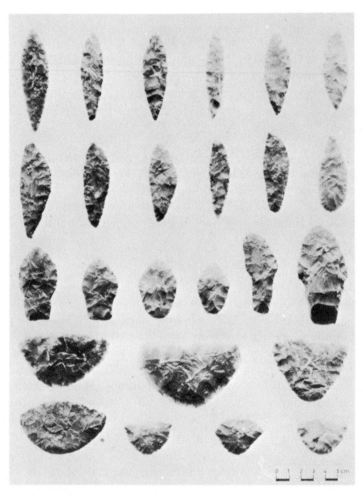

Fig. 37 - Flint implements of the Ipiutak culture: projectile points and scraper-like objects. Photo by courtesy of H. Larsen.

which had a broad handle of antler, frequently bearing fine decoration, and a bone point affixed in front.

Approximately 52% of all Ipiutak artifacts are of flint, using this term in an archeological rather than a mineralogical sense, to include various kinds of stone which can be flaked easily. This was available in unlimited quantities at Point Hope.

The carefully worked points and inset blades for arrowheads, harpoon heads, spear and lance heads, inset knives and skin-scrapers (Fig. 37), have already been mentioned. For the latter two objects discoidal blades were also suitable. There are large numbers of side- and end-scrapers, which according to Larsen and Rainey were mainly used to work bone, antler, ivory and wood. The number of drill points is on the other hand relatively small and it appears that these were exclusively used for hand drills; the bow drill was not known.

Finally, we may mention that apart from adzes and chisels, ground stone implements are very rare. Slate implements, such as the typical Eskimo women's knife or ulu are missing.

There are also objects connected with clothing and ornaments. The so-called 'ornamental bands', decorated antler or ivory bands, may have been fastened either to clothing, to a quiver, a tool bag, or to headgear. Another kind is thought to have been a head or brow band. A few stone and ivory labrets occur, and the purpose for which they were used is evident from some carved faces which also bear tattoo marks. There are no combs at all, but there is evidence of snow goggles. These show distinct connections with the Okvik culture and may have originated from it. The same applies to the fragments of two 'winged objects', one decorated in style 2 and the other in style 3 of the Okvik culture.

It will be apparent that nothing has been said about sherds of cooking-pots or of blubber lamps, which were presumably unknown to the inhabitants of the Ipiutak settlement. In most cases they must have used birch bark containers with a wooden base, of which a considerable number have been found at Deering. In these, liquids could be heated or brought to a boil with the aid of hot stones. This absence of pottery is certainly rather striking if we consider that clay vessels were in use on both sides of the Bering Strait at an earlier date.

But this is by no means the final enigma or the greatest surprise that Ipiutak culture holds in store. During the excavation season of 1940, with the help of virtually the entire population of Point Hope, Rainey finally succeeded in discovering the long sought-after burial-place of the Ipiutak settlement: it stretches east of the ruined houses along the shore of the great lagoon for a distance of approximately four kilometers. The graves can be identified on the surface by somewhat more plentiful vegetation. More than one hundred Ipiutak graves have been investigated but others may still lie concealed in the ground. In some cases the dead are interred lying extended in a log driftwood coffin at a depth of one half to one meter; and more rarely face down, or lying on one side, and in exceptional cases with flexed legs. In most instances the head faced to the west, less frequently to another cardinal point. The majority of the coffins contained only one skeleton, but some had two or even three. A little more than half the graves were equipped with a limited amount of grave goods (Fig. 38).

Other burials were placed directly beneath the sod or in the sod itself, probably as a result of the practice of exposing the corpse — interments where the body was left unprotected on the tundra and only after complete decomposition sank beneath the surface. Some of these burials, which usually consist of scattered human bones and grave goods, may have originally been enclosed in a log frame or have been covered by a pile of logs.

A particular characteristic of these surface burials is the presence of the strangest grave goods, such as are not encountered in coffin burials. Larsen and Rainey are therefore probably right in assuming that these burials were of a certain class of person with a high social status.

The grave goods have only a few parallels in the house ruins, but these suffice to show that settlement and cemetery belong together. The most peculiar custom, observed in three coffin burials, is the use of artificial ivory eyeballs with jade pupils placed in the eye sockets, from which the eye had probably been gouged out beforehand, or else between the eyelids (Fig. 38). An old Eskimo from Point Hope knew a legend which tells of a man with ivory eyes; possibly such a skull with artificial eyes may once have been found by some natives, so giving rise to the legend. One of the skulls mentioned also had in the

Fig. 38 - Ipiutak burials from Point Hope, northwestern Alaska. Above left:
coffin burial, skull with artificial eyes of ivory and jade. Above right:
detail. Below left: detail from a coffin burial containing two skeletons
(adult and child); with the adult skeleton, some vertebrae were im-
paled on an ivory rod, and the grave goods consisted of decorated
tubes of caribou-antler. Below right: coffin burial containing a man, a
woman and a small child, on whose chest was placed an ivory mask
consisting of several parts. Photo by courtesy of H. Larsen.

nasal cavity two small sculptured ivory nose-plugs, which show a bird-like head with inlaid eyes of jade. Another ivory carving is a mouth-cover representing lips which are sewn together. A similar mouth-cover was discovered in another burial, and a third one is less clearly identifiable.

This expresses a belief that the body openings had to be closed to prevent an evil spirit from molesting the deceased or else from bringing danger from the corpse upon the living.

The artificial eyes also recall similar finds encountered in the Kachemak culture. It is of interest that the skull of a loon, which was in one of the Ipiutak graves, likewise had eyes of ivory and jade. This conformity in the treatment of animal and human corpses also finds expression in the interment of a dog in one grave-like structure. Larsen and Rainey point out that there are numerous parallels in the Old World. There were also four perforated jaws of brown bears found in burials, which may suggest a bear cult.

Another curious fact came to light in one of the double coffin burials (adult and child): the adult's head had apparently been severed from the torso before interment and an ivory rod laid against the inner surface of the lumbar and thoracic vertebrae and inside the four uppermost cervical vertebrae. In this burial, which also contained the skull of the loon, were also found caribou-antler tubes decorated with stylized human faces, the significance of which is unknown (Fig. 38).

Some thin antler plates are also found covering the face of the dead and thus probably point to the presence of a ghost cult. One of these, with concentric circles arranged to represent eyes, was found placed upon a skull. Even more peculiar are two death masks pieced together of several parts. One of these was discovered in a coffin burial containing the skeletons of a man, a woman and a small child. On the child's chest were various carved and ornamented ivory plates which must have originally been attached to a wooden base and together formed a mask: four outer parts formed the outline of the face with mouth and eyebrows, a part in the center the nose, and two jade pieces probably the pupils of the eyes which were painted on or carved in the wooden support. It is striking that the mouth seems to represent lips, which are sewn together like the mouth-covers already mentioned. There are two large

labrets in the area of the chin and several more jade inlays.
The original location of two other accompanying ivory plates
and various pendants could no longer be established with
certainty (Fig. 38).

On the basis of this find it was possible to reconstruct a similar but more elaborately decorated ivory mask, the various
parts of which were no longer in their original arrangement. It
consists of seven individual pieces, some of which are held together by larvae-like cleats. The outside measurements are 14
by 16 centimeters (Fig. 39).

Fig. 39 - Mask-like set of ivory carvings from an Ipiutak burial on Point Hope,
northwestern Alaska. After H. Larsen and F.G. Rainey (1948).

Other items are anthropomorphic ivory and antler carvings,
some of which represent human heads and others, human
skulls (Fig. 42).

Coffin burials, and occasionally also the house ruins, yielded some naturalistic animal carvings. Most of these are renderings of polar bears and seals, more rarely of walrus and wolves.
The finest of all is the figure of a young walrus which, like
some other carvings, bears the so-called skeleton motif: a styl-

ized representation of the spine with ribs attached. Also striking are the pear-shaped bosses on each hip, a motif probably
derived from the crural spiral (Fig. 40). Both of these decorations resemble those that occur between 900 and 200 B.C. in
the Scytho-Siberian animal style of the region between the
Black Sea and the Ordos area of northern China, and in part
those of an even earlier date, in the La Tène style of the late
Iron Age in Central Europe. The frontal view of a bear on a

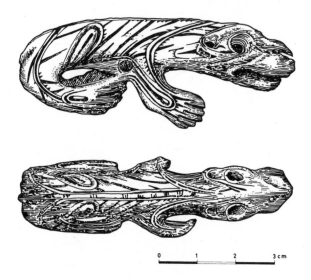

Fig. 40 - Young walrus. Ivory carving from an Ipiutak burial at Point Hope,
     northwestern Alaska. The skeleton motif can be easily recognized.
     After H. Larsen and F.G. Rainey (1948).

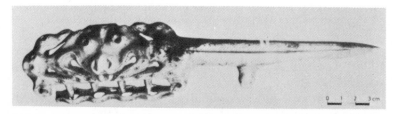

Fig. 41 - Ivory carving, the significance of which is unknown, from Point Spen-
     cer on the Seward Peninsula, Alaska. The stylized figure of the bear
     in the center is reminiscent of the Scytho-Siberian animal style. Pho-
     to by courtesy of Helge Larsen.

comb-like implement from Ipiutak also has common features with the Scytho-Siberian style (Fig. 41).

The same applies to the rendering of a bird's head, found in one of the houses, which can hardly be interpreted as anything else than a griffin. On the other hand, Larsen and Rainey also point to the fact that the skeleton motif was widely distributed in North America where the Tlingit and other Indians on the Northwest Coast used it in human and animal figures. It has been found in the Canadian Dorset culture, and representations of evil spirits known as *tupilak* in Angmagssalik, East Greenland, manifest it up to the present day. Thus the association between Ipiutak art and the Scytho-Siberian animal style need not have been direct, but the motifs concerned may have found their way into northwestern Alaska by devious routes.

Larsen and Rainey believe that some of the animal carvings mentioned here were attached to clothing around the shoulders. They point out that this was frequently the case among the shamans of Siberia and Mongolia.

The Ipiutak surface burials contained a fairly extensive group of peculiar carvings collectively termed 'open work carvings'. These are composed of three elements: highly stylized, fantastic animal figures (either as parts of other carvings or attached to them), swivels and chains (Fig. 42). The animals rendered in openwork carvings are invariably species that cannot be identified. Some are reminiscent of reptiles or amphibia. Others seem to be combinations of several animals or figments of imagination. They are among the oddest objects found at Ipiutak.

The second element of openwork carvings, the swivel, originally had a practical function: from Alaska to Greenland it is a part of the dogs' harness which serves to prevent the lines from tangling. We also find the swivel on harpoon lines or on floats. Some of the swivels discovered in Ipiutak surface burials, judging by their shape, could have been used for such purposes, but the size and elaborate decoration make this seem unlikely. In other cases a practical purpose is ruled out.

The third element, the carved ivory chain, is likewise fairly widely disseminated in the Eskimo area, especially in Alaska. But nowhere is it encountered as frequently as at Ipiutak. According to Larsen and Rainey it may be derived from metal models. They also point out that swivels and chains were often fastened as symbols to the clothing of Siberian and Central Asian shamans. It is entirely possible that these Ipiutak carvings were similarly employed.

Finally, we come to the openwork carvings proper, which usually combine several of the three elements described (Fig. 42). Almost 200 of these peculiar forms have been found, no two of which are identical. Since all these bizarre carvings, of outstanding technique of workmanship, were found in surface burials, the discoverers of the Ipiutak culture take the view that these burials were of a special class of persons, probably shamans.

What still remains to be discussed are the decorations attached to a large number of Ipiutak objects, to weapons and implements as well as ceremonial objects. Apart from some stylized renderings of human faces or of animal heads, these are in most cases geometric ornaments. Especially characteristic are straight or curved lines, which occur either by themselves or in combination with other motifs such as Y-shaped motifs, tridents, spurred lines resembling barbed wire, circles, ellipses, etc. Larsen and Rainey point to distinct parallels with the ornamentation of the Okvik and Old Bering Sea cultures.

Originally the Ipiutak culture was interpreted as the source of Eskimo culture and it was said to be derived from the Ob-Yenisei area some 5000 kilometers from Point Hope. This view is hardly tenable any longer. The Ipiutak culture was also at first assigned to too recent a period on the basis of certain radiocarbon analyses; this error was probably due to contamination of the wood samples examined. Recently Helge Larsen has assumed that Ipiutak must belong to the same period as the late Okvik and Old Bering Sea cultures, the dating of which, however, as we have seen is also not yet quite certain. A more recent radiocarbon dating, which represents an average of four Ipiutak samples, gives an age of 1619 $\pm$ 210 years and therefore belongs to the period from the second to the sixth century A.D. On the other hand, it must be borne in mind that at Ipiutak there is an absence of some vital elements such as pottery, ground slate implements and the blubber lamp, whereas these were present in the Okvik and Old Bering Sea cultures,

which clearly have strong links with Ipiutak. Another noteworthy relationship is the technique of stone-working with
that of the Denbigh Flint complex or with the American Epi-

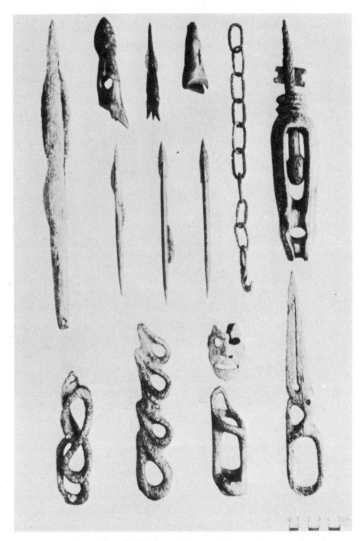

Fig. 42 - Lance-, harpoon- and arrowheads, openwork carvings and a small
anthropomorphic representation in antler and ivory, from Ipiutak on
Point Hope, northwestern Alaska. Photo by courtesy of K. Birket-
Smith.

Gravettian tradition in general. Moreover, the view of the Russian anthropologist G.F. Debetz that the skulls of Ipiutak skeletons have many features in common with those of the present-day Yukagir in northern Siberia is important. These together with other Paleo-Siberian peoples, and the Eskimos, seem to constitute a distinct ethnic group.

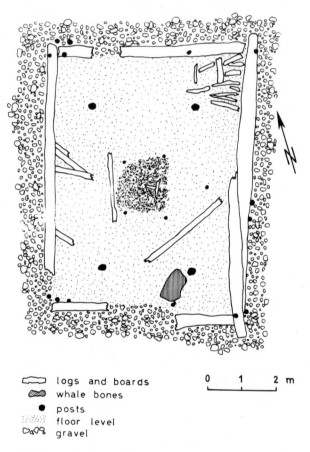

logs and boards
whale bones
posts
floor level
gravel

0   1   2 m

Fig. 43 - Ground plan of an Ipiutak house from Cape Krusenstern, northwestern Alaska. In the center is the open hearth. After J.L. Giddings and H.-G. Bandi (1962).

Ipiutak culture has also been found on Cape Krusenstern north of Kotzebue (Fig. 43). Here too the chronology of the

beach ridges (29th to 35th beach ridge) and radiocarbon analyses date it to the same period. The examination of a large Ipiutak meeting house, a *qualgi* measuring 8 by 12 meters, near
Deering in the north of the Seward Peninsula, was carried out
by Helge Larsen in 1950. This meeting house likewise yielded
neither pottery nor blubber lamps, and only a single piece of
ground slate was found, which of course may be interpreted as
an article of trade. But it is interesting to see that, in addition
to fragments of sleds, kayaks or canoes, there is evidence of
snowshoes, spear-throwers, fire drills and plaiting. Two radiocarbon analyses of Deering material give dates of 1380 $\pm$ 200
and 1290 $\pm$ 200 years, which tally with the dating of Ipiutak
mentioned above, but leave open the possibility of a later dating.

Finally, we may point once more to the Ipiutak influence
discovered by Larsen in the area between Nanvak Bay and
Chagvan Bay in the southern part of the Kuskokwim area,
southwestern Alaska.

The report on the Point Barrow expedition mounted by the
United States Army between 1881 and 1883 mentions a prehistoric Eskimo settlement identified as 'Perignax', 'Perigniak'
or 'Pergniak'. According to the present-day inhabitants of Barrow, it should be more correctly written 'Píg-i-nik'. The term
Birnirk culture used by archeologists goes back to Viljhálmur
Stefánsson who in 1912 encouraged the natives to dig at this
site and then bought their artifacts. Afterwards the Barrow Eskimos did not give up their archeological work at Birnirk and
other sites on Point Barrow, and thus it was possible for Knud
Rasmussen, W.B. Van Valin, A.H. Hopson and others to purchase further material; they also carried out some excavations
themselves. Systematic investigations were made by James A.
Ford in 1932 under the auspices of the United States National
Museum, but they have only recently been described in detail.

Birnirk is a group of 'dwelling mounds', a little less than one
kilometer northeast of Barrow. It is a place where a fairly considerable complex of refuse was formed as a consequence of
long settlement and the continuous construction of new buildings on the site of older ones, like the 'tells' in the Balkans or
Near East. There are 16 mounds in all, measuring from 60 cen-

timeters to 1 meter in height and from 15 to 36 meters in diameter, arranged in three rows running parallel to the present
shoreline (Fig. 44).

The Birnirk house is rectangular in plan and was built of
driftwood and an insulating layer of sod; whale bones also
served as a building material. The houses were semi-subterranean, with entrance passages which seem to have had no
cold trap, but led gently upwards into the house (Fig. 45). Also
noteworthy is a kind of 'skylight' covered by a gut-skin through
which some light could penetrate.

The population of the settlement at Birnirk gained their livelihood from hunting sea-mammals, and the whale now began

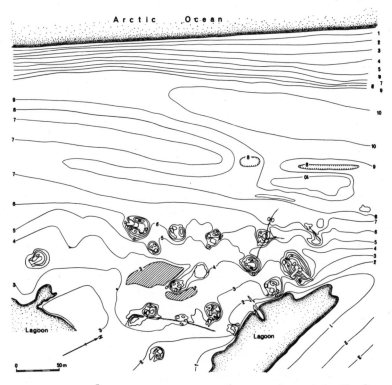

Fig. 44 - Plan of Birnirk settlement on Point Barrow, northern Alaska. The diagram shows the location of the individual 'dwelling mounds'. The
cross-hatched areas between the lagoons denote swampy terrain. Redrawn after J. Ford (1959).

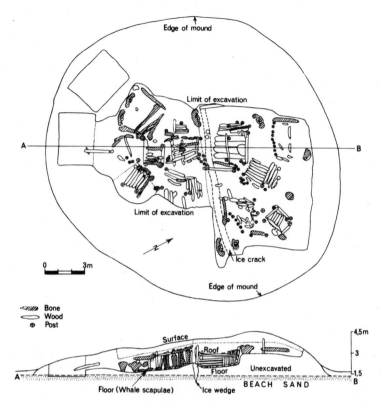

Fig. 45 - Ground plan and cross-section of excavations in a complex of houses at Birnirk. Redrawn after J. Ford (1959).

to play an important role as well as the seal and walrus. They also hunted land-mammals, caught birds, fished and collected shells, eggs, roots and berries. They possessed dog-drawn sleds, umiaks and kayaks.

The typical Birnirk harpoon head is made of antler and measures between 10 and 11 centimeters in length. Next to the open socket is a spur with one to three prongs. Above the line hole the harpoon head is rather flat but usually has a well-defined median ridge and on one side an inset blade of flint and on the other a barb. The relatively long fore part has no inset point in front. Most Birnirk harpoons bear simple decorations (Fig. 46).

In addition to the Birnirk type of harpoon head other types occur, of which only that of Naulock can be mentioned here. Measuring an average 9 centimeters in length, these harpoons are distinguished by a slightly bifurcated or multi-pronged spur, an open socket and a terminal inset point. Everything else that belongs to the harpoon equipment is of course also

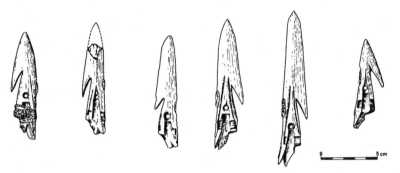

Fig. 46 - Birnirk harpoon heads. Redrawn from J. Ford (1959).

found in the Birnirk culture. Rather unusual is a kind of lance head, i.e. a long wooden shaft measuring approximately 40 centimeters in length, in one of the terminals of which a piece of flint is inserted, which is retouched ventrally and dorsally or, on the other hand, may be hardly worked at all. The proximal end is conical and fits into a hole in the socket-piece of the harpoon shaft that normally receives the foreshaft; a shallow notch on one edge of the lance made it possible to retain the line used to hold the lance head in place of the harpoon.

We need not deal in detail with the throwing-board, reflex bow, arrowheads made of antler with a characteristic tapering tang, bird darts, bolas, leisters and salmon spears, men's knives, and women's knives.

Birnirk pottery is made of clay, heavily tempered with sand and small gravel and is poorly fired. The walls of vessels range in thickness from 10 to 20 millimeters. Only two types could be determined: saucer-like lamps and cooking-pots with almost vertical sides which taper to a conical form at the bottom and terminate in a point. Frequently the vessels are decorated with curvilinear designs, produced with the aid of paddle-shaped whale bone stamps.

Only relatively few decorations appear on objects of bone, antler and ivory. Some of these are reminiscent of Punuk ornamentation. Also carvings such as small human figures made of bark or carved from sheets of baleeen are rather rare.

Ford assumes that the Birnirk culture was derived in the first place from impulses exerted by the Okvik and Old Bering Sea cultures. Other influences from Ipiutak and early Punuk also played a role. Outside Point Barrow the Birnirk culture has so far been established only sporadically. In America the limits of its spread extend eastward as far as Cape Parry, in the southwest of Amundsen Gulf, and also by way of Point Hope as far as Cape Prince of Wales on Seward Peninsula; in Asia they extend as far as Cape Baranov, east of the Kolyma estuary and to St. Lawrence Island. Ford is certain that chronologically Birnirk coincides with the final stage of the Old Bering Sea and the early Punuk cultures. Giddings assigns it to the period from 500 to 900 A.D., a view which has recently found support in radiocarbon analyses.

On Point Barrow traces of the Birnirk culture are not limited to the ruins at Birnirk itself. They are also found at Kugusugaruk, southwest of Barrow, where Van Valin discovered a large number of burials. Ford examined a number of other sites, one of which was Nunagiak, approximately 100 kilometers west of Barrow, near Point Belcher. He was also able to purchase artifacts which Eskimos had discovered in 1932 when some house ruins near Utkiavik, very close to Barrow, were explored. On the basis of these complexes, both of which, and especially Utkiavik, are more recent than Birnirk, he endeavored to show that a gradual development took place from Birnirk toward the Thule culture. He believes that the representatives of the Thule culture probably left Point Barrow approximately at the time when Nunagiak was settled, and then migrated to Arctic Canada, whence they went on to Greenland. This may have taken place around 900 A.D. On the other hand, W.E. Taylor believes, first, that the Birnirk culture had already spread as far as Cape Parry on Amundsen Gulf before 900 A.D.; secondly, that the development of the Thule culture took place in the entire coastal area to the west as far as Cape Prince of Wales at the furthermost point of Seward Peninsula; thirdly, that the Canadian Thule culture did not develop in Alaska but was derived from offshoots of Birnirk which spread as far as Amundsen Gulf.

The later cultural development in Arctic Alaska may best be described on the basis of some other discoveries which Helge

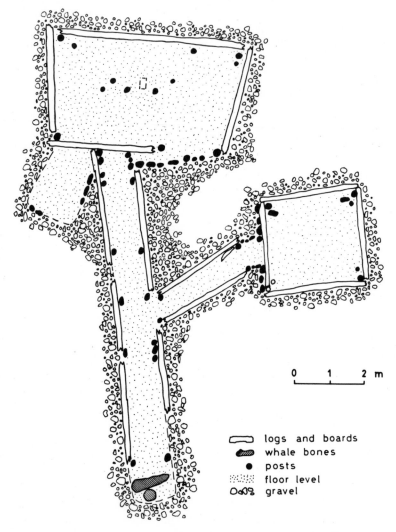

Fig. 47 - Ground plan of a house of the Western Thule culture on Cape Kru-senstern, northwestern Alaska. After J.L. Giddings and H.-G. Bandi (1962).

Larsen and Froelich G. Rainey made at Point Hope during their excavations at Ipiutak. They were able to identify the Birnirk culture there, although only in three graves. It was

Fig. 48 - Finds of the Western Thule culture on Cape Krusenstern, north-western Alaska. After J.L. Giddings and H.-G. Bandi (1962).

succeeded by a phase termed the Western Thule culture. The material concerned manifests connections both with Birnirk and with the Canadian or Eastern Thule culture (Figs. 47, 48, 49). The harpoon heads, like those from the Nunagiak phase at Point Barrow, resemble very closely those of Thule type 2: open socket, barbs on one or both sides, no inset point. The arrowheads, too, show a certain development compared to those of Birnirk. On the other hand a number of types are absent which are characteristic of the Eastern Thule culture, such as the snow knife, crescent-shaped blubber lamps and runners for sleds. According to Giddings, Western Thule must be dated between 900 and 1300 A.D. It is superseded by another phase which Larsen and Rainey term the Tigara culture, after the Eskimo name for the present-day settlements on Point Hope, partly because most of the finds originate from house

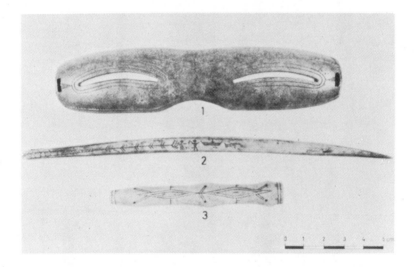

Fig. 49 - Ivory carvings of the Western Thule culture from Cape Krusenstern, northwestern Alaska: (1) snow goggles; (2) point with engraved hunting scene; (3) decorated needle-case. After J.L. Giddings and H.-G. Bandi (1962).

ruins and graves in the vicinity (more than 400 of which were examined!), and partly because this culture is to a great extent identical with that of the historic Tikerarmiut Eskimos. Among the harpoon heads one notices that there are less of the type with open sockets. Most numerous are those with closed sockets, two or more lateral barbs and no inset point. Also the terminals of the arrowheads have a somewhat different shape: between the body and the conical tang there is a sharply cut shoulder and the tang has a narrow, ridge-formed belt or four knobs. A novelty are the long, slender tanged flint arrow points. Some evidence, such as the appearance of flat sled runners, which are typical of the Eastern Thule culture, indicates the beginning of a movement from Arctic Canada back to Alaska. The Tigara phase, which we consider as a further development of the Western Thule culture, is assigned by Giddings to the period from 1300 to 1700 A.D.

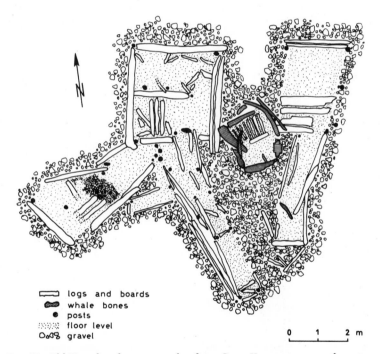

logs and boards
whale bones
posts
floor level
gravel

0   1   2 m

Fig. 50 - Old Kotzebue house complex from Cape Krusenstern, northwestern Alaska. The house on the left has a trapezoid kitchen annex; between the two houses is a storage cache made of whale bones. After J.L. Giddings and H.-G. Bandi (1962).

The development is brought to a close by a so-called modern phase. Here there is evidence not only of contact with the white man but also of a continuation of the 'feedback' movement from the Eastern Thule culture area just mentioned.

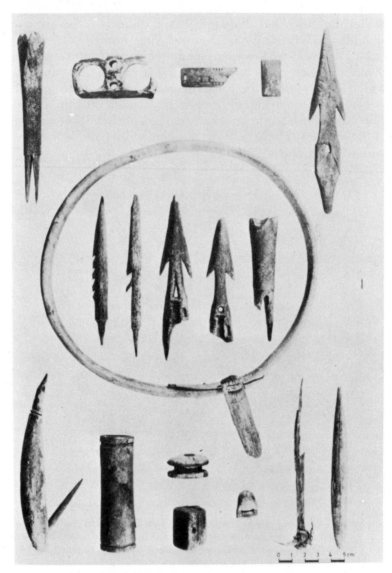

Fig. 51 - Artifacts of the Old Kotzebue culture from Cape Krusenstern, northwestern Alaska. Center: frame of a toy drum. After J.L. Giddings and H.-G. Bandi (1962).

Forms appear which developed there, such as the sealing stool and the seal indicator both of which were employed in breathing-hole hunting. On the other hand some fresh elements appear of Asiatic and southern Alaskan origin which suggest that contact with European culture and the consequent desire of the natives to obtain imported goods led to an intensification of barter trade between the various groups of Alaskan Eskimos. From other elements it can be inferred that local development continued to take place.

The development of Western Thule culture described very briefly here may have taken a similar course in other parts of Alaska north of the Bering Strait. Important evidence of this comes from the studies made by J.L. Giddings between 1940 and 1947 along the Kobuk River from Kotzebue Sound far into the interior. His excavations, which were combined with dendrochronological research, were mainly centered upon the following sites: Ahteut, a settlement on the middle Kobuk dating from the first half of the thirteenth century A.D.; Ekseavik, a small settlement a little further downstream, inhabited around 1400; Old and Middle Kotzebue (*circa* 1400/first half of sixteenth century), near the present-day settlement of the same name (Figs. 50, 51); and Ambler Island on the upper Kobuk, settled in the middle of the eighteenth century. There is scarcely any doubt that a development similar to the one described at Point Hope took place in the Kobuk area. As early as the so-called Western Thule phase an advance upstream can be established. Later this parallel between the coast and the interior must have continued, or even survived to the present day. Giddings gives the term 'Arctic Woodland culture' to the inland types of each phase of development, i.e. to the cultures of groups that do not live directly on the coast. But we should not imagine that there was a clear dividing line between the coastal and inland Eskimo; contact and exchanges were intensive; movements in both directions took place continuously.

Bibliography: Collins, 1954c; Debetz, 1959; Ford, 1959; Giddings, 1952a, 1957, 1962a, 1962b, 1962c, 1963, 1966, 1967; Giddings and Bandi, 1962; Larsen, 1952, 1954; Larsen and Rainey, 1948; Mason, 1930; Stefánsson, 1914; Wissler, 1916.

INTERIOR OF ALASKA

The references to the Arctic Woodland culture lead us to the interior of Alaska, which today can of course only to a limited extent be regarded as part of the 'Eskimo area', but bears traces suggesting that it was once inhabited by ancestors of the present-day Eskimos. This means that we now have to take a big step backward in time from the settlements on the Kobuk, some of which are very recent, back to sites whose material is from a much earlier period. We shall at first remain on the Kobuk, and then turn to the Brooks Range and to its northern foothills.

In 1941 J.L. Giddings, in the course of his investigations on the Kobuk, came across a site near Onion Portage, some 160 kilometers from the estuary as the crow flies, which appeared to him full of promise. In 1961 he resumed his studies there and soon established a sequence of cultures extending over a long period of time. After his death the excavations were continued by his collaborators, in particular Douglas Anderson. So far eight different cultural phases are said to have been distinguished, the relative antiquity of which was determined according to the level at which they lay buried in the river banks. Since no exact data have as yet been published, one may simply mention that the lowest stratum contained flint material with boat-shaped cores for which radiocarbon dating suggests an age of about 8000 years, and which can probably be considered as American Epi-Gravettian. Proceeding upwards, there is a layer containing material which resembles Palisades II on Cape Krusenstern. Denbigh material is only encountered further up, in association with a house of circular ground plan whose age is put at approximately 4000 years. This may suffice to indicate that this is an extremely important find. It is of particular significance that as early as 8000 years ago an industry appeared on the Kobuk in which the dissemination of the American Epi-Gravettian can be identified. As mentioned above, the Onion Portage site became even more important when, in the summer of 1967, it was discovered that below there is another layer with material reminiscent of the leaf-shaped point complex of the late Lower Paleolithic in northern Eurasia, with the addition of some elements of Upper Paleolithic character.

In 1949, just one year after J.L. Giddings had identified the Denbigh Flint complex, Ralph S. Solecki came across further traces of the American Epi-Gravettian tradition in the course of his exploration of the region of the Kukpowruk and Kokolik rivers, which rise on the northern slope of the Brooks Range, or to be more precise on their western spurs, the Delong Mountains, and flow toward the Arctic Ocean. On the Kukpowruk he discovered two sites with microblades as well as a large number of more recent sites — usually hunting camps used only for a short while — which probably originated from the same period as the remains of the settlements just mentioned in the Kobuk area. Solecki emphasizes that one of these two surface sites (No. 121) yielded cores which have common features with the boat-shaped nuclei from the College Campus site near Fairbanks. But the other one (No. 65) contained large cores that were more conical in shape. In addition both sites yielded end-scrapers and the usual refuse material.

Recently William N. Irving reported on the results of studies carried out in 1954 and 1961 in the Howard Pass area (between the upper Noatak and Colville). Near North Point (= Punyik Point) on Lake Itivlik he encountered the clearly identifiable ruin of a house, partly underground, with a low-lying entrance passage containing small-tool material. Not far from this he could also establish two different phases of the American Epi-Gravettian tradition, or as he puts it, the 'Arctic Small-Tool tradition, which was closely related to the Denbigh Flint complex'.

Earlier in 1950-51, the same scholar had come across small-tool industries further east in the area of Anaktuvuk Pass, one of the easiest ways across the central part of the Brooks Range, or to be more precise, in the Endicott Mountains. He mentions in particular the site of Imaigenik in Anaktuvuk Valley, the material of which has many features in common with that of the Denbigh Flint complex. On the other hand, he regards another small-tool site at Tuluak Lake as a little more developed, and from this infers that we must reckon with a gradual modification of the Epi-Gravettian tradition, as taking place parallel with its geographical dissemination.

In 1950 Robert J. Hackman discovered by Lake Natvakruak

north of Anaktuvuk Pass material which bears a striking similarity to the Denbigh Flint complex. Most of the forms described by Giddings are present, among them the pseudo-burin. On
the other hand one core resembles the College Campus site
type.

John M. Campbell mentions a number of other groups of
finds from the Anaktuvuk Pass area in addition to the Kogruk
complex mentioned in connection with possible traces of the
earliest immigrations into Alaska. The Kayuk complex is distinguished especially by so-called Lerma points belonging to
the Northern Point tradition, and is assigned to the period between 7000 and 5000 years ago. The Natvakruak complex has
common features with the Denbigh Flint complex, and is
estimated to be between 6000 and 4000 years old. The Tuktu
complex, too, reveals links with the American Epi-Gravettian
tradition. On the other hand, points with basal notches appear here, which is why we have already mentioned it in connection with the Old Whaling culture of the Bering Strait area.
It may go back to about 4000 or 3000 years ago. The cultural
and chronological position of a further complex, the Toyuk
complex, is not at all clear. It is succeeded by an Ipiutak variant, the Kavik complex, and the recent Nunamiut culture.
Some restraint will be necessary in evaluating these numerous
'complexes', which are mainly based upon surface finds or
have at least not been extracted from a complex stratigraphy.

Bibliography: Campbell, 1959, 1961a, 1961b, 1962b; Giddings, 1952a, 1962a; Hadleigh-West, 1965a; Irving, 1951,
1953, 1957, 1962a; Nelson, 1937; Rainey, 1939, 1940, 1953;
Skarland and Giddings, 1948; Solecki, 1950a, 1950b, 1951a,
1951b; Solecki and Hackman, 1951; Thompson, 1948.

Canada

Crossing the border into Canada (Fig. 52), one first enters
the northwestern part of Yukon Territory, where R.S. Mac
Neish explored near Engigstciak, in the Firth River area. In
this region the British Mountain complex and its associations
with a Mousterian-like technique are already familiar. Since

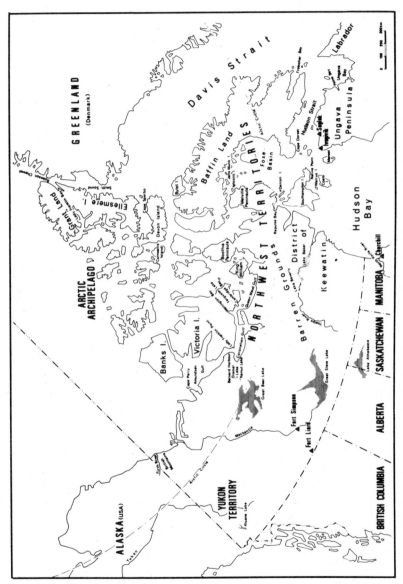

Fig. 52 - Map of northern Canada, showing places and sites mentioned in the text.

MacNeish is known for his tendency to be very free in drawing up new concepts, it is not surprising that in the Engigstciak area he distinguishes eight other complexes based upon further finds — most of them recovered on the surface or at a slight depth. British Mountain is followed first by the Flint Creek complex, which is correlated with the Northern Point tradition, and then by the New Mountain complex, dating from between 5000 and 4000 years ago, which belongs to the American Epi-Gravettian tradition and has two components. One of these is microlithic and comprises a large number of elaborately retouched inset pieces, arrowheads and pseudo-burins as well as small blades. The other is macrolithic, with larger projectile points, some of which MacNeish correlates with the Angostura type based on the Plano tradition of the western United States, as well as scrapers, end-scrapers etc. The animal bones discovered show that the principal game hunted was the caribou, in rarer instances the bison, musk-ox, deer and mountain sheep. Although it cannot be shown with absolute certainty that the two components of the New Mountain complex were contemporaneous, there is no doubt that MacNeish's discovery represents a further step in the development of the small-tool industries as they advanced from west to east. His six more recent Engigstciak complexes all contain pottery and can be regarded as parallels to the later development in northern Alaska.

Still within a radius of 800 kilometers from the Firth River, W.E. Taylor began exploration of the region between Cape Parry on Amundsen Gulf and Queen Maud Gulf in 1963. During the first summer he discovered a small-tool industry termed Pre-Dorset at Wellington Bay, on the south coast of Victoria Island. Early Dorset sites were found in the same area as well as near Bernard Harbor and at Wellington Bay; and finally, the Thule culture was identified near Cape Parry, at Lady Franklin Point, at Wellington Bay and Cambridge Bay. In 1964 further Pre-Dorset sites were added on the Ekalluk River, which links Ferguson Lake with Wellington Bay. In 1965 Taylor also localized on Banks Island a Pre-Dorset site which he called Umingmak. This Pre-Dorset can no doubt be incorporated in the general scheme of the American Epi-Gravettian and affords interesting evidence of this early immigration spreading in the direction of Greenland.

But first let us deal with the remaining areas of Arctic Canada. We encounter other early traces of occupation in the southeast of Great Bear Lake. MacNeish distinguishes there three complexes which he calls Franklin Tanks, Great Bear River and Northwest Territory Docks. The first two are characterized by projectile points, some of which according to MacNeish are of Paleo-Indian origin, so that we are dealing here with the Northern Point tradition. The third one seems to belong to the Epi-Gravettian. The question must however be raised whether it is correct to keep on drawing up new 'complexes' on the basis of surface finds. The large number of uncertainties involved result in a most confused and ambiguous picture. Restraint is even more in order when one hears that in 1949 in two months MacNeish explored the vast zone from Great Bear Lake up the Mackenzie as far as Great Slave Lake and from there as far as Athabaska Lake and also to the lakes on the upper Coppermine River. As he himself reports, he covered about 15,000 kilometers and discovered 40 sites with a total of 225 artifacts, which he subsequently classified in four complexes: Taltheilei and Artillery Lake as constituent parts of the Northern Point tradition, Lockhart River as a component of the American Epi-Gravettian tradition, and Whitefish Lake, a late prehistoric group.

This does not mean that MacNeish was not on the right track. But if one considers how many archeological problems in Europe could be solved only after decades of intensive study, one wonders whether a more cautious judgment of new finds in the Arctic might not be wiser.

Further to the northeast, approximately midway between Great Bear Lake and Coronation Gulf, Elmer Harp carried out explorations in the area of Dismal Lake and Kamut Lake, which have to be mentioned here. The sites Dismal 1a and 1b at the western end of the lake are distinguished by projectile points, lanceolate or corner-notched, as well as by knives, end-scrapers and broad scrapers. Small-tool material is absent, but this has been authenticated at two other sites: Dismal 2, not far from the southeastern end of the lake (Fig. 53), and at the northeastern end of Kamut Lake. This includes microblades, retouched burins and pseudo-burins as well as small scrapers. But both sites also have a relatively abundant amount of large

Fig. 53 - Small-tool material from Dismal 2, Arctic Canada. Photo by courtesy of E. Harp.

material: lanceolate points, knives and scrapers. On the other hand Harp emphasizes that there are various differences between Dismal 2 and Kamut Lake; for example, the ratio between microlithic and macrolithic material amounts to 4:1 in the former case and 1:4 in the latter. But we must not overlook

the fact that these are all surface sites, so that we have to reckon with the possibility of components from more than just one
chronological period. As far as our problem is concerned, it is
of particular importance that the American Epi-Gravettian tradition has been established in this area as well.

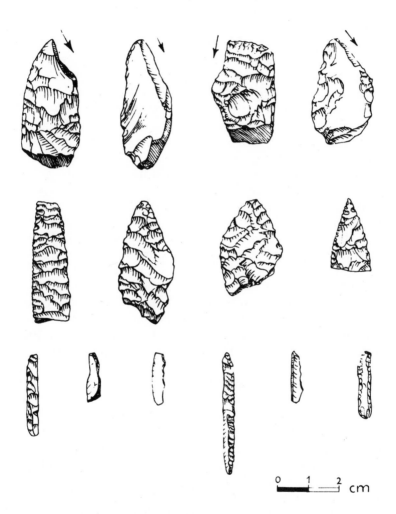

Fig. 54 - Stone tools (burins, projectile points with retouched surfaces and
pseudo-burin spalls), from Thyazzi on North Knife River west of
Churchill, Manitoba. Redrawn after J.L. Giddings (1956b).

With MacNeish's explorations of Athabaska Lake in northern Alberta and Saskatchewan, the provinces of central Canada have been reached. If from there another jump of 700 kilometers to the southeast is made, we reach the western shore of Hudson Bay, near Churchill in Manitoba. In doing so no doubt a large number of prehistoric sites in the Barren Grounds, the endless tundra regions, have been skipped simply because they are still awaiting discovery. At Churchill we once again come across traces left by J. Louis Giddings: when he explored this area in 1953 he heard from an Indian of a flint site called Thyazzi near North Knife River, west of Churchill. Indeed it turned out that at the spot designated, numerous artifacts and flakes were lying about (Fig. 54). Even Giddings must have been surprised that these types bore considerable resemblances to those of his Denbigh Flint complex. Thus in the eastern Arctic he once again encountered traces of the American Epi-Gravettian tradition. Prominence must be given to the occurrence of retouched and pseudo-burins, as well as to elaborately worked points and lateral inset blades for arrowheads; on the other hand so far no microblades or appropriate cores have been discovered. It will be seen that this material also bears a resemblance to that of the Pre-Dorset culture to be discussed below. Elmer Harp points to common features between the Thyazzi material and that of Dismal 2 and Kamut Lake.

From these data it can be inferred that the early immigrants with their small-tool flint material gradually spread from Alaska across Arctic Canada and finally reached Hudson Bay. Hitherto only the individual landmarks along their long and widely spread route were known. But these suffice to show that they conquered almost the entire Arctic in the course of several waves of migration, offshoots of which we shall also encounter in Greenland. The people concerned were evidently capable of mastering the harsh conditions of life in the interior. They were able to adapt themselves to life on the coast in the east, just as well as at Cape Denbigh in the west. This is apparent from the Pre-Dorset culture. Originally the relevant finds in the Canadian Arctic were termed Sarqaq, by association with a site in the Disko Bay area, West Greenland. But in the meantime Sarqaq has been identified as a Greenland group which probably was derived from the Pre-Dorset culture, as

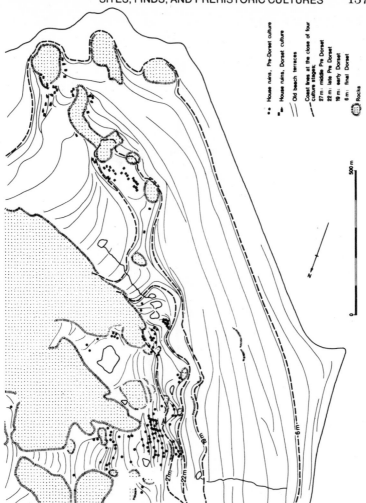

Fig. 55 - Topography of the Jens Munk site, on the island of that name off the
      north of Melville Peninsula near the coast of Baffin Land. Redrawn
      after J. Meldgaard (1960a).

did the Dorset culture itself. This is likewise a branch of the
American Epi-Gravettian. At first Pre-Dorset was known mainly from studies carried out in 1954 and 1957 by Jørgen Meldgaard, in the north of Melville Peninsula, under the auspices
of the Danish National Museum. He concentrated upon three
sites north of Fox River basin: Alarnerk, a summer settlement

of the Igloolik Eskimos on the mainland (Fig. 11), Parry Hill
(= Kaleruserk) on Igloolik Island, and Jens Munk (=Kapuivik)
on Jens Munk Island, near the opposite shore of Baffin Land.
At these sites Meldgaard was able to establish extensive sequences of beach terraces containing archeological remains.

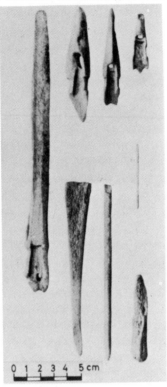

Fig. 56 - Pre-Dorset finds from the Jens Munk site on Jens Munk Island (Baffin Land), 23 meter terrace (about 1000 B.C.). Of special interest are
the harpoon heads which have features in common with the much
more recent Thule culture. After J. Meldgaard (1960a).

It showed that the upper terraces bear traces of the Pre-Dorset
culture, the middle ones those of the Dorset culture, and
the lower ones have been occupied from Thule times to the
present day. On Jens Munk the Pre-Dorset sites are situated
51 to 23 meters and the Dorset ones from 22 to 6 meters above
sea level, while the Thule ones are lower down (Fig. 55).
    Of prime interest are the facts which Meldgaard was able to

ascertain with regard to the Pre-Dorset people. These not only provide information about their dwellings but also add to our knowledge about their culture, since the extremely dry climate in the Igloolik area allowed organic remains to survive. The ruins of their houses are circular or oval in ground plan; they were built of sizeable blocks of stone with a hearth in the center. Pottery appears to be completely absent. The Igloolik finds are predominantly animal bones and implements made of them. They indicate that the Pre-Dorset culture was by that time already clearly oriented toward life on the coast. It is surprising to find harpoon heads present which have features in common with those of the much more recent Thule culture (Fig. 56). Bows and arrows were also well known and dogs were kept. Stone implements were made of flint. From the formation of the shoreline and radiocarbon datings it can be inferred that the Pre-Dorset culture lasted approximately from 4000 to 2800 years ago. It changed surprisingly little during this period. The only striking feature is that the craftsmanship of the more recent artifacts was less elaborate and clumsier. Another point to note is that hitherto no skeletons of the Pre-Dorset people have been found. L. Oschinsky takes the view that they were of the Arctic Mongoloid type.

In the course of research carried out in 1958 along Thelon River, in the region between Baker Lake and Beverly Lake in the center of the Keewatin district, west of Hudson Bay, Elmer Harp established *inter alia* an infiltration which he associates with the middle and later phases of the Pre-Dorset culture in the Igloolik area. He believes that this began around 3000 years ago.

On Jens Munk and at other places in the Igloolik area there appeared, shortly after the Pre-Dorset inhabitants — or possibly ousting them — a population whose culture was different. The name given them is derived from Cape Dorset in the southwest of Baffin Land. For a very long time our information about the Dorset culture was very scanty. But thanks to Meldgaard's studies near Alarnerk it is possible to identify five different phases, spread over the period between 700 B.C. and 1300 A.D. These are associated with over 200 house ruins distributed over a number of beach terraces. Conditions were similar at Parry Hill and Jens Munk.

But first of all some general observations are in order about the Dorset culture, as it is known from earlier finds made in an area extending from Newfoundland in the south by way of the Hudson Bay area to the Arctic Archipelago and across to Greenland. A particularly large number of Dorset settlements are to be found in the region between the Hudson Strait, Fox Basin and Boothia Peninsula (Fig. 57).

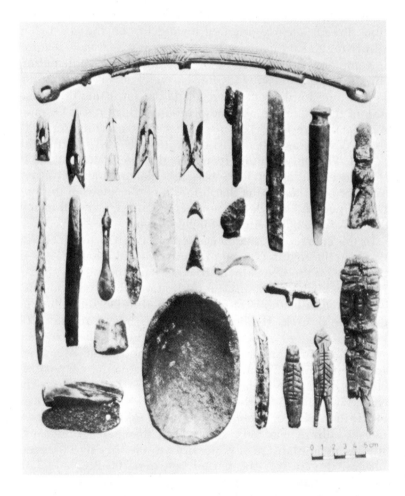

Fig. 57 - Dorset finds from Arctic Canada and North Greenland. Photo by courtesy of K. Birket-Smith.

The Dorset people lived by hunting seal, walrus, polar bear, caribou, foxes and hares, as well as by catching birds and fishing. Whaling was not known. Dogs were not to be had so there were no dog-drawn sleds. Small hand sleds had to suffice. In this connection one may also note the use of ice-creepers, made of bone, which were fastened to the feet. For travel by water kayaks may have been employed. The settlements are always situated on the coast and frequently at the same places that later were selected by the Thule people. Generally speaking, these settlements consisted of semi-subterranean rectangular houses measuring 4 by 5 meters, and in addition to these there also were large meeting houses measuring some 7 by 14 meters. Little is known about the construction of the walls and roof. As a rule pieces of sod were probably piled upon one another and covered with skin, but stone structures also occurred. Inside were benches for sitting and sleeping upon, which ran along the side walls, as well as small open hearths. Entrance passages and cold traps appear at a later stage, when the Dorset people established contact with the Thule culture; simultaneously their houses became narrower; adjoining rooms were added for the hearth and storage purposes; the benches were moved to the rear wall. During the summer the Dorset people presumably lived in skin-covered tents.

In addition to the open hearths, oval or triangular stone lamps served as a source of light and heat. Cooking-pots were made of the same material — varieties of soapstone which could be worked easily. Pottery seems to have been unknown.

The characteristic Dorset harpoon head is a type with a swallow-tailed base, and a closed foreshaft socket; the latter is rectangular due to ignorance of the drill in the Dorset culture, which meant that holes had to be cut or gouged out. This is also the case with the line hole, which either runs parallel to the rectangular foreshaft socket through the harpoon head, or else there are two line holes opposite one another and placed vertically to the socket. In front, these harpoon heads either terminate in a point or else they are round with a slot to receive a stone point (Fig. 57). Besides this type and its variants there are a number of others. For example, harpoon heads similar to those of Thule type 2, differing only in that the line hole is not placed in the center but laterally, and is once again cut or gouged out. Wherever inset points are employed, they almost invariably consist of retouched flint, and only in rare instances of ground slate; they are mostly triangular with a concave base; occasionally pieces are to be found with basal notches. In the case of the larger specimens, some of which are tanged, it is difficult to distinguish whether these are lance points or knife blades.

Other implements are bird darts and leisters, some of which have barbs on either side; men's knives with blades of retouched flint (occasionally also of ground slate), affixed laterally or at the end of a bone or ivory handle; many such knife blades are asymmetrical in shape. Ulus also occur. Scrapers made of flint-like material are found in various types. Axe or adze blades, which occur occasionally, are only polished on the cutting edge. Characteristic also are whetstones made of quartziferous sandstone. Among the implements of organic material are flint-flakers, awls and needles with eyes, kept in cylindrical cases; a few snow knives also seem to occur. From time to time solid copper and meteoritic iron were worked, but of course only by hammering.

Ornaments comprise pendants of bone, ivory or wood, which occasionally bear engraved decorations; necklaces are pieced together from perforated animal teeth or small stone discs. Utensils were occasionally ornamented with x-shaped or linear designs.

Ivory or bone animal figures are usually small; some of them are naturalistic, while others are more or less stylized or have a grotesque appearance. Frequently they bear the skeleton motif which has already been encountered in the Ipiutak culture; with it often goes an x-shaped sign placed on the back of the head (Fig. 58).

Small human figures likewise can be naturalistic or grotesque caricatures and without exception they are most original works. For these also the skeleton motif is used as well as tattoo-marks. Particularly characteristic are curious carvings of antler or wood featuring a number of human faces — in one case as many as 28. Collins takes the view that these are not Eskimo or Indian faces but definitely European (Fig. 66a and b). In Greenland it was quite possible for the Dorset people to have made contact with the inhabitants of the medieval Norse settlements on the southwestern coast. The corresponding finds in Canada could perhaps be traced back to the Vikings who are supposed to have journeyed across the Davis Strait. Recently evidence has actually come to light of Viking settlements in Newfoundland: excavations by H. Ingstad in an area spotted by J. Meldgaard near Cape Bauld have yielded artifacts which

Fig. 58 - Polar bear swimming. Ivory carving of the Dorset III phase (approx. 500 A.D.), from Alarnerk in the north of Melville Peninsula. Photo by courtesy of J. Meldgaard.

are considered as Norse. It is, however, somewhat strange that both in Canada and Greenland contact with the white man should have led Dorset artists to carve human faces clustered together like grapes.

There is still more to be said about the burials of the Dorset people. According to Meldgaard three types can be established so far. The first one consists of a circular grave-pit lined with stones, where the grave goods seem to have been placed inside without any particular system. The second one has a mound of stones on top of the interment; in this case, the grave goods were not only added with greater care but also included decorated objects, frequently broken or unfinished, which probably had a symbolic character. More recent is the third type of burial, which is regarded as an imitation of the large stone cists of the Thule culture.

To return to Meldgaard's findings in the Igloolik area, which have so far only been touched upon, he distinguishes five phases, the criteria being the way in which Dorset houses are distributed on the various beach terraces and the artifacts discovered in them. What we have so far described as the Dorset culture is a late phase of this development, roughly corresponding to Melgaard's fourth phase.

It is extremely surprising that, as one goes back to the earlier phases, one gets further and further away from this picture. But there is no doubt that there is here a continuous development, during which the typical forms of harpoon heads and retouched flint implements of the late Dorset culture gradually evolved.

The earliest phase is characterized by large harpoon heads and lance points with the shaft socket open or only partly closed, and by a greater proportion of ground slate implements than of retouched flint ones. The soapstone lamps are square in form. Another point is that during the first two phases of the Dorset culture in the Igloolik area, which can be dated approximately to the period between 700 B.C. and 500 A.D., no art was produced (Fig. 59). It is not until phase 3 that there is evidence of sculpture (Fig. 58). Simultaneously a level of development was reached entirely adapted to life on the coast, with walrus-hunting as the main means of livelihood. Hunting from the edge of the ice seems to have played an important role, and it is conceivable that igloos made of snow came into use in this connection; they may have derived from domed wooden houses covered with skins and snow. In phase 4, which corresponds to the Dorset culture as described, earlier development reached its climax; particularly surprising is the almost explosive force with which art appears on the scene. In phase 5, to

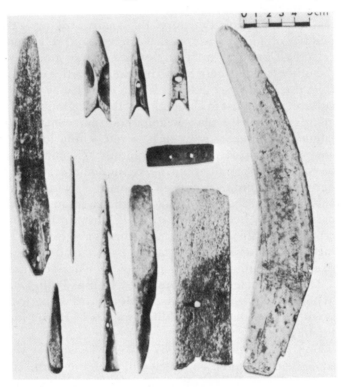

Fig. 59 - Artifacts of Dorset II from Jens Munk site on Jens Munk Island (Baffin Land), 22 meter terrace (about 800 B.C.). After J. Meldgaard (1960a).

which radiocarbon analysis gives an age of 600 ± 150 years, it is possible to establish evidence not only of an influence from the Thule culture, but also of a certain deterioration of climatic conditions, which may have been a contributory factor in the ousting of the Dorset culture from the Igloolik area, or its extinction, around 1300 A.D.

Igloolik is by no means the only area where an early phase of the Dorset culture could be established. In 1954-5 similar observations were made by Henry B. Collins near Native Point, in the southeast of Southampton Island; he called the locality 'T 1 site', a designation derived from Tuneriut, the Eskimo name for Native Point. Since this material has already been published, it is known that the early Dorset culture has a distinct small-tool admixture. Especially striking is the large number of microblades, so that on one hand 'T 1' material re-calls the Denbigh Flint complex and related groups, while on the other it differs both from Thyazzi on North Knife River and from the Pre-Dorset culture. In the early facies of the Dorset culture, in contrast to Denbigh and the two groups of finds just mentioned, burins play no important part. Small points and lateral inset blades with surface retouching for arrowheads are partly comparable to Ipiutak forms. Also noteworthy is the occurrence of so-called burin-like implements, which may be derived from ordinary or pseudo-burins. As with the latter, the chisel-like cutting edge is not at right angles to the surface but parallel to it; but in contrast to all burins it is produced by grinding. Collins points to similar implements in the Old Ber-ing Sea culture and at Ipiutak. It is certain that these burin-like implements are characteristic of the Dorset culture.

The 'T 1' material was termed by Collins Proto-Dorset (not to be confused with Pre-Dorset). Meldgaard seems to compare it with the second phase of his complex of Dorset finds from Igloolik.

One further point: in 1957-8 W.E. Taylor likewise came across early material on Ungava Bay, on the south side of the Hudson Strait. Among other things he established for the first time Dorset inland settlements on Payne Lake in the interior of Ungava Peninsula. He further reports that he found a skele-ton 'in what was almost certainly a Dorset culture context' at Imaha, on Payne Bay in the west of Ungava Bay. According to Oschinsky, an examination showed beyond all doubt that it was of the Eskimo type. The same can be said of skeletons from Dorset sites on Mansel Island and near Sugluk on Hudson Strait. Meldgaard was able to recover some skeletons at Alar-nerk, but it is not yet known what results their analysis has produced.

This brings us to a much disputed problem: the origin of the Dorset culture and the racial origin of its representatives. For a long time two opposing concepts have been advanced. According to one, the Dorset culture is of Indian origin and gradually penetrated northwards from the Great Lakes and the St. Lawrence area. Adaptation to the tundra and to the Arctic coast is said to have led to its becoming 'Eskimoized'. According to the other theory the Dorset culture is an Eskimo phenomenon, originating in Alaska or some other part of the Western Arctic, with roots going back to a hypothetical Pre-Okvik stage. Adherents of this hypothesis also usually recognize a certain Indian influence.

New investigations which throw a rather different light on the origins of the Dorset culture enable one to come nearer to solving the problem. Meldgaard says that 'a number of new traits in the early Dorset culture smell of the forest': in this connection he mentions wood carvings, caribou hunting, fishing and the bear cult. He claims to have identified parallels with 'Late Archaic' and 'Early Woodland' cultures further south in the Indian area, somewhere between the Great Lakes, James Bay south of Hudson Bay, and Newfoundland, from approximately 1000 A.D. 'This, however, does not necessarily mean that the Dorset people were Indians wandering out on the Arctic barrens from the forest, but it does indicate very strong influences from the area.' Let us draw attention to one detail which he emphasizes in this connection: at various early Dorset sites small points were noted on which, after careful chipping on both surfaces, two long blades were pressed from the point on the same surface, each removing approximately one half of the chipped area, giving this surface of the blade a keeled or fluted appearance. This peculiar procedure seems to have had two purposes: to make the edges as sharp as possible and the front part of the point thin. Meldgaard seeks to link this technique with that of Paleo-Indian projectile points with fluted shafts, and points out that this technique occurs most frequently at early Dorset sites in Newfoundland but is met with more rarely further north, and is not present at all in Greenland. In regard to the origin of the Dorset culture he also bases his view upon legends related by present day Igloolik Eskimos. These provide interesting evidence of the significance of the mythical Tunit people, who are well-known throughout the Eastern Eskimo area. Originally the Tunit were thought to be Indians, but later the view prevailed that they were Eskimos of the Thule culture. According to the Igloolik natives, however, the Tunit had nothing to do with the Thule people, with whose remains — especially of house ruins — they are quite familiar and which they ascribe to their own ancestors. On the contrary, they associate the Tunit with other places, and these are always Dorset settlements. In legends the Tunit are described as good caribou hunters who were armed only with a spear. In winter they caught seals at breathing-holes; walrus-hunting was also of importance. Finally, the Tunit are said to have been driven out by ancestors of the Igloolik Eskimos after several battles.

Meldgaard's views as to the origin of the Dorset culture and of its links with the Indian area are by no means generally shared. But Henry B. Collins, too, thinks it possible that the Dorset culture was derived from the Arctic Small-Tool tradition, or according to my broader terminology, from the American Epi-Gravettian tradition and that it was influenced by Indian cultures further south, either by the Old Copper culture or by other Archaic groups.

As W.E. Taylor emphasizes, today there are good reasons to assume that the Dorset culture has its roots in the American Epi-Gravettian tradition. He thinks it feasible that the starting point may have been, for example, the Lockhart River complex in the interior of Arctic Canada, established by MacNeish. The Dorset culture is then said to have begun to crystallize from approximately 3000 years ago, at first in the form of a Pre-Dorset stage, later in that of classical Dorset. The fact that Dorset has a distinctly more Eskimo character and lasted longer than the small-tool cultures he explains as due to continuous influences from the Western Eskimo center. This does not seem to me necessarily so, since we know that the Pre-Dorset already had a tendency toward Eskimo culture. The development from Pre-Dorset to Dorset may not, however, have taken place in the Igloolik area, where Meldgaard established a marked difference between the two, but instead further south. On the other hand, the Igloolik finds show that the early phases of the Dorset culture contained the seeds from which later development sprang. Taylor is convinced that in the near future it will be generally accepted that the Dorset population belonged to the Eskimo race and to the Eskimo-Aleut linguistic family.

It should be borne in mind that parts of the American Epi-Gravettian tradition in the interior must have been in contact with the Indian elements, so that intermingling and influences were possible. This may have been the reason why the Dorset culture, which should be regarded as basically Eskimo, bears a certain Indian imprint.

It is already known that in about 1300 A.D. the Dorset people in the Igloolik area, in the north of Melville Peninsula, came into contact with the newly-arrived Thule culture. If Meldgaard's interpretation of the Tunit legends is correct, the Dorset people must have been driven out by ancestors of the present-day Central Eskimos. Thus, contrary to earlier opinions, the Igloolik Eskimos and other groups of the present-day Central Eskimos in the Canadian Arctic would be descendants of the Thule people.

Let it be recalled, moreover, that in northern Alaska, and possibly further east as far as Amundsen Gulf as well, a development can be identified in the latter half of the first millennium A.D. which led from the Birnirk to the Thule culture by way of intermediary stages. On the other hand the Pre-Dorset culture established in the Igloolik area as early as about 2000 B.C. contained some elements which distantly anticipated the Thule culture. This suggests that the roots of the Thule culture in the Western Arctic go back long before Birnirk.

Yet it is certain that only in association with Birnirk did an advanced form of the Thule culture begin to crystallize over wide areas along the Arctic coast, which then spread rapidly eastwards. As has been shown, it continued to develop in the Central areas so that, when a feedback movement to the west occurred at a relatively late period, new elements were introduced to Alaska which left a particular imprint on the Western Thule culture in that area.

The term Thule culture is derived from the fact that the first reliable find was made in 1916 in connection with the Second Thule Expedition near Thule in North Greenland. Our knowledge about the Thule culture is mostly due to the Fifth Thule Expedition in the early 20's. The settlement of Thule has in the meantime been moved to the north of Inglefield Bay, whereas its former location appears on new maps under the name 'Dundas'; in our map (Fig. 62) this change has not been taken into consideration. When Therkel Mathiassen published his fundamental work on the Thule culture in 1927, he was unable to say anything definite about its absolute age. In the meantime Meldgaard has ascribed the earliest Thule traces in the Igloolik area to the period around 1300 A.D. On the other hand, it will be seen later when dealing with Greenland that the Thule culture was introduced into this area earlier, probably in the eleventh century, or at the latest the twelfth.

Mathiassen's field work during the Fifth Thule Expedition was centered upon the following areas: Repulse Bay, in the south of Melville Peninsula where the site of Naujan was investigated especially closely, the east coast of Melville Peninsula, Southampton Island in the north of Hudson Bay, northern Baffin Land including Bylot Island, and King William Island in the Arctic Archipelago. Subsequent studies by Henry B. Collins and Canadian archeologists have shown that in Arctic Canada the Thule culture extends over almost every stretch of coast on the mainland and the islands, as well as on Labrador. It was wholly oriented to whaling and in this respect was clearly distinguished from the present-day Central Eskimo.

The settlements are invariably situated on the seashore, and consist of permanent winter houses, some of them semi-subterranean. They were built of whale bones, skin and sod; the roof, too, was generally supported by a structure of whale ribs and jawbones. In ground plan they were usually round, and entrance was always gained through a passage with a cold trap. Sometimes several house ruins have a communal entrance passage, so that in plan the entire complex forms a cloverleaf. There are also rectangular houses. In the interior of the Thule houses there was, along the rear wall, an elevated bench for sitting and sleeping. Two-shouldered snow knives, frequently slightly bent, and in most cases made of whale bone, rarely of antler or ivory, were clearly used to build snow houses during winter journeys. Knowledge of these was probably derived from the Dorset culture. On the other hand stone circles suggest that in summer conical skin tents were used.

The inhabitants of these dwellings hunted whale, seal, walrus, polar bear, caribou, musk-ox and smaller mammals: the catching of birds, fishing, collecting of mussels and edible plants likewise contributed to their subsistence. Kayaks and umiaks were used, and in winter they had dog-drawn sleds.

The Thule culture, as one might expect, has numerous parallels with Birnirk. On the other hand it continued to develop after it found its way into the Central areas, so that it acquired its own individual character (Fig. 61). First of all mention may be made of the harpoon heads, which can be classified in different types. Mathiassen designates as type 1 harpoon heads with open socket, lateral spur without a barb, and without inset point; type 2 likewise has an open shaft socket and lateral spur, no inset point, but two barbs opposite one another— rarely one; type 3, in which the shaft socket is again open and the spur situated laterally, has no barb, but does have an inset point (Fig. 60). In addition to smaller harpoon heads for sealing and walrus-hunting larger ones were made for whaling.

The inset points for harpoon heads consist of bone or ground

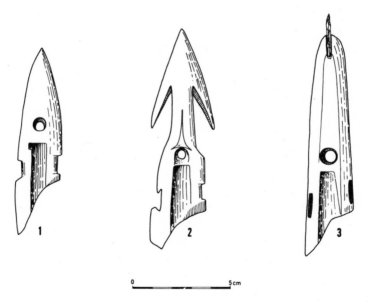

Fig. 60 - Thule harpoon heads: types 1 - 3.

slate, rarely of flint. Moreover, in association with harpoons we may mention the following: foreshafts, shaft sockets, finger-rests, ice picks, and mouthpieces of floats. The throwing-board was probably also used for so-called bladder darts.

Lance heads with open socket, detachable from the shaft, likewise have points of ground slate or bone. These were fastened in a way strangely similar to that of Paleo-Aleut prong harpoons: the stone point was placed in a kind of recess on the lance head and (in this differing slightly from Aleut forms) fixed by means of one or more perforations. In addition to these there are lance heads which are fastened tightly to the shaft. Among other implements essential in hunting walrus from the edge of the ice, or seal at breathing-holes in the ice, were wound plugs, flipper-like scratchers for baiting seals, indicators which immediately reveal the arrival of a seal, and small hunting stools. With regard to bows and arrows it must be emphasized that, in addition to wooden bows, there also occur those made of baleen and that the antler arrowheads with barbs in front have two wart-like knobs, recalling similar types of the Birnirk culture. For working on sinew the sinew-twister, a flat little S-shaped bone instrument, was used. Other equipment of the Thule hunter included bird darts and bolas, leisters and fish-hooks, hooks for catching sea gulls, and various kinds of traps. In addition he used the men's knife, of which there are many varieties.

Among the tools used are whetstones, bow drills and hand drills, adzes, picks, wedges, hammerstones and flint-flakers. In their activities women used the ulu, with a blade of ground slate, skin-scrapers of bone, awls, sewing needles, kept in so-called winged needle-cases, thimbles of leather, and thimble-holders. The soapstone lamp particularly characteristic was the crescent- shaped type which had on the inside a number of elevations where wicks were placed. The same material was also used for making cooking-pots, usually oval in shape. Badly-fired pottery seldom occurs. Other household goods are cups and saucers of wood or baleen, spoons and ladles, marrow-extractors, blubber-pounders, fire drills or pyrite, and baleen mats; the latter were placed on the benches for sitting and sleeping.

Little clothing has survived, but in this connection buttons

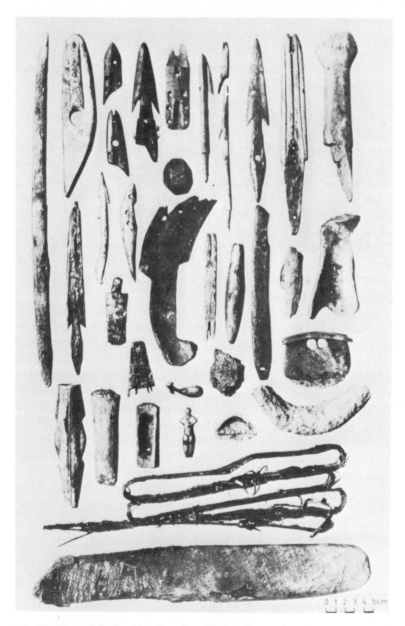

Fig. 61 - Typical finds of the Canadian Thule culture. Photo by courtesy of K. Birket-Smith.

and other kinds of fasteners, snow goggles, combs and ornaments should be mentioned. The latter consisted of perforated animal teeth, carved ivory pendants, bone beads and stone pendants.

Finally there is Thule art, which seems rather poor by comparison with that of other Eskimo cultures. Characteristic are small ivory figures of swimming birds. Since they frequently have a woman's head, they may have had a magical significance. Meldgaard, on the other hand, wonders whether they may not have been some kind of piece used in dice games. Also in the case of small human ivory or wooden sculptures it is not possible to identify with certainty the purpose for which they were used. The ornamentation of utensils is limited to occasional engraved lines, with or without spurs, and Y-shaped signs.

Thule burials are rectangular, lined with stones and covered with huge slabs. In these megalith-like stone cists, the dead were buried together with their personal belongings. Finally, the grave was covered with boulders.

As Therkel Mathiassen has summarized, Thule culture may be considered a highly developed and specialized Eskimo culture. It was created by a people who lived in permanent winter houses along the coast, and temporarily in snow huts, and who in summer had conical tents. They hunted sea-mammals including the whale, and land animals, and supplemented this by catching birds and fishing. All the typical Eskimo weapons, implements and equipment were present. It undoubtedly had a great influence upon later cultural development in the Eskimo area. According to Collins, in some areas it has been able to survive in a slightly modified form down to the present day in Labrador, on Southampton Island and Baffin Land, as well as among the Polar Eskimos of the Thule district in North Greenland, and at Point Barrow in northwestern Alaska. As regards the presence of the Thule culture in Alaska, it has been suggested that some time between 1300 and 1700 A.D. a 'feedback' movement took place from the Central areas of Arctic Canada, which found expression in the appearance of typical Eastern Thule elements in the Western Thule culture in Alaska. No doubt the Thule culture in Alaska—Western Thule influenced by the more advanced Eastern Thule—forms the basis of subsequent cultural development in this region. The situation is different in the Central areas where the Thule culture had a flourishing period during the fourteenth century: then it disappeared again, a process which has so far not been satisfactorily explained. It is not convincing to assume that the Thule people were compelled to migrate on account of an advance by more primitive groups from the interior, whose last survivors would be the Caribou Eskimos. A more likely hypothesis is that the abandonment of the coast of the Central areas might be connected with a deterioration of the climate in the fifteenth century. Subsequently tribes from the interior may have advanced in the direction of the coast. But it remains to be explained what kind of people they were and what kind of culture they had. Were they representatives of a much less advanced branch of the Thule culture, or were they descendants of the Pre-Dorset population, who were driven into the interior when the Dorset people arrived in the Central areas about 700 A.D.? The latter assumption would come close to Birket-Smith's view, namely that the Caribou Eskimos should be regarded as the last relic of a very ancient Proto-Eskimo stratum. One may rule out the possibility of derivation from the Dorset population, as relevant cultural indications of this are completely absent. A final answer to these problems cannot as yet be given. The only certain fact is that in the Central areas a cultural form prevails which, in contrast to the Thule culture, is not oriented exclusively towards coastal life, but in part bears the imprint of the interior.

The traces of the Thule culture can now be followed in a northeasterly direction as well. By doing so, however, it would be realized that Greenland must have been reached before the area which has just been discussed. From this it can be inferred that migrations took place along the Arctic coast which did not immediately lead into the Igloolik area. But it is better if we first consider the preceding infiltrations from Arctic Canada into Greenland.

We may note that in 1960 G.R. Lowther came across traces of the American Epi-Gravettian tradition near Cape Sparbo on Devon Island, north of Baffin Land. It included microblades, pseudo-burins and inset blades which no doubt belong to this complex. On the other hand it has not hitherto been possible to make equivalent discoveries on Ellesmere Land, which forms a bridgehead in the direction of Greenland. Moreau S. Maxwell, who in 1958 worked in the northern part of the island, in eastern Grant Land, established that the earliest finds were middle or late Dorset culture. But he expressed the view that in future explorations it should be borne in mind that at the time when the American Epi-Gravettian tradition infiltrated into Greenland the conditions of settlement on Ellesmere Land were entirely different from what they are today. At that time the water level of the lakes was higher by 1.8 to 15 meters, and that of the sea by 18 to 27 meters, which of course affected the location of settlements. The possibility that earlier sites exist on Ellesmere Land or Grant Land is suggested by the fact that in Hall Land — part of North Greenland, separated from Grant Land only by the 25-kilometer-wide Robeson Channel — Eigil Knuth encountered in 1958, near the site of Solbakken, at 17 to 20 meters above sea level, traces of the Independence culture to be described later, which is linked with a relatively early advance of the American Epi-Gravettian into this area.

Bibliography: Bird, 1945; Birket-Smith, 1929; Byers, 1962; Collins, 1950, 1951b, 1952, 1953b, 1955a, 1955b, 1956a, 1956b, 1957, 1958a, 1958b; Giddings, 1956b; Harp, 1951, 1953, 1958, 1959a, 1959b, 1960, 1961, 1962, 1964; Ingstad, 1964; Jenness, 1923, 1925, 1941; Johnson, 1946; Johnson and Raup, 1964; Laughlin and Taylor, 1960; Leechmann, 1943; Lowther, 1960; MacNeish, 1951, 1953, 1954, 1955, 1956a, 1956b, 1960, 1962a, 1962b, 1964; Martijn (MS.); Mathiassen, 1927; Maxwell, 1960, 1962; Meldgaard, 1955, 1960a, 1960b, 1962; O'Bryan, 1953; Oschinsky, 1964; Quimby, 1962; Rowley, 1940, 1950; Taylor, 1958, 1959a, 1959b, 1960a, 1960b, 1962a, 1962b, 1962c, 1963a, 1963b, 1964a, 1964b, 1964c, 1967a, 1967b; Taylor and Swinton, 1967; Wintemberg, 1939.

Greenland

Today it is absolutely certain that immigration into Greenland took place at an early date (Fig. 62). As early as 1907, O. Solberg pleaded for a 'Greenland Stone Age' on the basis of surface finds from the Disko Bay area on the west coast. In 1922 Lauge Koch encountered traces of the Dorset culture in Ellesmere Land opposite Hall Land. In 1934 Henry B. Collins also came out in support of a Dorset migration into West Greenland. But it is only in the last fifteen years that early infiltrations could be determined with certainty.

In 1947 Eigil Knuth resumed the exploration interrupted by the Second World War in Peary Land and on Danmark Fjord between latitudes 81° and 84° North, namely north and south of Independence Fjord, as well as other places in North and Northeastern Greenland. This area is characterized by an alteration of four and a half months of continuous darkness and five months of continuous daylight and receives a great quantity of driftwood which comes from Siberia and finds its way right into the interior of many fjords. Thanks to Knuth's admirable tenacity, we today know of several migrations into this area. Like Meldgaard in the Igloolik area later, Knuth found that the sites where he worked were situated at various levels on the ancient beach terraces. In the meantime some radiocarbon datings have been added as well. The earliest ones are the Independence I and II cultures, named after Independence Fjord on Peary Land. The site of Deltaterrasserne on Jørgen Brønlund Fjord, an arm of Independence Fjord, yielded for an early phase (Independence IA) a radiocarbon dating of 4676 ± 120 years and other dates (Independence IB) which are between 4300 and 3700 years old. The age of Independence IC is given as 3389 ± 130 years. As these tests were made on driftwood, the dates were questionable at first, but after four charcoal tests on Arctic willow, made in 1963, yielded an average age of 3975 years for Independence I, these may be considered reliable. Apart from this it was observed that the Independence I sites are situated on beach terraces between 21 and 8 meters above the present-day sea level (Independence IA at 21 to 19 meters, Independence IB at 15 to 11 meters, and Independence IC at 11 to 8 meters), while those of Independence

II are at a level of 7 to 3 meters. More recent finds were encountered below the 3 meter level. Independence I culture seems to have reached Peary Land during a period when the climate was relatively favorable, which finds expression in the number and size of settlements. Pearylandville on Nedre Midsommer Sø, for example, has 27 house ruins. On the basis of the animal bones discovered Knuth regards the Independence

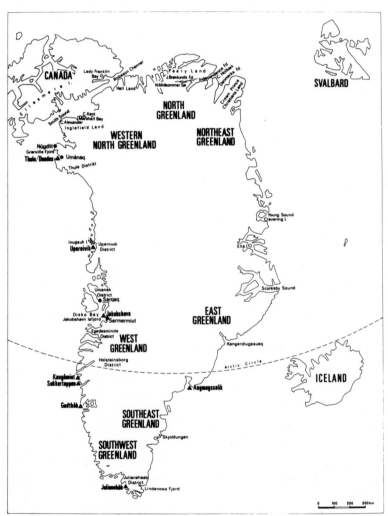

Fig. 62 - Map of Greenland showing places and sites mentioned in the text.

people as definitely hunters of musk-ox; the bones of these animals, rich in fat, may have played an important part as fuel, and their dung was presumably used as well. Besides the musk-ox, walrus and seal were probably hunted from the ice. There are at first only very few finds from the early phases of the Independence culture, but on the basis of microblades it is possible to identify a link between them and the American Epi-Gravettian tradition. The same is true of the subsequent stages, in which we also find retouched burins, some of them fairly long, and pseudo-burins. Combined with these are, however, relatively large flint implements, such as leaf-shaped and tanged projectile points, knives with surface retouching and scrapers. According to Knuth the size of the implements is due to the fact that they were used for skinning and cutting up musk-ox. Furthermore, it is striking that in the Independence I cul-

Fig. 63 - Ground plan of an Independence I dwelling (tent house) from Delterrasserne on Jørgen Brønlund Fjord, North Greenland. Photo by courtesy of E. Knuth.

ture cores occur which are reminiscent of the boat-shaped types of the Epi-Gravettian. On the basis of excavations in the summer of 1963, Knuth is of the opinion that there are certain similar features between Independence I and the Sarqaq culture of West Greenland. On the other hand he points to the following differences: the absence in Independence I of lamps and ground pseudo-burins; the frequent occurrence there of microblades and basal notches on burins, scrapers and projectile points (Fig. 64); the considerable size of most of the stone implements; the elliptical form of the fairly small dwellings, which have a central passage and hearth, and are compared by Knuth to the Lapp *gamme*. The ground plan is indicated by fairly large stones. According to Knuth the so-called tent house of Independence II is derived from the typical house of Independence I (Fig. 63), although not without some (Paleo)-Indian influence. It is not yet clear where this development took place. In ground plan it is likewise elliptical; but the central passage and hearth are formed here by stone slabs, squared off toward the wall. Knuth thinks that he can identify in these tent houses common features with the Indian tepee.

Lamps have not been authenticated either. Knuth infers from this that at the time of the Independence culture the polar basin contained far less ice, so that huge quantities of driftwood reached the coastal areas of North Greenland from Siberia. His most recent investigations here, incidentally, have shown that in both Independence I and II at least three different types of house or tent were known, which were erected and used according to the season. Identical dwellings are said to occur also in Arctic Canada, i.e. on Ellesmere Land, Cornwallis Island, Boothia Peninsula and in the Igloolik area.

As a result of radiocarbon analysis Independence II is ascribed to the period around 3000 years ago, i.e. approximately one thousand years later than Independence I; from a site on Cape Holbaeck, at the mouth of Danmark Fjord, there are radiocarbon datings suggesting an age of 3200 to 3000 years. According to Knuth the stone material of this culture has features in common with forms of the Pre-Dorset culture in the Igloolik area and those of the T 1 site on Southampton Island (Fig. 64). In his illustrations it is possible to identify microblades and large projectile points or knives with two lateral basal notches. In addition to these there are bone lance points with a horseshoe-shaped base and a massive lateral inset blade. Some harpoon heads discovered in the summer of 1963 call to mind pieces which Meldgaard found in the Igloolik area some 30 to 23 meters above sea level, at relatively late Pre-Dorset

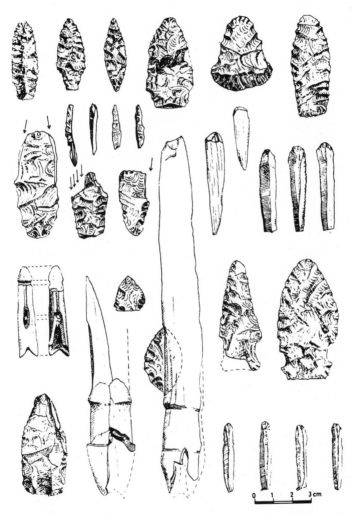

Fig. 64 - Artifacts of the Independence culture from Danmark Fjord, North Greenland. Above: Independence I; below, Independence II. After E. Knuth (1958).

sites. As mentioned, Knuth was able to show that the musk-ox hunters of Independence found their way into Greenland from the area of Lady Franklin Bay, in the northeast of Ellesmere Land, by way of the Robeson Channel. H.P. Steensby had long ago referred to this route purely theoretically as 'the musk-ox route' and associated it with the earliest immigrations into North Greenland. In a southerly direction they do not seem to have penetrated beyond Inglefield Land, since it was always difficult to pass Cape Alexander, which was surrounded at all times by open water. On the other hand they did follow the route along the north coast, and finally reached Northeastern Greenland.

Near Nûgdlît at the mouth of Grandville Fjord, northwest of former Thule in the western part of North Greenland, Knuth likewise came across small-tool material. An earlier group may be ascribed to a late period of Independence I and forms a link between it and Sarqaq in West Greenland. A more recent one, it seems, ought to be assigned to the period after Independence II and seems to have parallels in North and Northeastern Greenland. Pear-shaped ground plans of tents are regarded as characteristic.

The name of the Sarqaq culture in West Greenland derives from a site near Sarqaq on the northern shore of Disko Bay. It was here that in 1948 Hans Moosegaard discovered some flint material which a little later was published by Jørgen Meldgaard. Sarqaq finds, it was held, suggest that this is a branch of the American Epi-Gravettian and appears to have had fairly close links with the Canadian Pre-Dorset.

The Sarqaq people are considered by Knuth as definitely caribou hunters, and he presumes that their migration route ran from Ellesmere Land across Smith Sound to the area south of Cape Alexander. It is in any case certain that the Sarqaq culture found its way into West Greenland. In 1953 Helge Larsen and Jørgen Meldgaard, together with other Danish archeologists, went to the Disko Bay area. As a result of the explorations they carried out there, an extremely informative stratigraphy was established at Sermermiut on the mouth of Jakobshavn Isfjord (Fig. 13), and various other sites were discovered in the Disko Bay area.

At Sermermiut, not far from a vast prehistoric settlement,

possibly the largest in the whole of Greenland, a stratigraphic sequence was excavated in which it was possible to identify clearly Sarqaq, Dorset, Thule and more recent deposits (Fig. 65). These excavations were continued in 1955 by Therkel Mathiassen, who confirmed these results. A date between 800 and 500/400 B.C. is assigned to the Sarqaq stratum, which must have been formed during a period when the climate was at first warm and dry but later became damp. The stratum of the settlement lies upon virgin soil of gravel and contains primarily artifacts made of *'angmak'*, a kind of chert. Predominant is

Fig. 65 - Profile at Sermermiut on Jakobshavn Isfjord, Disko Bay area (West Greenland). It contains a sequence of finds from the following cultures (from the bottom upwards): Sarqaq, Dorset, Thule, and more recent phases. Photo by courtesy of J. Meldgaard.

the pseudo-burin, partly produced by grinding; in addition to these there are inset points with a chipped surface, frequently tanged, which, to judge from their size, must have been used mainly as spear points but also as arrow points. Furthermore there are small symmetrical double points and asymmetrical pieces, both of which are retouched on the surface, and short stumpy adze-blades and scrapers of almost triangular shape, made from larger blades. These forms bear a striking resemblance to those of Ipiutak and other Alaskan cultures. Although microblades are absent, there is no doubt that they were linked with groups of the American Epi-Gravettian tradition recognized further west, such as the material from North Knife River. On the other hand, Meldgaard is not inclined to derive the

Fig. 66a See over.

Sermermiut Sarqaq from the Igloolik area. Helge Larsen was able to establish traces of the Sarqaq population at 22 other places in the Disko Bay area, almost invariably succeeded by Dorset sites. Other Sarqaq sites and finds have been localized further south, in the Egedesminde and Holsteinsborg district, and as far south as the Godthaab area. Subsequently this culture seems to have found its way around the southern tip of Greenland to the east coast as far as the Angmagssalik area. Larsen assumes that this was the terminus of its spread. Individual related elements further north, as far as Northeastern Greenland, he associates with influences radiating in the opposite direction from the Independence culture.

It is known from the *Islendigabók* that Erik the Red came across remains of settlements, boats and stone tools when he explored the fjords of Southwestern Greenland for favorable places where Norse colonies could be set up. It may very well be the case that these were traces of the Sarqaq people, if in-

Figs. 66a, b - 'Cluster of faces'. Wood carving from Upernivik area, West Greenland. Twenty faces in all can be identified on the four sides of the piece represented here. Dorset culture. Photo by courtesy of the National Museum, Copenhagen.

deed they are not of the Dorset culture.

As early as 1922 Lauge Koch encountered Dorset finds in Hall Land on the Robeson Channel in North Greenland. Also the 'Greenland Stone Age' postulated in 1907 by Solberg is based upon traces of the Dorset culture in the Disko Bay area. In the meantime the researches of Larsen and Meldgaard, continued by Mathiassen, have demonstrated beyond all doubt

that the Dorset culture did not find its way into Greenland until the second immigration wave. At Sermermiut it was separated from the Sarqaq culture beneath it by a sterile stratum of
turf, approximately 15 centimeters thick. All Sarqaq elements
are absent from this Dorset stratum, which can be dated to the
first half of the first millennium A.D., during a period when the
climate was warm and dry. For stone implements preference
was given to chalcedony, but in addition flint was used, and
'angmak' (chert) only rarely. Microblades prevail; there also
occur asymmetrical implements with surface retouching and
basal notches which could be used as projectile points or
knives; some of the scrapers are very small. Another characteristic are burin-like implements such as were encountered in
the early Dorset material excavated by H.B. Collins at the site
of T 1 on Southampton Island. Meldgaard states that the Dorset culture which found its way into Disko Bay belonged to a
relatively early phase. It is comparable to the third stage of the
Dorset culture in the Igloolik area, which does not yet show
any signs of development into 'classical' Dorset.

As mentioned before, the Dorset culture has been established at several other places on Disko Bay. Although scholars
have only just begun to trace its spread toward the south, its
vestiges can be followed as far as Southwestern Greenland,
and from there even as far as Angmagssalik on the east coast.
It is not impossible that these Dorset immigrants were still
able to establish contact with Norse colonists, since it took
them some time to advance from the Disko Bay area to Southwestern Greenland. Collins thinks that the strange carved
'clusters of faces' discovered at Dorset sites both in Canada
and in West Greenland — one sample in the Disko Bay area
and another in the Upernivik district (Figs. 66 a, b) — may suggest such early contacts with the white man.

To the north of Disko Bay, apart from Lauge Koch's find in
Hall Land, the Dorset culture is known mainly from the studies of Erik Holtved in the Thule district. Here this Danish archeologist found traces of it in particular in three kitchen middens near Inuarfigssuaq on Marshall Bay in Inglefield Land.
In part, these reveal a fully developed Dorset culture, from
which it may probably be deduced that a second wave arrived
at the time of 'classical' Dorset; in part there already seems to

have been some influence from the Thule culture. Inuarfigssuaq does indeed have a large Thule settlement, which can be
assigned to an early date. From here the Dorset culture, influenced by Thule, crosses North Greenland in the direction
of Northeastern Greenland. Eigil Knuth was able to trace vestiges of it across Peary Land all the way to Young Sound (74°
30'N.). Offshoots could even be identified on Scoresby Sound.

This leads to the problem of the significance of the Thule
culture for Greenland. We have already encountered in Alaska
and Arctic Canada this widely disseminated culture, which

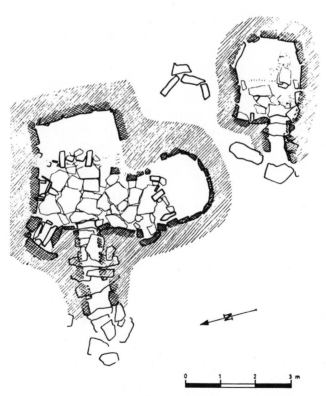

Fig. 67 · Ground plans of Thule houses, from Cape Kent in Inglefield Land,
North Greenland. After E. Holtved (1964).

greatly influenced the subsequent development of Eskimo civilization. It is assumed that the Eskimos who introduced the Thule culture into Arctic Canada left northern Alaska about 900 A.D., or that by this time they had already advanced as far as Cape Parry on Amundsen Gulf. But it remains an open question whether the culture they represented made the transition

Fig. 68 - Wooden frame of an umiak belonging to Thule immigrants to North Greenland. This boat was discovered in 1949 by Eigil Knuth on the beach at Herlufsholm, in the easternmost part of Peary Land; he had it brought to Copenhagen, where it is now displayed in the National Museum. Radiocarbon datings suggest that it made the journey around North Greenland 474 ± 100 years ago. Photo by courtesy of E. Knuth.

from Birnirk to Thule exclusively in northern Alaska, or whether this process took place simultaneously in many places along the Arctic coast, so that the Eastern Thule culture originated with a branch of the Birnirk culture that had penetrated far to the east. This movement from Arctic Alaska along the shore of the Arctic Ocean and through the Arctic Archipelago must have reached North Greenland relatively quickly, probably during and just after the eleventh century. Holtved is of the opinion that in Inglefield Land early Thule culture acquired all its distinctive features during the twelfth and thirteenth centuries at the latest. His studies show that this branch of the Thule culture differs in some elements from that which Mathiassen covered in Arctic Canada, where the flourishing height of its development occurred in the fourteenth century. These elements are regarded as ancient, either because of their dissemination or because they are not yet fully oriented toward life on the coast. The houses of this early Thule culture in North Greenland are usually round in ground plan but there is also the tendency to erect square buildings. The latter finds expression particularly on Cape Kent in the eastern part of Inglefield Land, where Holtved discovered some large rectangular houses (Fig. 67).

On the basis of non-meteoritic pieces of iron chains, lance heads, link armor etc., it must be assumed that at a surprisingly early stage contacts took place between the Thule people in Inglefield Land and the Norse colonists at least 1500 kilometers away to the southeast.

After the early Thule immigrants had begun to advance eastward, via North Greenland (Fig. 68), and southward, along the west coast (as Meldgaard established at Sermermiut, they found their way into the Disko Bay area about 1250 A.D.), they were succeeded by a further wave of immigrants in the north about 1300. Holtved established traces of this new infiltration chiefly on Ruin Island, off Inuarfigssuaq in Marshall Bay. Although the culture of these new immigrants has distinct connections with Thule, Holtved thinks he can identify a strong Punuk substratum, i.e. he assumes that the group of people concerned left Alaska with a Punuk-like culture and were greatly influenced by Thule culture on their way east. A striking feature is the great importance of whaling. Finds of Norse objects in the houses on Ruin Island show that this group, too, came into contact with the Vikings at an early stage.

During 1946-7, in the course of his further work in the Thule district, Holtved discovered near Nûgdlît, northwest of former Thule, a related group whose links with the west were even more distinct, whereas Norse objects were missing. It may be that this is a somewhat earlier phase of this immigration, which took place around 1300.

After the new arrivals had in due course likewise turned southward, and had come in contact with the Inugsuk culture, they became — according to Holtved — the driving force in the annihilation during the fourteenth century of the western Norse settlements on Godthaab Fjord ('western' by contrast with the 'eastern' colony on Julianehaab Bay, a little further south).

Fig. 69 - Finds from Inugsuk showing links between Eskimo and Norse settlers in Southwestern Greenland. Above: Wooden figurine carved by Eskimo, representing Norsemen (left: possibly a woman). Below: A European face, probably also carved by an Eskimo, and a spindle whorl of Norse origin made of whale bone with a wooden handle. Redrawn after Th. Mathiassen (1930a).

This brings up the term Inugsuk culture. It has already been mentioned that the Thule culture, which had infiltrated into North Greenland at an early stage, gradually shifted over to the west coast. As early as 1929, in the course of his excavations near Inugsuk in the Upernivik district, on the northern third of the west coast, Therkel Mathiassen was able to establish that in the twelfth and thirteenth centuries the Thule culture continued to develop and the result of this was the Inugsuk culture. A similar development took place in the Thule district. The Inugsuk culture is distinguished by a vast increase in hunting by means of the kayak and in the implements required for this. In addition to harpoon heads with open sockets, which tally with those of the Thule culture, there are also those with closed sockets. Another characteristic feature is the appearance of elements which are obviously due to Norse influence (Fig. 69). This is particularly true of the production of small wooden containers by the coopering technique, with strips of baleen serving instead of metal for the hoops. On the other hand, there is a complete absence of pottery.

Norse influences and the contacts already mentioned with the Ruin Island people as they advanced south were to make a considerable contribution to the flourishing of Inugsuk culture in the Thule district about 1400, and also to its advance still further southward beyond Upernivik district. Besides climatic changes and the loosening of ties with Europe, this must have been one reason, as we have seen, for the destruction of the 'western' Norse settlement on Godthaab Fjord between 1350 and 1360 A.D. A little further to the north, near Kangamiut, not far from Sukkertoppen, Mathiassen examined in 1930 an Inugsuk settlement from the period between 1350 and 1500. The next area he explored was in the Julianehaab district, just south of the 'eastern' Norse settlements. These were wiped out some time around 1500, but we do not know exactly how. At that time the Inugsuk migrants had already left the southern tip of Greenland behind and advanced into the Angmagssalik area on the east coast. In the sixteenth century offshoots of the Inugsuk culture which continued to advance on the east coast from south to north infiltrated as far as Crown Prince Christian Land in the northern part of the east coast.

Offshoots of the Independence Culture and those of a Dorset facies influenced by Thule, as well as the pure Thule culture from the north arrived in Northeast Greenland, according to Holtved, during the 14th century. To these was added the Inugsuk culture, advancing from the south. Thus a peculiar hybrid culture was formed in Northeast Greenland. It is called 'Northeast Greenland mixed culture' and has two phases. The first may have taken place during the sixteenth century A.D.;

Fig. 70 - Ruins of a winter house of the Northeast Greenland mixed culture, at Dødemandsbugten, Clavering Island. Photo (taken before excavation) by courtesy of Helge Larsen.

Fig. 71 - The interior of a winter house of the Northeast Greenland mixed culture, at Dødemandsbugten, Clavering Island. View from the rear wall, showing in the middle the edge of the bench on which the inhabitants sat and slept, raised above the paved floor; to the right is the original location of the lamp; the entrance passage (top, center) not yet unearthed. Photo by courtesy of H. Larsen.

the second occurred in the seventeenth and eighteenth centuries. This may best be observed in the settlement of Dødemandsbugten on Clavering Island, where in 1931-2 Larsen carried out investigations on a grand scale which Jørgen Meldgaard and I were later able to bring to a conclusion (Figs. 12, 70-72).

But as early as 1600 A.D. the individual areas of Inugsuk cul-

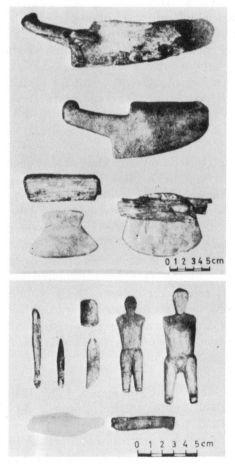

Fig. 72 - Objects of the Northeast Greenland mixed culture from Dødemandsbugten, Clavering Island. Above: snow knife and ulu; below; toy implements and wooden figurines. After H.-G. Bandi and J. Meldgaard (1952).

ture along the coasts of Greenland were beginning to lose contact with one another. This occurred first between the Thule district and West Greenland. Then the southern part of the east coast became depopulated – except for the Angmagssalik and Kangerdlugssuaq areas, as we know from where excavations were carried out by Therkel Mathiassen and Helge Larsen, respectively. During the eighteenth century the culture in the Angmagssalik area acquired an individual character; it has already been noted that among its distinguishing features are sculptures which curiously enough recall the Dorset culture. The Kangerdlugssuaq settlement became extinct and the Northeast Greenland mixed culture, which had hitherto maintained a link between its several parts, now broke up. During the eighteenth and nineteenth centuries the descendants of the Inugsuk Eskimo came into contact with the white man on the west as well as on the east coast – this time with whale hunters who periodically sought out the waters around Greenland.

Then the bell tolled for the Eskimo of Northeast Greenland. As late as 1823 Captain Douglas Charles Clavering encountered a small group of natives on the island that now bears his name. But when the Second German Arctic Expedition under Captain Karl Koldeway penetrated into this area again in 1869-70, it was found to be completely deserted. Even today we still do not know whether the abandonment of Northeast Greenland is linked with the almost simultaneous departure of the caribou or with other events. Just as the first appearance of the Eskimos in the west, on the Bering Strait, raises many questions that still cannot be answered, so also the disappearance of their latterday descendants far to the east, in Northeast Greenland, remains an enigma.

Bibliography: Bandi and Meldgaard, 1952; Degerbøl, 1936; Glob, 1935, 1946; Holm, 1883; Holtved, 1944-54; Johnson, 1933; Knuth, 1952, 1954, 1958, 1965, 1966/67; Koch, 1945; Larsen, 1934, 1938, 1960b; Larsen and Meldgaard, 1958; Mathiassen, 1928, 1929, 1930a, 1930c, 1931, 1933, 1934a, 1934b, 1936, 1958; Mathiassen and Holtved, 1936; Meldgaard, 1952, 1967; Nørlund, 1937; Porsild, 1915; Richter, 1934; Solberg, 1907; Thomsen, 1917; Thostrup, 1911; Wissler, 1918.

CONCLUSION: A MOSAIC WITH MANY GAPS

We have endeavored to give an outline of Eskimo prehistory in the various parts of the Arctic in accordance with the present state of our knowledge. The reader will now expect a final summary presenting the picture as a whole. There are good reasons for hesitation on this score, since much has still to be clarified. Two courses are open, neither of which is completely satisfactory.

One is to evaluate the frequently contradictory views of various authors, and to supplement them by personal opinions. Many scholars have already tried to analyze the development of Eskimo culture as a whole or in its principal parts. One may mention the works by Henry B. Collins, Kaj Birket-Smith, Helge Larsen and Froelich G. Rainey, Erik Holtved, Frederica de Laguna, J.L. Giddings, Elmer Harp, Richard Mac-Neish and D.E. Dumond. Many of their views are endorsed by the present author, while others arouse scepticism or can be rejected. But there is no doubt that a discussion of the various opinions expressed would go beyond the scope of this book and probably confuse many readers, as it would be necessary to deal with a number of detailed points. Nevertheless various charts are given in the Appendix to indicate how developments are regarded by some of the scholars listed.

The second possibility would be a concise summary. This, however, necessarily involves a certain element of subjectivity, as one naturally emphasizes whatever one finds convincing. The entire process may also be made to appear more simple than it actually is. Nevertheless preference is given to this option, fully aware that the picture presented is a mosaic with many gaps, a sketch that will still undergo many alterations.

It is not necessary to deal again with the problem of early migrations from the Old World to the New. Eskimo prehistory obviously began only when there arrived in Arctic North America late offshoots of the Siberian Gravettian, in other words Epi-Gravettian people. Exactly when this happened we still do not know; the date might be anywhere between 15,000 and 10,000 years ago. Let it be recalled in this connection that the finds from Anagula in the eastern Aleutians and from Onion Portage on the Kobuk, which according to our terminology are to be classed as American Epi-Gravettian, could be dated to a period some 8000 years ago. The same is true for the famous Campus site. W.S. Laughlin also supposes that as early as 15,000 - 10,000 years ago, a population which I like to call 'Epi-Gravettian' inhabited both the Pacific coast of Siberia and the region along the southern shore of the Bering land bridge. I am, however, inclined to think that this population not only remained in the coastal area of the land bridge but was probably oriented primarily toward the interior, and that adaptation toward life on the coast set in only gradually. It seems to me unlikely that the hinterland of the land bridge was, as Laughlin presumes, in those days still an area frequented by Paleo-Indians, whom he terms Proto- or Semi-Mongoloids.

According to Laughlin the Epi-Gravettian people belonged to a Mongoloid, or let us say Arctic-Mongoloid, racial group, from which sprang both the Eskimo and Aleut as well as various Paleo-Siberian groups. This view is also shared by Oschinsky. It is conceivable that the gradual diminution and final interruption of the land bridge led a considerable number of this Epi-Gravettian population to infiltrate into Alaska. When this happened cannot yet be ascertained with certainty. We have seen that (leaving aside a possible flooding at the time of the Two Creeks oscillation, 12,000 - 11,000 years ago) towards the end of the final stage of the late Neopleistocene some 10,000 years ago the Bering land bridge, which was becoming ever narrower, must have finally been interrupted. About 8000 years ago the coastline was already very similar to that of today. At approximately the same time an ice-free corridor may also have opened up again between Alaska and the southern part of the United States. It is conceivable that hunters of the interior, whose traces we find at such sites as Teklanika in Mount McKinley National Park or at the Campus site near Fairbanks, had advanced as far as Central Alaska at a time when other Epi-Gravettian groups were living on Anangula and on the Kobuk; but it may also be possible that Teklanika and the College Campus site must be ascribed to a slightly more recent period than Anangula. But there is also the estimated date of about 10,000 B.C. for the so-called Denali complex in Central Alaska. We shall only know more about this if other relevant complexes can be dated by radiocarbon analysis.

The advance into Alaska made by Epi-Gravettian hunters living on the land bridge was presumably most likely in the area where natural routes led into the interior: from Southwestern Alaska along the vast river systems of the Yukon-Tanana and Kuskokwim, up which we may presume that small groups of hunters gradually and successively made their way.

The culture of these migrants is termed by various authors the 'Northwest Microblade tradition', to distinguish it from a more recent phase, the 'Arctic Small-Tool tradition'. These are both referred to by the collective term 'American Epi-Gravettian', since we endorse the views of H.B. Collins and J.B. Griffin that the differences are not very serious.

In the beginning the inventory of stone implements of the American Epi-Gravettian is distinguished by the fact that microblades always occur which were detached from boat-shaped or conical cores; the fairly numerous scrapers are mostly rather short and stumpy; burins seem to play only a subordinate part, a fact which is difficult to explain. In general the material varies quite significantly from one site to another. Frequently it is possible to identify influences exerted by Paleo-Indian or Archaic groups, which shows that approximately at the time when the Epi-Gravettian infiltrated into Alaska there must have been a feedback movement from the southern part of the United States, the area where specialized Paleo-Indian hunter cultures had developed, northwards into this region. I call this phenomenon the 'Northern Point tradition'. Between this and the American Epi-Gravettian there seems to have been a large amount of overlapping, influence and intermingling.

Whether and to what extent elements of the Epi-Gravettian people advanced from Alaska southwards cannot as yet be assessed with certainty. But there can scarcely be any doubt that Epi-Gravettian influences found their way into the Paleo-Indian area, as is suggested, for example, by the appearance of true burins in the southwestern United States. What is of particular interest here is that the majority of these immigrants spread across the Subarctic and Arctic areas to the east and northeast. So far we cannot follow this process in detail. But it seems certain that it took place in several waves, differing chronologically and culturally; with advances in various directions; that contact was established in many places with representatives of the Northern Point tradition, which likewise was by no means uniform, but may be regarded as thoroughly Indian; that the Epi-Gravettian continued to develop over the course of time, which is why the more recent phase is described by many writers as the Arctic Small-Tool tradition. It is also possible that this development was influenced by some new impulses from Siberia. Besides microblades there are only characteristic small burins or pseudo-burins, inset points and lateral inset blades for arrowheads. But not all these small-tool elements occur at each site of the more recent American Epi-Gravettian; occasionally one or the other is missing. Moreover, it must be borne in mind that besides these there are also to be found larger artifacts of flint-like material which are worked less well. It might have been possible to identify further links or differences if objects of organic material had survived as well.

Of importance is the fact that we have some clues about the arrival of individual groups of the American Epi-Gravettian tradition in the eastern Arctic. This is true, for example, of the Independence culture in Northern Greenland, the earliest stage of which, Independence IA, probably appeared there as early as about 4500 years ago. The boat-shaped cores, similar to those at the College Campus site near Fairbanks and at Ralph Solecki's site no. 121 in the Kukpowruk area of the northwestern Brooks Range, lead to the assumption that one relatively early migration route of the American Epi-Gravettian ran fairly far to the north.

This assumption is also supported by W.E. Taylor's recent Pre-Dorset finds in the Arctic Archipelago. An early advance in the direction of the eastern Arctic is also suggested by the Pre-Dorset finds in the Igloolik area, in the north of Melville Peninsula, dating from approximately 4000 years ago. It is important that in this case one is also familiar with the bone and antler objects; the appearance of harpoon heads is particularly striking, since these not only suggest the hunting of sea-mammals but also distantly anticipate the Thule culture. I am convinced that this is due to influences from the west and for this reason assume that somewhere in the Bering Strait area there were early tendencies of development toward the true Eskimo culture as represented much later by the Thule culture.

Dorset, too, which superseded the Pre-Dorset culture in the Igloolik area during the eighth century B.C., must somehow be linked with the Epi-Gravettian tradition that came from Alaska. But it appears that the Dorset groups at first lived relatively far to the south and were influenced to a greater or lesser degree by Indian elements. Thanks to the Igloolik finds it is known that in this area the early stages of the Dorset culture were clearly oriented toward life on the coast. This is further proof that representatives of the American Epi-Gravettian tradition were able to adapt themselves to the typical Eskimo way of life. Why therefore should it not be assumed that they were Eskimos? Such a conclusion is also suggested by recent finds of skeletons which indicate that the Dorset people were ethnically Eskimos.

It is not necessary to describe once again the further dissemination of the American Epi-Gravettian and Dorset in the direction of Greenland; it has been seen that both cultures had a considerable power of expansion.

It can also be observed from the Denbigh Flint complex that the representatives of the American Epi-Gravettian tradition who originally lived in the interior made a partial readjustment to life on the coast, and obtained their livelihood from hunting sea-mammals: this relatively late phase, in which elements of the American Epi-Gravettian tradition appear both in specialized form and to a large extent fused with those of the Northern Point tradition, is definitely no longer oriented exclusively toward the interior. This gradual adaptation would, however, be even clearer if more were known about the relevant items of equipment made of organic material.

In Alaska the development appears to have continued, either from the Denbigh Flint complex or from the presumably slightly earlier group of finds at the base of the Trail Creek Caves, in the direction of such cultures as Choris, Norton and Near Ipiutak. Ipiutak, too, may have received stimuli from this quarter, especially in regard to stoneworking techniques. It is still not clear by which route knowledge of pottery production, authenticated from Choris onward, reached Alaska at the beginning of the last millennium B.C. J.B. Griffin, who studied this problem thoroughly, points to linear- and check-stamped pottery in the Lena valley in Siberia in the period between 3500 and 3000 years ago.

The common features between early sites on Hokkaido and Sakhalin, and at other places along the Pacific coast of Siberia, and the beginnings of the American Epi-Gravettian tradition in Alaska make it likely that the culture of the population who inhabited this vast area between approximately 15,000 and 10,000/8000 B.P. had a relatively uniform character. It must be kept in mind that the Bering land bridge formed a connecting link between the two areas. About the further development on the Asiatic side after the opening of the Bering Strait, hardly anything is known so far. If we assume that here, too, various small-tool industries experienced a development which was generally speaking similar to that of the American Arctic but differed from it in detail, then we have to presume that there is a gap in the finds; for hitherto there has been a complete absence of industries which in their chronology and pattern of development would correspond to the American Epi-Gravettian tradition down to the Denbigh Flint complex and the cultures derived from it. These still have to be discovered. If this possibility is excluded then a considerable hiatus appears between the Epi-Gravettian of the Asiatic side and the Okvik culture which appeared there much later.

This question is rather important, in view of the problem of whether the Okvik-Old Bering Sea-Punuk sequence may be rooted in a development which occurred on the Asiatic or the American side of the Bering Strait. If the center which may

have existed was not located in Siberia, then we shall have to
look for it in Alaska. The most likely area would be Southwestern Alaska, the district between Norton Sound and Bristol
Bay, the archeology of which is still considerably less familiar
than that of other coastal areas. Linguistic and ethnographic
conditions suggest that crucial processes may have taken place
here in prehistoric times. Chester S. Chard is likewise inclined to believe that in Southwestern Alaska, and especially in
the area between Bristol Bay and the Alaskan Peninsula, a development began around 2000 B.C. which led to the appearance of highly specialized Eskimo cultures of sea-mammal
hunters. In this connection he points to the extremely favorable environmental conditions in this area. Laughlin thinks it
possible that the dynamic dissemination which began a little
later and was mainly oriented toward the Bering Strait, may
be due to a sudden large increase in the population. Finally,
it must be remembered that in Southwestern Alaska there are
sporadic finds which point to links with groups living in the
north, such as Norton, Near Ipiutak and Ipiutak, as well as
those living on the Aleutian Islands and Central Southern
Alaska.

In this connection one should also mention the problem of
the settlement of the Aleutian Islands (where at an early stage,
as is well-known, Epi-Gravettian people left their traces at
Anangula), of Kodiak Island and Central Southern Alaska. There
is much evidence that points to various infiltrations into this
region, and the question thus remains open whether these
later migrants still came across any remnants of the Epi-Gravettian population. On Kodiak Island the Ocean Bay I phase,
as we have seen, may be dated back to the fourth millennium
B.C. The Paleo-Aleut wave of migration is ascribed to the period around 2000 B.C. and in Central Southern Alaska Kachemak I seems to have commenced shortly after 1000 B.C. We
may well assume that all these impulses originated in Southwestern Alaska. Curious, however, are the common features
between some Paleo-Aleut cultural elements and certain
phenomena in northern Japan and on Sakhalin, whereas corresponding evidence is so far lacking further to the north; are
these not perhaps influences exerted along the Aleutian chain?
On the other hand the fact that the late Kachemak culture in

Central Southern Alaska has some common features with Ipiutak in Northwestern Alaska suggests that Southwestern Alaska played the role of an intermediary: for example, in the custom of burying the dead with artificial ivory or jade eyes, which has been recognized in both areas.

We do know that on the Asiatic side of the Bering Strait there suddenly appeared during the last millennium B.C. a highly specialized and richly developed Eskimo culture: Okvik. A little later, possibly as early as about 300 B.C., it was succeeded by the Old Bering Sea culture, which in turn, in association with fresh influences from the Siberian hinterland, produced the Punuk culture around the middle of the first millennium A.D. How can this be explained? I am convinced that the Okvik culture must have had preliminary stages; it is impossible that it could have arisen out of virtually nothing. The first obvious place to look for such a development is on the Asiatic side. It could, for example, be thought that those groups of the Epi-Gravettian tradition which, according to Laughlin, withdrew to St. Lawrence Island and the Siberian mainland when the Bering land bridge was flooded, survived there for a long time and finally developed their culture to a surprisingly high level. But in spite of relatively plentiful excavations in these areas, there are as yet no clues to support this hypothesis. On examining it more closely, one has to reckon seriously with the possibility that it developed in Alaska — probably in connection with the dissemination mentioned above, which started about 2000 B.C. in Southwestern Alaska in the direction of the Bering Strait. Then, during the second millennium B.C., a movement may have begun from there westwards, which brought Eskimo elements to the Asiatic side of the Bering Strait; they probably went by way of the Seward Peninsula and across the Bering Strait to the Siberian mainland, and from there also to St. Lawrence Island. On the Asiatic side of the Bering Strait the culture of these immigrants must have developed almost with explosive force, on account of the favorable environmental conditions which they enjoyed there. Just as a caprice of nature sometimes gives unusually colorful blossoms to an otherwise scraggy plant, which then wither again, so too in this case peculiarly luxuriant cultures seem to have developed which did not last for very long. It remains to be clarified whether, as D. Jenness has presumed, external stimuli also played a part here, in connection with the relatively late immigration of a population from the Asiatic mainland in the direction of the American Northwest Coast, where the highly specialized Indian culture of this area was developed.

Another flourishing culture was Ipiutak, from the first half of the first millennium A.D. But in spite of distinct links with the Bering Strait area, its development must have been different. This can be inferred—last but not least—from the lack of pottery, ground slate implements and blubber lamps. For this reason it may have branched off a little earlier than Okvik. Where and how this happened again is not known. The fact that at Ipiutak new impulses may be noted from the Siberian interior or northern China—in particular the Scytho-Siberian animal style—seems to point to the Asiatic side of the Bering Strait, especially the hinterland. But it must be remembered, first, that relevant evidence is so far lacking, and secondly, that we have Ipiutak-like finds from Southwestern Alaska. Moreover, we also have to bear in mind that the Ipiutak technique of working stone seems to have been influenced by Denbigh; that links with the Kachemak Bay culture exist; and that Ipiutak carvings even show some common features with objects from the Fraser River delta near Vancouver from the last millennium B.C. Finally, it is difficult to find an explanation as to why the Ipiutak culture should have been transplanted to Northwestern Alaska from somewhere across the Bering Strait, although it must be admitted that there are also obstacles to the assumption that it derived from a hitherto undiscovered center in Southwestern Alaska.

The same is probably true of the Birnirk culture of the latter half of the first millennium A.D., although this could not develop so fully or in such a bizarre way as did the Bering Strait and Ipiutak cultures.

We are thus faced with the fact that, during the two millennia before and after the beginning of the Christian era, astonishing cultures developed on the Asiatic side of the Bering Strait and in Northern Alaska, which originated from a center that has not yet been localized with certainty but was presumably situated in Southwestern Alaska. These cultures—Okvik, Old Bering Sea, Punuk and Birnirk—are definitely oriented toward life on the coast, whereas Ipiutak occupies something of a special position by virtue of its partial orientation towards the interior.

On the other hand, we know that some Thule elements already appeared earlier, and others simultaneously, at various places in the Eskimo area: in the Pre-Dorset culture of the Igloolik area in Arctic Canada around 2000 B.C., and at Kachemak I in Central Southern Alaska during the last millennium B.C. At Birnirk this tendency can be seen particularly clearly, whereas on the other hand it is possible to identify here pronounced links with Okvik and the Old Bering Sea culture.

All this seems to us to suggest that for a long time true Eskimo or Thule tendencies were latent in the center of development thought to have existed in Southwestern Alaska, whence presumably the decisive impulses originated that gave birth to Okvik and Birnirk. But it was not until the end of Birnirk, during the tenth and eleventh centuries A.D., that they at last managed to break through fully. It is not certain whether Birnirk gave the stimulus to this, or whether this culture was merely in close proximity to the development that led to Thule. Nor is it possible as yet to answer the question in which way Thule elements reached Northern Alaska, via Northwestern Alaska, before setting out on their triumphal march across the Arctic. It is certain that the Thule culture first appeared in Northern Alaska, where we encountered it as Western Thule, and from there it also seems to have radiated influences to Siberia, and to have influenced late Punuk or partially superimposed itself upon it. But the main point is that from Northern Alaska the Thule culture developed and spread unflaggingly towards the east, like the emptying of a blocked reservoir. In many places earlier groups were probably either driven out or assimilated. The first advance seems to have taken place during the eleventh century in the north, from Arctic Canada by way of the Arctic Archipelago to North Greenland. From there it continued, first, southwards down the west coast, where the Inugsuk culture was formed during the twelfth and thirteenth centuries, and secondly, across North Greenland to the northeastern part of the island. Later waves of Thule migrants took possession of extensive areas of Arctic Canada, where they experienced a considerable development during the fourteenth century.

Thus, finally, a remarkable degree of unification was attained, a dissemination of the Thule culture (or at least elements of it) from the eastern tip of Siberia to the east of Greenland. Later developments, however, partially obliterated this picture of unity, since the links were broken at many places and individual areas developed along lines of their own. The greatest breach was in the central areas, from which the Thule people withdrew relatively late, some time between 1300 and 1700 A.D. The gap was filled by groups with a slightly less developed culture which nevertheless also contained Thule elements. It is still uncertain whether these were descendants of the Pre-Dorset population which had been driven into the interior by the Dorset people, or of earlier Thule groups who had abandoned life on the coast on account of the vast stocks of caribou available in the Barren Grounds.

These considerations lead to the conclusion that the subsequent development of Eskimo culture at the Thule level existed in embryo at a very early stage. Since Thule forms occur in the Canadian Pre-Dorset, it was presumably latent in the American Epi-Gravettian tradition. But from this it should not be deduced that development took place in a straight line from the Epi-Gravettian tradition to Thule. No doubt there were several ramifications and separate lines of development, which in the case of Okvik or Ipiutak, for example, were so strong that they almost obscured for a time the main wave of movement towards Thule. This is probably one of the reasons why so much is still rather unclear. But in my view it is possible to trace the development toward Thule, and thus toward the typical Eskimo coastal culture, like a red thread that runs across vast areas of territory and over long stretches of time.

This account has of course deliberately simplified the process of development to a very great extent. But we have chosen this course rather than follow many specialists in Eskimo archeology in drawing up almost incomprehensibly complicated schemes. Not long ago Frederica de Laguna pointed out very justly that descriptions and interpretations of finds can occasionally be understood only by 'the active lodge members of the inner circle'. I know of cases where not even this was possible! De Laguna also cautioned scholars against introducing new 'industries', 'complexes' or 'cultures' into the literature each time they discovered a handful of material at some former camp site, and on top of this giving it as difficult a name as possible. It is also a great disadvantage that in most cases only preliminary reports are published, and that full and extensive accounts of the material discovered are often long delayed or never appear at all. This 'Arctic Small-Paper tradition', as one might call it, has had a very harmful effect.

Thus in this final chapter and in the diagram given in the Appendix an attempt has been made to represent Eskimo prehistory simply – in many respects no doubt too simply. Everything of secondary importance has been omitted and only the main lines of development have been included as they appear today. It is obvious that these views will not meet with general agreement. But it ought to be borne in mind that this is only an attempt at an interpretation, and these hypotheses would be amended without hesitation wherever necessary in the light of new discoveries. And finally it should be said to the skeptics that probably no one individual today is able to provide final explanations of all the events that occurred in the prehistory of the Eskimo area. Much field work and intensive study will be required before we can see matters with due clarity and bring the various interpretations that have been made closer together.

In 1958, carrying out a plan put forward by Knud Rasmussen, Kaj Birket-Smith and Helge Larsen invited American, Canadian and Russian scholars, together with Scandinavian experts to participate in a 'Circumpolar Conference' in Copenhagen. These discussions and contacts were useful and most promising. Let us hope that they will be continued and expanded in the future, so that by fruitful international collaboration – even across the Bering Strait – an ever more comprehensive picture may be gained of the prehistory of the Eskimo area.

Bibliography: Birket-Smith, 1929, 1930, 1937, 1948, 1951, 1959; Borden, 1962; Campbell, 1962a; Chard, 1958, 1960; Collins, 1937b, 1940, 1943, 1951a, 1953a, 1954a, 1954b, 1960, 1962, 1964; Debetz, 1960; Dumond, 1965; Giddings, 1960a, 1960b, 1961, 1963, 1964; Griffin, 1962; Hammerich, 1958, 1960; Irving, 1962b; Jenness, 1928b, 1933; de Laguna, 1946,

1947, 1962; Larsen, 1960a; Laughlin, 1962b, 1963b; Leroi-Gourhan, 1946; Levin, 1960; MacNeish, 1959a, 1959b, 1963; Mathiassen, 1930b; Rainey and Ralph, 1959; Ritchie, 1962; Rudenko, 1961; Swadesh, 1962; Taylor, 1959, 1963.

APPENDIX

The following diagrams give an idea of the views of some experts on the origin, development and dissemination of Eskimo culture. The last diagram illustrates my own opinions.

Diagram 1 is due to F. de Laguna, who designed it in 1947, showing that it is a compromise between the estimates of chronology made by various writers.

Diagram 2 was published in 1948 by H. Larsen and F.G. Rainey in their monograph on Ipiutak. Generally speaking, it accords with ideas still valid today, the only difference being that the relationship between the Ipiutak, Near Ipiutak, Okvik and Old Bering Sea cultures has been shifted somewhat in the meantime.

Diagram 3, compiled by H.B. Collins in 1954, deserves special attention. Due to the discovery and publication by this date of the Denbigh Flint complex, as well as of similar finds in the interior of Alaska and Arctic Canada, the development is here shown in greater depth.

Diagram 4 was published for the first time in 1948 by Birket-Smith in the Swiss edition of his book on the Eskimo. He reproduced it in a slightly modified form in the second edition of the English translation in 1959. Noteworthy here is the distinction between Proto-, Paleo- and Neo-Eskimo stages, which stems from H.P. Steensby. The expressions 'Paleo-' and 'Neo-' do not seem to me a fortunate choice, as they could lead to erroneous associations with Paleolithic and Neolithic. Moreover, we have seen that the American Epi-Gravettian people, who would correspond to the Proto-Eskimo of Birket-Smith, had a certain tendency toward adaptation to life on the coast, i.e. that Sarqaq (Pre-Dorset) and Dorset, which are placed here with the Paleo-Eskimo stage, had strong connections with the American Epi-Gravettian. I also doubt whether the Ipiutak and Old Bering Sea cultures can be assigned to two different stages of cultural development, all the more so since some interlocking is evident, and it is becoming increasingly apparent that Ipiutak must be assigned to a relatively late period.

Diagram 5, by R.S. MacNeish, was produced in 1963. In it a distinction is drawn between various stages of development, referred to as 'traditions'. The British Mountain tradition, as mentioned, hardly needs to be taken into account as far as the development of Eskimo culture is concerned. The 'Cordilleran tradition' and 'Northern Plano tradition' correspond to my collective term 'Northern Point tradition'; the 'Northwest Microblade tradition' and 'Arctic Small-Tool tradition' I have combined under the term American Epi-Gravettian tradition. The groups of sites and cultures listed are only partly to be found in our text, since it would have been too confusing to include all discoveries, which are frequently rather uncertain. Moreover, some of them have been inserted erroneously – as, for example, Palisades II, a group of sites so far poorly defined, but which definitely does not belong to the 'Northwest Microblade tradition', i.e. to the American Epi-Gravettian.

Diagram 6 is a legacy of J.L. Giddings, who published it in 1964, shortly before his death, in his great monograph on Cape Denbigh. It shows how this outstanding specialist on the archeology of the Eskimo area judged the development in the various regions.

Another attempt to represent cultural development over the entire Eskimo area is diagram 7 published by D.E. Dumond in 1965. This has the advantage that the most recent finds and linguistic differences have also been taken into consideration.

The last diagram, number 8, is my own which agrees with the text of this volume. I have tried to include as far as possible the entire area where the development of Eskimo culture took place, from the Bering land bridge, which is no longer in existence today, as far as Northeastern Greenland. It illustrates my opinions: first, that the American Epi-Gravettian spread across Southwestern Alaska into the interior of Alaska and subsequently, in various waves and directions, as far as the Eastern Arctic; secondly, that Southwestern Alaska appears to have been the starting point of all important developments, which brought about both the appearance of peculiar and highly specialized cultures in the Bering Strait and in Northwestern and Northern Alaska as well as the final breakthrough of the Thule culture.

Southeastern Alaska	Northern Alaska	St. Lawrence Island	Arctic Canada	Greenland (Northern west coast)	Newfoundland
Modern: Russian, Tlingit and Athabaskan expansion (Bering, 1741)	Modern (Beechey, 1826)	Modern: Russo-Siberian expansion (Bering, 1728)	Modern: expansion from Barren Grounds to Coast	Modern: Contact with European whalers and Danish administration	Micmac
......A.D. 1700......	......A.D. 1700......	......A.D. 1700......			......A.D. 1830......
					Beothuk (Eskimo in Gulf of St. Lawrence, Champlain 1603)
late	Protohistoric: Thule return	Protohistoric: influenced by Thule return	(Hudson 1610)	......A.D. 1650......	
				Protohistoric: adaptation to environment	
Kachemak Bay III: developed	......A.D. 1400......	......A.D. 1400......	......A.D. 1500......		......A.D. 1500......
sub-III		Punuk	Thule	......A.D. 1400......	Dorset with Thule influence (Dorset Eskimo in "Markland," Southeast Labrador, Thorfinn Karlsefni 1003–6
	Thule? (found only at Cape Prince of Wales)			Inugsuk: contact with Normemen	
				......A.D. 1200......	
......A.D. 1000......	......A.D. 1000......		......A.D. 1000......	Thule: Migration from Canada	A.D. 1000 or earlier?
Kachemak Bay II			Thule and Dorset	......A.D. 1000...... (Erik the Red, 983)	
Migration to Canada early in this period			......A.D. 800......	Dorset?	? ?
			Dorset	? ?	
......A.D. 500......	......A.D. 500......	......A.D. 500......			
Kachemak Bay I	Birnirk	Early Punuk	? ?		
	......A.D. 100......	......A.D. 100......			
	......A.D. 1......				
	Old Bering Sea? Ipiutak at Point Hope, and something else?	Old Bering Sea			
......A.D. 1......					
......B.C......	......B.C......	......B.C......			

Diagram 1.   Eskimo archeology. After F. de Laguna (1947).

	Southeast Alaska	Bering Strait	North Alaska	Arctic Canada	Greenland
1900 A.D.	Modern	*Modern*[a]	*Modern*	Central Eskimo	*Modern*
					Intermediate
1500 A.D.	Kachemak Bay III	*Recent Prehistoric*	*Tigara*	*Eastern Thule*	*Inugsuk*
					Eastern Thule
1000 A.D.	Kachemak Bay II	*Punuk*	*Western Thule*	Dorset and *Western Thule*	Dorset?
		Early Punuk	*Birnirk*		
500 A.D.	Kachemak Bay I	*Old Bering Sea*	?	Dorset	
			Near Ipiutak		
		Okvik	Ipiutak		
1 A.D.					

Diagram 2. The position of the Ipiutak culture in the relative time sequence of Eskimo culture. After H. Larsen and F. G. Rainey (1948).

[a] Italics indicate phases of the Neo-Eskimo or Arctic Whale Hunting culture.

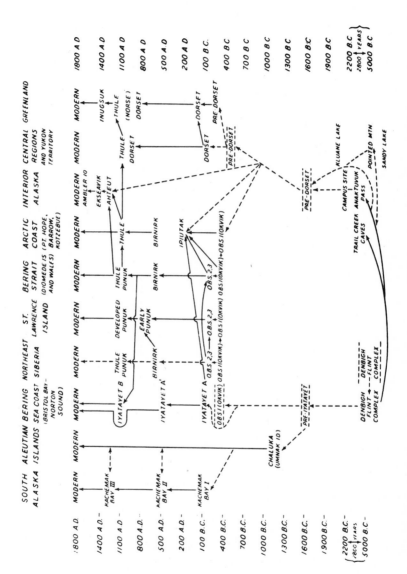

Diagram 3.   Known and postulated culture stages in the Eskimo area. After
H. B. Collins (1954a).

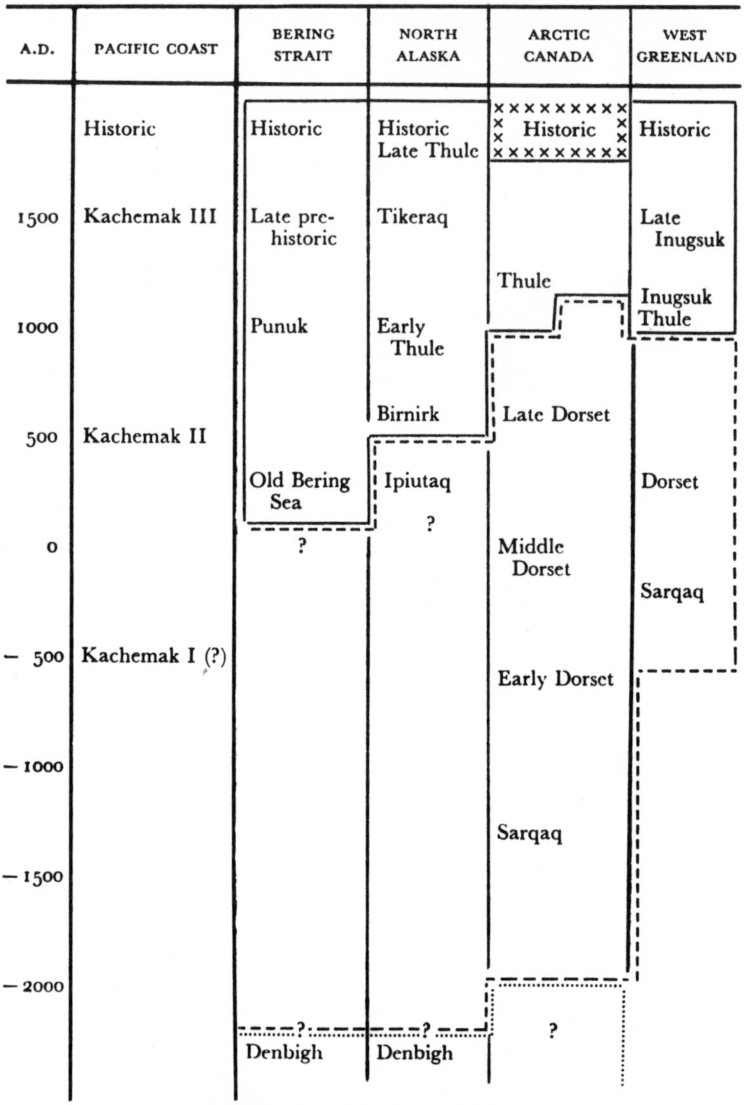

A.D.	PACIFIC COAST	BERING STRAIT	NORTH ALASKA	ARCTIC CANADA	WEST GREENLAND
	Historic	Historic	Historic Late Thule	Historic	Historic
1500	Kachemak III	Late pre-historic	Tikeraq	Thule	Late Inugsuk
1000		Punuk	Early Thule		Inugsuk Thule
500	Kachemak II		Birnirk	Late Dorset	
0		Old Bering Sea ?	Ipiutaq ?	Middle Dorset	Dorset Sarqaq
— 500	Kachemak I (?)			Early Dorset	
— 1000					
— 1500				Sarqaq	
— 2000				?	
		Denbigh	Denbigh		

× × × × × × Eschato-Eskimos (advance of inland tribes).
————— Neo-Eskimos (further adaptation to the sea: whaling).
— — — — Palaeo-Eskimos (adaptation to the sea: sealing).
················ Proto-Eskimos (inland hunters and fishermen).

Diagram 4. Cultural stages of the Eskimo culture. After K. Birket-Smith (1959).

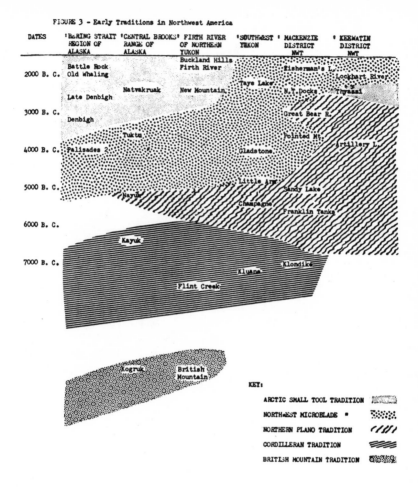

FIGURE 3 - Early Traditions in Northwest America

Diagram 5.   Early Man in the Western American Arctic. After R. S. Mac-
Neish (1963).

| | Greenland | Canada | | | Central Brooks Range | Other Kobuk | Onion Portage | Point Hope | Battle Rock | Cape Krusenstern | Alaska | | | | | | | Asia | |
	Greenland (Many sites)	Igloo-lik	Dismal Lake	Engigstciak							Trail Creek	Choris Peninsula	Cape Espenberg	Cape Prince of Wales	Cape Denbigh	Aleutians	Cook Inlet	Coast	Interior
1000 A.D.	Eskimo	Eskimo	Eskimo (Indian?)	Eskimo (Indian?)	Eskimo (Indian?)	Eskimo	Eskimo	Eskimo	Eskimo	Eskimo	Eskimo	Eskimo	Eskimo	Eskimo	Eskimo Nukleet	Aleut	Atha-pascan	Chukchi-Eskimo	Many tribes
	Thule	Thule						Western Thule	Western Thule	Western Thule Birnirk	Western Thule			Western Thule Birnirk			Kachemak Bay III	Punuk	
A.D. B.C.	Dorset	Dorset					Upper Middle	Ipiutak Near Ipiutak	Ipiutak Near Ipiutak	Ipiutak Near Ipiutak	Ipiutak	Flint Stations	Singauruk II Singauruk I Kugzruk	Singauruk II	Norton		Kachemak Bay II	Old Bering Sea Okvik	Meral Ages
							Lower Middle		Battle Rock	Norton			Norton-Choris	Kugzruk			Kachemak Bay I		
1000 B.C.	Sarqaq	(Sarqaq?) pre-Dorset					(Choris?)			Choris	Large diagonally flaked points	Choris	Choris						Kitoi
										Trail Creek-Choris									
2000					Several "small tool" sites		Old Hearth			Old Whaling									Serovo
	Independence I		Dismal II	Long, undated sequence, not yet clearly isolated by stratigraphy	Undated sites and cultural phases	Little Noatak			Denbigh Flint Complex	Denbigh Flint Complex	Denbigh Flint Complex	Denbigh Flint Complex	Denbigh Flint Complex	Denbigh Flint Complex	Denbigh Flint Complex	Paleo- to Neo-Aleutian physique and culture			
3000							Frozen In 1961			Lower Bench Palisades II	Microblades and hafts								Isakovo
4000					Undated sites and cultural phases	Kiana Bench										Microblades (?)			
Much older				Chemically changed flints?	Chemically changed flints					Palisades I									

Diagram 6.   Cultural phases of the Arctic. After J. L. Giddings (1965).

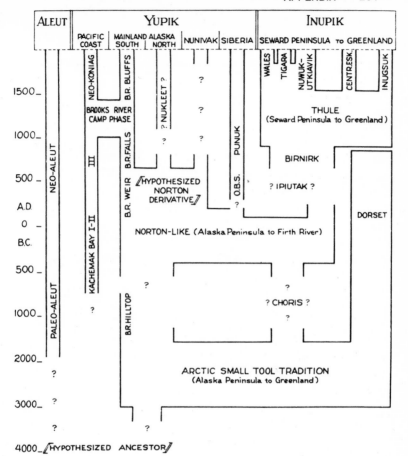

Diagram 7. Schematic diagram of suggested archeological relationships in the Eskimo area. After D. E. Dumond (1965).

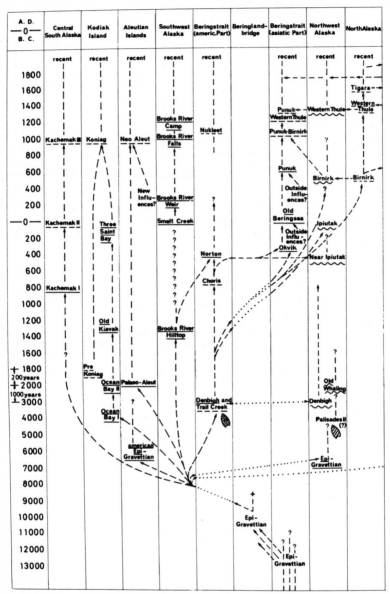

Diagram 8.   Outline of cultural sequences in the entire Eskimo area according
to the author's view expressed in this book.

Southern Central Alaska	Northern Central Alaska	Arct.Canada North (Centr.Reg.)	Arct.Canada Interior	Arct.Canada Hudson Bay Region	North Greenland	West Greenland	Southwest Greenland	Southeast Greenland	Northeast Greenland	A.D. 0 B.C.
	recent	recent	recent (Caribou Eskimos)	recent	+	recent	recent	recent	+ Mixed Culture	
	?←		?		+				Inugsuk	1800
→?			?→?				+	Inugsuk	Thule ?	1600
?←	Thule	? ? ? ?	Thule		Inugsuk	Inugsuk	Inugsuk	Dorset/Thule ?	1400
				Thule	Thule				1200
	Birnirk		+	Thule	+	Northmen		?	1000
				Dorset	+			Independence	800
					?	?			600
							Dorset?		400
						Dorset?			200
					?	Dorset?			0
					Dorset				200
					?	?			400
			Dorset			?	Sarqaq		600
				+?	Sarqaq	Sarqaq			800
				Independence II					1000
									1200
	?	?							1400
									1600
? ? ? ?	Tuktu	Epi-Gravettian	Epi-Gravettian	Pre-Dorset	Independence I					1800 / 200 years / 2000 / 1000years / 3000
									4000
Epi Gravettian									5000
									6000

Method of dating:

— by C 14

∿∿∿ by historical events

∿ by beach ridges

⊔⊓⊔ by beach sequences

- - - estimated by help of strati-
graphical, geological and other
indications or supposed on the
basis of comparison with
similar complexes in other
parts of the Eskimos area

⬮ influences of the "Northern
point tradition" (Palaeoindian)

- - → directions of diffusion and influences

········ connecting lines

— — supposed or verified roots or
extensions

+ no continuation

| 7000 |
| 8000 |
| 9000 |
| 10000 |
| 11000 |
| 12000 |
| 13000 |

BIBLIOGRAPHY

Abbreviations

AA   American Antiquity
A Anthr   American Anthropologist
AINA   Arctic Institute of North America
AMNH-AP   American Museum of Natural History, Anthropological Papers
APUA   Anthropological Papers, University of Alaska
ARAN   Arctic Anthropology
MoG   Meddelelser om Gronland
NMC   National Museum of Canada, Annual Report
Sm Misc.   Smithsonian Institution, Miscellaneous Publications
Sm R   Smithsonian Institution, Report
SWJA   Southwestern Journal of Anthropology

Ackerman, Robert E. *Archaeological Investigations into the Prehistory of St. Lawrence Island, Alaska.* University Microfilms Inc. (61-3480) Ann Arbor, 1961.
   Culture Contact in the Bering Sea: Birnirk-Punuk Period. AINA, Technical Papers, No. 11, pp. 27-34, 1962.
   Prehistory in the Kuskokwim-Bristol Bay Region, Southwestern Alaska. Laboratory of Anthropology, Washington State University, Pullman, Washington, 1964.
   Prehistoric Art of the Western Eskimo. The Beaver, Autumn, pp. 67-71, 1967.
Aigner, Jean S. *Bone Tools and Decorative Motifs from Chaluka, Umnak Island.* ARAN, Vol. 3, No. 2, pp. 57-83, 1966.
Amdrup, Georg Carl *Report on the Danmark Expedition to the Northeast Coast of Greenland.* MoG, Vol. 41, No. 1, Copenhagen, 1913.
Anderson, D. *A Stone Age Group Site at the Gateway to America.* Scientific American, Vol. 218, No. 6, pp. 24-33, 1968.
Arutyunov, S. A. and D. Sergeyev *New Finds in the Old Bering Sea Cemetery at Uelen.* AINA, Anthropology of the North: Translations from Russian Sources, No. 5, pp. 327-332, Toronto, 1964.
Arutyunov, S. A., M. G. Levin and D. A. Sergeyev *Ancient Burials on the Chukchi Peninsula.* AINA, Anthropology of the North: Translations from Russian Sources, No. 5, pp. 333-346, Toronto, 1964.
Bandi, Hans-Georg *The Burins in the Eskimo Area.* APUA, Vol. 10, No. 2, pp. 19-28, 1963.
Bandi, Hans-Georg and Jorgen Meldgaard *Archaeological Investigations on Clavering Island, Northeast Greenland.* MoG, Vol. 126, No. 4, Copenhagen, 1952.
Bank, Theodore *Cultural Succession in the Aleutians.* AA, Vol. 19, pp. 40-49, 1954.
Befu, Harumi and Chester S. Chard *Preceramic Cultures in Japan.* A Anthr, Vol. 62, pp. 815-849, 1960.

Beregovaia, N. A. *Extrémités de Harpons des anciennes populations du Cap Beranov. (Harpoon Points of the Ancient Populations of Cape Baranov). (Fouilles de l'expedition de la Kolyma en 1946.)* IN: Okladnikov, Aleksei P. (Ed.) Paléolithique et Néolithique de L'U.R.S.S., pp. 354-381, Gap, 1957.

Bergsland, K. *The Eskimo-Uralic Hypothesis.* Journal de la Société Finno-Ougrienne, Vol. 61, 1959.

Bird, Junius *Archaeology of the Hopedale Area, Labrador.* AMNH-AP, Vol. 39, Pt. 2, New York, 1945.

Birket-Smith, Kaj *The Caribou Eskimos.* Report of the 5th Thule Expedition, 1921-1924, Vol. 5, Parts 1, 2, Copenhagen, 1929.

    The Question of the Origin of Eskimo Culture: a Rejoinder. A Anthr, N.S., Vol. 32, No. 4, pp. 508-525, 1930.

    Eskimo Cultures and their Bearing upon the Prehistoric Cultures of North America and Eurasia. IN: George G. MacCurdy (Ed.), Early Man, London, 1937.

    Recent Achievements in Eskimo Research. Journal of the Royal Anthropological Institute, Vol. 77, 1947, pp. 145-157, London, 1951.

    The Eskimos. 2nd ed., London, 1959.

Boas, Franz *The Eskimo.* Proceedings and Transactions of the Royal Society of Canada, Vol. 5, Section 2, 1888.

Borden, Charles E. *West Coast Crossties with Alaska.* AINA, Technical Papers, No. 11, pp. 9-19, 1962.

    Radiocarbon and Geological Dating of the Lower Fraser Canyon Archaeological Sequence. Proceedings, 6th International Conference, Radiocarbon and Tritium Dating, Washington State University, pp. 165-178, Pullman, Washington, 1965.

Bosch-Gimpera, Pedro *Die erste Besiedlungswellen auf dem amerikanischen Kontinent. (The first waves of settlement on the American Continent).* Saeculum, Vol. 13, No. 2, pp. 121-131, 1962.

Bushnell, Geoffrey and Charles McBurney *New World Origins Seen from the Old World.* Antiquity, Vol. 33, pp. 93-101, 1959.

Butler, B. Robert *The Old Cordilleran Culture in the Pacific Northwest.* Occasional Papers of the Idaho State College Museum, No. 5, Pocatello, Idaho, 1961.

Byers, Douglas S. *The Bering Bridge-Some Speculations.* Ethnos, Vol. 1-2, pp. 20-26, 1957.

    New England and the Arctic. AINA, Technical Papers, No. 11, pp. 143-155, 1962.

Campbell, John M. *The Kayuk Complex of Arctic Alaska.* AA, Vol. 25, No. 1, pp. 94-105, 1959.

    The Kogruk Complex of Anaktuvuk Pass, Alaska. Anthropologica, N.S., Vol. 3, No. 1, pp. 1-18, 1961a.

    The Tuktu Complex of Anaktuvuk Pass. APUA, Vol. 9, No. 2, pp. 61-80, 1961b.

    (Ed.) Prehistoric Cultural Relations between the Arctic and Temperate Zones of North America. AINA, Technical Papers, No. 11, 1962a.

Cultural Succession at Anaktuvuk Pass, Arctic Alaska. AINA, Technical Papers, No. 11, pp. 39-54, 1962b.

Ancient Alaska and Paleolithic Europe. APUA, Vol. 10, No. 2, pp. 29-49, 1963.

Chard, Chester S. *Eskimo Archaeology in Siberia.* SWJA, Vol. 11, No. 2, pp. 150-177, 1955.

The Oldest Sites of Northeast Siberia. AA, Vol. 21, No. 4, pp. 405-409, 1956.

An Outline of the Prehistory of Siberia, Part 1: The Pre-Metal Periods. SWJA, Vol. 14, No. 1, pp. 1-33, 1958a.

Mesolithic Sites in Siberia. Asian Perspectives, Vol. 2, No. 1, pp. 118-127, 1958b.

New World Migration Routes. APUA, Vol. 7, No. 1, pp. 23-26, 1958c.

The Western Roots of Eskimo Culture. Actas del 33 Congreso Internacional de Americanistas 1958, Vol. 2, pp. 81-87, San Jose, 1959a.

New World Origins: a Reappraisal. Antiquity, Vol. 33, pp. 44-49, 1959b.

Maritime Culture in the North Pacific: Age and Origin. Akten d. 34. Internationalen Amerikanistencongresses, pp. 279-283, Vienna, 1960.

The Old World Roots: Review and Speculations. APUA, Vol. 10, No. 2, pp. 115-121, 1963.

Clark, Donald W. *Two Late Prehistoric Pottery-Bearing Sites on Kodiak Island, Alaska.* ARAN, Vol. 3, No. 2, pp. 157-184, 1966.

Colinvaux, P. A. *The Environment of the Bering Land Bridge.* Ecological Monographs, Vol. 34, No. 3, pp. 297-329, 1964.

Collins, Henry B. *Archeology of the Bering Sea Region.* Sm R for 1933, pp. 453-468, Washington, 1935.

Archeology of St. Lawrence Island, Alaska. Sm Misc., Vol. 96, No. 1, Washington, 1937a.

Culture Migrations and Contacts in the Bering Sea Region. A Anthr, Vol. 39, No. 3, pp. 375-384, 1937b.

Outline of Eskimo Prehistory. Sm Misc., Vol. 100, pp. 533-592, Washington, 1940.

Eskimo Archaeology and its Bearing on the Problem of Man's Antiquity in America. Proceedings of the American Philosophical Society, Vol. 86, No. 2, pp. 220-235, 1943.

Excavations at Frobisher Bay, Baffin Island, Northwest Territories. NMC for 1948-49, Bulletin 118, pp. 18-43, Ottawa, 1950.

The Origin and Antiquity of the Eskimo. Sm R for 1950, pp. 423-467, Washington, 1951a.

Excavations at Thule Culture Sites near Resolute Bay, Baffin Island, Northwest Territories. NMC for 1949-50, Bulletin 123, pp. 49-63, Ottawa, 1951b.

Archaeological Excavations at Resolute, Cornwallis Island. NMC for 1950-51, Bulletin 126, pp. 48-63, Ottawa, 1952.

Radiocarbon Dating in the Arctic. AA, Vol. 18, No. 3, pp. 197-203, 1953a.

Recent Developments in the Dorset Culture Area. Mem. of the Society for American Archaeology, No. 9, pp. 32-39, 1953b.

Archaeological Research in the North American Arctic. Arctic, Vol. 7, No. 3-4, pp. 296-306, 1954a.

Arctic Area. Instituto Panamericano de Geografia e Historia, Program of the History of America, Vol. 1, No. 2, Mexico, 1954b.

The Position of Ipiutak in Eskimo Culture-Reply. AA, Vol. 20, No. 1, pp. 79-84, 1954c.

Archaeological Work on Southampton and Walrus Island, Hudson Bay. Year Book of the American Philosophical Society, pp. 341-344, 1955a.

Excavation of Thule and Dorset Culture Sites at Resolute, Cornwallis Island, Northwest Territories. NMC for 1953-54, Bulletin 136, pp. 22-35, Ottawa, 1955b.

The T 1 Site at Native Point, Southampton Island, Northwest Territories. APUA, Vol. 4, No. 2, pp. 63-89, 1956a.

Archaeological Investigations on Southampton and Coats Island, Northwest Territories. NMC for 1954-55, Bulletin 142, pp. 82-113, Ottawa, 1956b.

Archaeological Work in Arctic Canada. Sm R for 1956, pp. 509-528, Washington, 1957.

Archaeological Investigations on Southampton and Walrus Islands, Northwest Territories. NMC for 1955-56, Bulletin 147, pp. 22-61, Ottawa, 1958a.

Present Status of the Dorset Problem. Proceedings of the 32nd International Congress of Americanists, 1956, pp. 557-560, Copenhagen, 1958b.

An Okvik Artifact from Southwest Alaska and Stylistic Resemblances between Early Eskimo and Paleolithic Art. Polar Notes, Occasional Publications of the Stefánsson Collection, Dartmouth College Library, Vol. 1, pp. 13-27, Hanover, N.H., 1959.

Recent Trends and Developments in Arctic Archeology. Actes du VIe Congres International des Sciences Anthropologiques et Ethnologiques, Vol. 2, pp. 373-377, Paris, 1960.

Bering Strait to Greenland. AINA, Technical Papers, No. 11, pp. 126-139, 1962.

Paleo-Indian Artifacts in Alaska: An Example of Cultural Retardation in the Arctic. APUA, Vol. 10, No. 2, pp. 13-18, 1963.

The Arctic and Subarctic. IN: Jennings, Jesse D. and Edward Norbeck (Eds.), Prehistoric Man in the New World, Chicago, 1964.

Cranz, D. *History of Greenland.* London, 1767.

Cressman, Luther S. and D. E. Dumond *Research on Northwest Prehistory: Prehistory in the Naknek Drainage, Southwestern Alaska.* Eugene, 1962.

Dall, William H. *On the Succession in the Shell-heaps of the Aleutian Islands.* Contributions to North American Ethnology, Vol. 1, pp. 41-91, Washington, 1877.

Davis, Wilbur A. *Archaeological Investigations of Inland and Coastal Sites of the Katmai National Monument, Alaska.* Microcard Publications in Archaeology and Anthropology, No. 4, University of Wisconsin Press, 1954.

Dawkins, Boyd *Cave Hunting*. London, 1874.

Debetz, George F. *The Skeletal Remains of the Ipiutak Cemetery*. Actas del 33 Congreso Internacional de Americanistas 1958, pp. 57-64, San Jose, 1959.

    Problems of Physical Anthropology in Arctic Regions. Acta Arctica, Vol. 12, pp. 61-66, 1960.

Degerbol, Magnus *The Former Eskimo Habitation in the Kangerdlugssuak District in East Greenland*. MoG, Vol. 104, No. 10, Copenhagen, 1936.

Denniston, Glenda B. *Cultural Change at Chaluka, Umnak Island: Stone Artifacts and Features*. ARAN, Vol. 3, No. 2, pp. 84-124, 1966.

Dikov, N. *The Stone Age of Kamchatka and the Chukchi Peninsula in the Light of New Archaeological Data*. ARAN, Vol. 3, No. 1, pp. 10-25, 1965.

Dumond, D. E. *Two Early Phases from the Naknek Drainage*. ARAN, Vol. 1, No. 2, pp. 93-104, 1963.

    A Note on the Prehistory of Southwestern Alaska. APUA, Vol. 12, No. 1, pp. 33-45, 1964.

    On Eskaleutian Linguistics, Archaeology and Prehistory. A Anthr, Vol. 67, No. 5, Part 1, pp. 1231-1257, 1965.

Ford, John *Eskimo Prehistory in the Vicinity of Point Barrow*. AMNH-AP, Vol. 47, Pt. 1, New York, 1959.

Geist, Otto and Froelich G. Rainey *Archaeological Excavations at Kukulik*. Miscellaneous Publications of the University of Alaska, Vol. 2, Washington, 1936.

Giddings, James Louis *Early Flint Horizons on the North Bering Sea Coast*. Journal of the Washington Academy of Sciences, Vol. 39, No. 3, pp. 85-90, 1949.

    Early Man on the Bering Sea Coast. Annals of the New York Academy of Sciences, Series 2, Vol. 13, No. 1, pp. 18-21, 1950.

    The Denbigh Flint Complex. AA, Vol. 16, No. 3, pp. 193-203, 1951.

    The Arctic Woodland Culture of the Kobuk River. Philadelphia, 1952a.

    Ancient Bering Strait and Population Spread. IN: Collins, Henry B. (Ed.), Science in Alaska, AINA Special Publication, No. 1, pp. 85-102, Washington, 1952b.

    The Denbigh Flint Complex Is Not Yet Dated. AA, Vol. 20, No. 4, pp. 375-376, 1955.

    The Burin Spall Artifact. Arctic, Vol. 9, No. 4, pp. 229-237, 1956a.

    A Flint Site in Northernmost Manitoba. AA, Vol. 21, No. 3, pp. 255-268, 1956b.

    Round Houses in the Western Arctic. AA, Vol. 23, No. 2, pp. 121-135, 1957.

    The Archeology of Bering Strait. Current Anthropology, Vol. 1, No. 2, pp. 121-138, 1960a.

A View of Archeology about Bering Strait. Acta Arctica, Fasc. 12, pp. 27-34, 1960b.

Cultural Continuities of Eskimos. AA, Vol. 27, No. 2, pp. 155-173, 1961.

Onion Portage and Other Flint Sites of the Kobuk River. ARAN, Vol. 1, No. 1, pp. 6-27, 1962a.

Seven Discoveries of Bering Strait. Proceedings of the American Philosophical Society, Vol. 106, No. 2, pp. 89-93, 1962b.

Side-Notched Points Near Bering Strait. AINA, Technical Papers, No. 11, pp. 35-38, 1962c.

Some Arctic Spear Points and Their Counterparts. APUA, Vol. 10, No. 2, pp. 1-12, 1963.

The Archaeology of Cape Denbigh. Providence R.I., 1964.

Cross-Dating the Archaeology of Northwestern Alaska. Science, Vol. 153, No. 3732, pp. 127-135, 1966.

Ancient Men of the Arctic. New York, 1967.

Gjessing, Gutorm *Circumpolar Stone Age.* Acta Arctica, Fasc. 2, Copenhagen, 1944.

Some Problems in Northeastern Archaeology. AA, Vol. 13, No. 4, pp. 298-302, 1948.

Glob, Peter V. *Eskimo Settlements in Kempe Fjord and King Oscar Fjord.* MoG, Vol. 102, No. 2, Copenhagen, 1935.

Eskimo Settlements in Northeast Greenland. MoG, Vol. 144, No. 6, Copenhagen, 1946.

Greenman, E. F. *The Upper Palaeolithic and the New World.* Current Anthropology, Vol. 4, No. 1, pp. 41-92, 1963.

Griffin, James B. *A Preliminary Statement on the Pottery from Cape Denbigh, Alaska.* IN: Asia and North America: Transpacific Contacts, Memoirs of the Society for American Archaeology, Vol. 9, pp. 40-42, 1953.

Some Prehistoric Connections between Siberia and America. Science, Vol. 131, No. 3403, pp. 801-812, 1960.

A Discussion of Prehistoric Similarities and Connections between the Arctic and Temperate Zones of North America. AINA, Technical Papers, No. 11, pp. 154-163, 1962.

Haag, William *The Bering Strait Land Bridge.* Scientific American, Vol. 206, No. 1, pp. 111-123, 1962.

Hadleigh-West, Frederick *Leaf-shaped Points in the Western Arctic.* APUA, Vol. 10, No. 2, pp. 51-62, 1963a.

(Ed.) Early Man in the Western American Arctic: a Symposium. APUA, Vol. 10, No. 2, 1963b.

Archaeological Survey and Excavations in the Proposed Rampart Dam Impoundment, 1963-1964. (Manuscript), 1965a.

Excavations at Two Sites on the Teklanika River, Mt. McKinley National Park, Alaska. (Manuscript), 1965b.

The Donnelly Ridge Site and the Definition of an Early Core and Blade Complex in Central Alaska. AA, Vol. 32, No. 3, pp. 360-82, 1967.

Hammerich, L. *The Origin of the Eskimo.* Proceedings of the 32nd International Congress of Americanists, pp. 640-644, Copenhagen, 1958.

Some Linguistic Problems in the Arctic. Acta Arctica, Vol. 12, pp. 83-89, 1960.

Harp, Elmer *An Archaeological Survey in the Strait of Belle Isle Area.* AA, Vol. 16, No. 3, pp. 203-220, 1951.

New World Affinities of Cape Dorset Culture. APUA, Vol. 1, No. 2, pp. 37-54, 1953.

Prehistory in the Dismal Lake Area, N.W.T., Canada. Arctic, Vol. 11, No. 4, pp. 219-249, 1958.

The Moffatt Archaeological Collection from the Dubawnt Country. AA, Vol. 24, No. 4, pp. 412-422, 1959a.

Ecological Continuity on the Barren Grounds. Polar Notes, Occasional Publications of the Stefánsson Collection, Dartmouth College Library, Vol. 1, pp. 48-56, Hanover, N.H., 1959b.

Archaeological Evidence Bearing on the Origin of the Caribou Eskimos. Actes du VIe Congres International des Sciences Anthropologiques et Ethnologiques, Tome II (1er vol.), pp. 409-413, Paris, 1960.

The Archaeology of the Lower and Middle Thelon, Northwest Territories. AINA, Technical Papers, No. 8, 1961.

The Culture History of the Central Barren Grounds. AINA, Technical Papers, No. 11, pp. 69-75, 1962.

The Cultural Affinities of the Newfoundland Dorset Eskimo. Ottawa, 1964.

Hatt, Gudmond *Kyst-og inlandskultur i det arktiske.* Geografisk Tidsskrift, Vol. 23, Copenhagen, 1916.

Heizer, Robert F. *Archaeology of the Uyak Site, Kodiak Island, Alaska.* Berkeley and Los Angeles, 1956.

Holm, G. *Beskrivelse of ruiner i Julianehaabs Distrikt, undersogte i Aaret 1880.* MoG, Vol. 6, pp. 57-145, Copenhagen, 1883.

Holtved, Erik *Archaeological Investigations in the Thule District. Pt. 1, Descriptive Part,* MoG, Vol. 141, No. 1, Copenhagen, 1944; *Pt. 2, Analytical Part,* MoG, Vol. 146, No. 3, Copenhagen, 1954.

Hopkins, David M. *Cenozoic History of the Bering Land Bridge.* Science, Vol. 129, No. 3362, pp. 1519-1528, 1959.

Hopkins, David M. and J. L. Giddings *Geological Background of the Iyatayet Archaeological Site, Cape Denbigh, Alaska.* Sm Misc., Vol. 121, No. 11, pp. 1-33, Washington, 1953.

Hopkins, David M., F. S. MacNeil, R. L. Merklin, O. M. Petrov *Quaternary Correlations across Bering Strait.* Science, Vol. 147, No. 3662, pp. 1107-1114, 1965.

(Ed.) The Bering Land Bridge. Stanford, 1967a.

The Cenozoic History of Beringia-A Synthesis. IN: Hopkins, D. M., The Bering Land Bridge, pp. 451-481, Stanford, 1967b.

Hrdlicka, Ales *The Anthropology of Kodiak Islands.* Philadelphia, 1944.

The Aleutian and Commander Islands and their Inhabitants. Philadelphia, 1945.

Humphrey, Robert L. *The Prehistory of the Utakok River Region.* Current Anthropology, Vol. 7, No. 5, pp. 586-588, 1966.

Ingstad, Helge *Vinland Ruins Prove Vikings Found the New World.* National Geographic, Vol. 126, No. 5, pp. 708-734, 1964.

Irving, William N. *Archaeology in the Brooks Range of Alaska.* AA, Vol. 17, No. 1, pp. 52-53, 1951.

   Evidence of Early Tundra Cultures in Northern Alaska. APUA, Vol. 1, No. 2, pp. 55-85, 1953.

   An Archaeological Survey of the Susitna Valley. APUA, Vol. 6, No. 1, pp. 37-52, 1957.

   1961 Field Work in the Western Brooks Range, Alaska: Preliminary Report. ARAN, Vol. 1, No. 1, pp. 76-83, 1962a.

   A Provisional Comparison of Some Alaskan and Asian Stone Industries. AINA, Technical Papers, No. 11, pp. 55-68, 1962b.

   Northwest North America and Central United States: A Review. APUA, Vol. 10, No. 2, pp. 63-71, 1963.

Jenness, Diamond *Origin of the Copper Eskimos and Their Copper Culture.* Geographical Review, Vol. 13, pp. 540-51, 1923.

   A New Eskimo Culture in Hudson Bay. Geographical Review, Vol. 15, pp. 428-437, 1925.

   Archaeological Investigations in Bering Strait. NMC for 1926, Bulletin 50, Ottawa, 1928a.

   Ethnological Problems of Arctic America. American Geographical Society, Special Publication No. 7, pp. 167-175, 1928b.

   The Problem of the Eskimo. IN: Jenness, Diamond (Ed.), The American Aborigines, their Origin and Antiquity, pp. 373-396, Toronto, 1933.

   Prehistoric Culture Waves from Asia to America. Journal of the Washington Academy of Sciences, Vol. 30, No. 1, 1940.

   An Archaeological Collection from the Belcher Islands in Hudson Bay. Annals of the Carnegie Museum, Vol. 28, pp. 186-206, Pittsburgh, 1941.

Jennings, Jesse D. and Edward Norbeck (Editors) *Prehistoric Man in the New World.* Chicago, 1964.

Jochelson, Waldemar *Archaeological Investigations in the Aleutian Islands.* Carnegie Institution, Publication 367, Washington, 1925.

   History, Ethnology & Anthropology of the Aleut. Ibid, Publication 432, Washington, 1933.

Johnson, D. Mc D. *Observations on the Eskimo Remains on the East Coast of Greenland between 72° and 75° North Latitude.* MoG, Vol. 92, No. 6, Copenhagen, 1933.

Johnson, F. *An Archaeological Survey along the Alaska Highway.* AA, Vol. 11, No. 3, pp. 183-186, 1946.

Johnson, F. and Henry M. Raup *Investigations in Southwest Yukon.* Geobotanical and Archaeological Reconnaissance, Papers of the Robert S. Peabody Foundation for Archaeology, Vol. 6, No. 1, Andover, 1964.

Knuth, Eigil *An Outline of the Archaeology of Peary Land.* Arctic, Vol. 5, No. 1, pp. 17-33, 1952.

The Paelo-Eskimo Culture of Northeast Greenland Elucidated by Three New Sites. AA, Vol. 19, No. 4, pp. 367-381, 1954.

Archaeology of the Farthest North. Proceedings of the 32nd Congress of Americanists, Copenhagen 1956, pp. 561-573, Copenhagen 1958.

Pearyland's Arkaeologi I & II. Naturens Verden, June, pp. 170-184, 1965; September, pp. 266-279, 1965.

The Ruins of the Musk-ox Way. Folk, Vol. 8-9, pp. 191-219, 1966-67.

Koch, Lauge *The East Greenland Ice.* MoG, Vol. 130, No. 3, Copenhagen, 1945.

Krieger, Alex D. *The Earliest Cultures in the Western United States.* AA, Vol. 28, No. 2, pp. 138-143, 1962.

Laguna, Frederica de *A Comparison of Eskimo and Palaeolithic Art, Pt. 1-2.* American Journal of Archaeology, Vol. 36, No. 4, pp. 477-511, 1932; Vol. 37, No. 1, pp. 77-107, 1933a.

Peintures Rupestres Eskimo. Journal de la Société des Américanistes, N.S., Vol. 25, pp. 17-30, 1933b.

The Archaeology of Cook Inlet, Alaska. Philadelphia, 1934.

Eskimo Lamps and Pots. Journal of the Royal Anthropological Institute, Vol. 70, Part 1, pp. 53-76, 1940.

The Importance of the Eskimo in Northeastern Archaeology. IN: Man in Northeastern North America, Papers of the Robert S. Peabody Foundation for Archaeology, Vol. 3, pp. 106-142, bibliography, pp. 307-348, 1946.

The Prehistory of Northern North America as Seen from the Yukon. Mem. of the Society for American Archaeology, Vol. 12, No. 3, Part 2, 1947.

Chugach Prehistory: The Archaeology of Prince William Sound, Alaska. Seattle, 1956.

Intemperate Reflections on Arctic and Subarctic Archaeology. AINA, Technical Papers, No. 11, pp. 164-169, 1962.

Laguna, Frederica de and Francis A. Riddle, D. F. McGeein, K. S. Lane and J. A. Freed *Archaeology of the Yakutat Bay Area, Alaska.* Smithsonian Institution, Bureau of American Ethnology, Bulletin 192, Washington, 1964.

Larsen, Helge *Dodemandsbugten: An Eskimo Settlement on Clavering Island.* MoG, Vol. 102, No. 1, Copenhagen, 1934.

Archaeological Investigations on Knud Rasmussen's Land. MoG, Vol. 119, No. 8, Copenhagen, 1938.

Archaeological Investigations in Southwestern Alaska. AA, Vol. 15, No. 3, pp. 177-186, 1950.

De Dansk-amerikanske Alaska-ekspeditioner 1949-1950. Geografisk Tidsskrift, Vol. 51, pp. 63-93, 1951.

The Ipiutak Culture: Its Origin and Relationships. IN: Tax, Sol (Ed.), Indian Tribes of Aboriginal America, Proceedings of the 29th International Congress of Americanists, Vol. III, pp. 22-34, Chicago, 1952 (with discussion by Diamond Jenness).

Archaeological Investigations in Alaska Since 1939. Polar Record, Vol. 6, No. 45, pp. 593-607, 1953.

The Position of Ipiutak in Eskimo Culture. AA, Vol. 20, No. 1, pp. 74-79, 1954.

(Ed.) The Circumpolar Conference in Copenhagen, 1958. Acta Arctica, Fasc. 12, Copenhagen, 1960a.

Eskimo-Archaeological Problems in Greenland. Acta Arctica, Fasc. 12, pp. 11-16, Copenhagen, 1960b.

Archaeology in the Arctic, 1935-1960. AA, Vol. 27, No. 1, pp. 7-15, 1961.

The Trail Creek Caves on Seward Peninsula, Alaska. Akten des 34. Internationalen Amerikanisten Kongresses, pp. 284-291, Vienna, 1962.

Near Ipiutak and Uwelen-Okvik. (In Press)

Larsen, Helge and Jorgen Meldgaard *Palaeo-Eskimo Cultures in Disko Bugt, West Greenland.* MoG, Vol. 161, No. 2, Copenhagen, 1958.

Larsen, Helge and Froelich G. Rainey *Ipiutak and the Arctic Whale Hunting Culture.* AMNH-AP, Vol. 42, New York, 1948.

Laughlin, William S. *Notes on an Aleutian Core and Blade Industry.* AA, Vol. 17, No. 1, pp. 52-55, 1951.

The Aleut-Eskimo Community. APUA, Vol. 1, No. 1, pp. 25-46, 1952.

Neo-Aleut and Palaeo-Aleut Prehistory. Proceedings of the 32nd International Congress of Americanists, Copenhagen 1956, pp. 516-530, Copenhagen, 1958.

Generic Problems and New Evidence in the Anthropology of the Eskimo-Aleut Stock. AINA, Technical Papers, No. 11, pp. 100-112, 1962a.

Bering Strait to Puget Sound: Dichotomy and Affinity between Eskimo-Aleuts and American Indians. Ibid, pp. 113-125, 1962b.

The Earliest Aleuts. APUA, Vol. 10, No. 2, pp. 73-91, 1963a.

Eskimos and Aleuts: Their Origins and Evolution. Science, Vol. 142, No. 3593, pp. 633-645, 1963b.

Human Migration and Permanent Occupation in the Bering Sea Area. IN: Hopkins, D. M., The Bering Land Bridge, Stanford, pp. 409-450, 1967.

Laughlin, William S. and Jean S. Aigner *Preliminary Analysis of the Anangula Unifacial Core and Blade Industry.* ARAN, Vol. 3, No. 2, pp. 41-56, 1966.

Laughlin, William S. and Gordon H. Marsh *A New View of the History of the Aleutians.* Arctic, Vol. 4, No. 2, pp. 74-88, 1951.

The Lamellar Flake Manufacturing Site on Anangula Island in the Aleutians. AA, Vol. 20, pp. 27-39, 1954.

Laughlin, William S., Gordon H. Marsh and John W. Leach *Supplementary Note on the Aleutian Core and Blade Industry.* AA, Vol. 18, pp. 69-70, 1952.

Laughlin, William S. and W. G. Reeder (Editors) *Studies in Aleutian-*

Kodiak Prehistory, Ecology and Anthropology. ARAN, Vol. 3, No. 2, 1966.

Laughlin, William S. and William E. Taylor *A Cape Dorset Culture Site on the West Coast of Ungava Bay.* NMC, Bulletin 167, pp. 1-28, 1960.

Leechman, Douglas *Two Cape Dorset Sites.* AA, Vol. 8, No. 4, pp. 363-375, 1943.

Leroi-Gourhan, A. *Archéologie du Pacifique-Nord.* Paris, 1946.

Levin, Maksim G. *Ancient Cemetery in Uelen (Chukotka).* Actas del 33 Congreso Internacional de Americanistas 1956, pp. 565-711, San Jose, 1959.

Problems of Arctic Ethnology and Ethnogenesis. Acta Arctica, Fasc. 12, pp. 47-60, 1960.

An Early Eskimo Cemetery at Uelen: A Preliminary Report on the Excavations of 1958. AINA, Anthropology of the North: Translations from Russian Sources, No. 5, pp. 305-318, Toronto, 1964.

Levin, Maksim G. and L. P. Popatov (Editors) *The Peoples of Siberia.* Chicago and London, 1956.

Levin, Maksim G. and D. Sergeyev *The Penetration of Iron into the Arctic: The First Find of an Iron Implement, in a Site of the Old Bering Sea Culture.* AINA, Anthropology of the North: Translations from Russian Sources, No. 5, pp. 319-326, Toronto, 1964.

Lowther, G. R. *An Account of an Archaeological Site on Cape Sparbo, Devon Island.* NMC, Bulletin 180, Contribution to Anthropology, Part 1, 1960.

McCartney, A. D. and C. G. Turner II *Stratigraphy of the Anangula Unifacial Core and Blade Site.* ARAN, Vol. 3, No. 2, pp. 28-40, 1966.

MacNeish, Richard S. *An Archaelogical Reconnaissance in the Northwest Territories.* NMC for 1949-50, Bulletin 123, pp. 24-41, Ottawa, 1951.

Archaelogical Reconnaissance in the Mackenzie River Drainage. Ibid, for 1951-52, Bulletin 128, Ottowa, 1953.

The Pointed Mountain Site near Fort Liard, N.W.T., Canada. AA, Vol. 19, No. 3, pp. 234-253, 1954.

Two Archaeological Sites on Great Bear Lake, N.W.T., Canada. NMC for 1953-54, Bulletin 136, pp. 54-84, Ottawa, 1955.

Archaeological Reconnaissance of the Delta of the Mackenzie River and Yukon Coast. NMC for 1954-55, Bulletin 142, pp. 46-81, Ottawa, 1956a.

The Engigstciak Site on the Yukon Arctic Coast. APUA, Vol. 4, No. 2, pp. 91-111, 1956b.

Men Out of Asia: As Seen from the Northwest Yukon. APUA, Vol. 7, No. 2, pp. 41-70, 1959a.

A Speculative Framework of Northern North American Prehistory as of April 1959. Anthropologica, N.S., Vol. 1, No. 2, pp. 1-17, 1959b.

Problems of Circumpolar Archaeology: As Seen from Northwest Canada. Acta Arctica, Vol. 12, pp. 17-26, 1960.

Recent Finds in the Yukon Territory of Canada. AINA, Technical Papers, No. 11, pp. 20-26, 1962a.

The Great Lakes to the Barren Lands. Ibid, pp. 140-142, 1962b.

The Early Peopling of the New World—As Seen from the Southwestern Yukon. APUA, Vol. 10, No. 2, pp. 93-106, 1963.

Investigations in Southwest Yukon. Archaeological Excavations, Comparisons, and Speculations. Papers of the Robert S. Peabody Foundation for Archaeology, Vol. 6, No. 2, Andover, 1964.

Martijn, Charles A. *Canadian Eskimo Carving in Historical Perspective.* Anthropos, Vol. 54, pp. 546-596, 1965.

Mason, John Alden *Excavations of Eskimo Thule Culture Sites at Point Barrow, Alaska.* Proceedings of the 23rd Congress of Americanists, pp. 383-394, New York, 1930.

Mason, Ronald J. *The Paleo-Indian Tradition in Eastern North America.* Current Anthropology, Vol. 3, No. 3, pp. 227-278, 1962.

Mathiassen, Therkel *Archaeology of the Central Eskimos.* Report of the 5th Thule Expedition, 1921-24, Vol. 4, Copenhagen, 1927.

Eskimo Relics from Washington Land and Hall Land. MoG, Vol. 71, No. 5, Copenhagen, 1929.

The Archaeological Collection of the Cambridge East Greenland Expedition 1926. MoG, Vol. 74, No. 9, Copenhagen, 1929.

Inugsuk, a Medieval Eskimo Settlement in Upernivik District, West Greenland. Ibid, Vol. 77, No. 4, Copenhagen, 1930a.

The Question of the Origin of Eskimo Culture. A Anthr, N.S., Vol. 32, No. 4, 1930b.

Archaeological Collections from the Western Eskimos. Report of the 5th Thule Expedition, 1921-24, Vol. 10, Copenhagen, 1930c.

Ancient Eskimo Settlements in the Kangamiut Area. MoG, Vol. 91, No. 1, Copenhagen, 1931.

Prehistory of the Angmagssalik Eskimos. Ibid, Vol. 92, No. 4, Copenhagen, 1933.

Contributions to the Archaeology of Disko Bay. Ibid, Vol. 93, No. 2, Copenhagen, 1934a.

Eskimo Finds from the Kangerlugssuaq Region. Ibid, Vol. 104, No. 9, Copenhagen, 1934b.

The Former Eskimo Settlements on Frederick VI's Coast. Ibid, Vol. 109, No. 2, Copenhagen, 1936.

The Sermermiut Excavations, 1955. Ibid, Vol. 161, No. 3, Copenhagen, 1958.

Mathiassen, Therkel and Erik Holtved *The Eskimo Archaeology of Julianehaab District with a Brief Summary of the Prehistory of the Greenlanders.* Ibid, Vol. 118, No. 1, Copenhagen, 1936.

Maxwell, Moreau S. *An Archaeological Analysis of Eastern Grant Land, Ellesmere Island, Northwest Territories.* NMC, Bulletin 170, Ottawa, 1960.

Pre-Dorset and Dorset Sites in the Vicinity of Lake Harbour, Baffin Land, N.W.T. National Museum of Canada, Bull. 180, Part 1, 1962.

McCartney, A. P. and C. G. Turner II *Stratigraphy of the Anangula Unifacial Core and Blade Site.* ARAN, Vol. 3, No. 2, pp. 28-40, 1966.

Meldgaard, Jorgen *A Paleo-Eskimo Culture in West Greenland.* AA, Vol. 17, No. 3, pp. 222-230, 1952.

Dorset Kulturen. Den dansk-amerikanske ekspedition til Arktisk Canada 1954. Kuml, Aarbog for Jysk Arkaeologisk Selskab, pp. 158-177, 1955.

Origin and Evolution of Eskimo Cultures in the Eastern Arctic. Canadian Geographical Journal, Vol. 60, No. 2, pp. 64-75, 1960a.

Prehistoric Culture Sequences in the Eastern Arctic as Elucidated by Stratified Sites at Igloolik. Selected Papers, 5th International Congress of Anthropological and Ethnological Sciences, Philadelphia, 1956, pp. 588-595, 1960b.

Eskimo Sculpture. London, 1960c.

On the Formative Period of the Dorset Culture. AINA, Technical Papers, No. 11, pp. 92-95, 1962.

Traditional Sculpture in Greenland. The Beaver, Autumn, pp. 54-59, 1967.

Michael, Henry N. *The Neolithic Age in Eastern Siberia.* Transactions of the American Philosophical Society, N.S., Vol. 48, Pt. 2, Philadelphia, 1958.

(Ed.) The Archaeology and Geomorphology of Northern Asia. AINA, Anthropology of the North: Translations from Russian Sources, No. 5, Toronto, 1964.

Mitchell, D. *Preliminary Excavations at a Cobble Tool Site (DjRi 7) in the Fraser Canyon, British Columbia.* NMC, Anthropological Papers, No. 10, pp. 1-20, 1965.

Moberg, C. *On Some Circumpolar Arctic Problems in North European Archaeology.* Acta Arctica, Fasc. 12, pp. 67-74, 1960.

Morlan, R. E. *The Preceramic Period of Hokkaido: An Outline.* ARAN, Vol. 4, No. 1, pp. 164-220, 1967.

Movius, Hallam L. *The Mousterian Cave of Teshik-Tash, Southeastern Uzbekistan, Central Asia.* Bulletin, American School of Prehistoric Research, Vol. 17, pp. 11-71, 1953.

Müller-Beck, Hansjurgen *Paleohunters in America: Origins and Diffusion.* Science, Vol. 152, No. 3726, pp. 1191-1210, 1966.

On Migrations of Hunters across the Bering Land Bridge in the Upper Pleistocene. IN: Hopkins, D. M. (Ed.), The Bering Land Bridge, pp. 373-408, Stanford, 1967.

Murdoch, John *Henry Rink: The Eskimo Tribes: a Review.* A Anthr, Vol. 1, pp. 125-133, 1888.

Narr, Karl J. *Das jungpleistozäne Bering-Land und die Erstbesiedelung Amerikas.* Forschungen and Fortschritte, 38th Jahrg, Fasc. 9, pp. 277-282, 1964.

Nelson, Edward W. *The Eskimo about Bering Strait.* 18th Annual Report, Bureau of American Ethnology, Part 1, 1899.

Nelson, Nels C. *Notes on Cultural Relations between Asia and America.* AA, Vol. 2, No. 4, pp. 267-272, 1937.

Norlund, P. *Wikingersiedelungen in Gronland.* Leipzig, 1937.

O'Bryan, Deric *Excavation of a Cape Dorset Eskimo Site, Mill Island, West Hudson Strait.* NMC for 1951-52, Bulletin 128, pp. 40-57, Ottawa, 1953.

Okladnikov, Aleksei P. *Archaeology of the Soviet Arctic.* Acta Arctica, Fasc. 12, pp. 35-46, 1960.

Okladnikov, A. P. and I. A. Nekrasov *New Traces of an Inland Neolithic Culture in the Chukotsk (Chukchi) Peninsula.* AA, Vol. 25, No. 2, pp. 247-256, 1959.

Oschinsky, Lawrence *The Most Ancient Eskimos.* Ottawa, 1964.

Oswalt, Wendell *The Archaeology of Hooper Bay Village, Alaska.* APUA, Vol. 1, No. 1, pp. 47-91, 1952.

　Prehistoric Sea Mammal Hunters at Kaflia, Alaska. APUA, Vol. 4, No. 1, pp. 23-61, 1955.

Péwé, Troy, David M. Hopkins and James L. Giddings *The Quaternary Geology and Archaeology of Alaska.* IN: Wright, H. and D. Frey (Eds.): The Quaternary of the United States, Princeton, 1965.

Porsild, Morten *Studies on the Material Culture of the Eskimo in West Greenland.* MoG, Vol. 51, Copenhagen, 1915.

Quimby, George I. *Periods of Prehistoric Art in the Aleutian Islands.* AA, Vol. 11, No. 2, pp. 76-79, 1945a.

　Pottery from the Aleutian Islands. Fieldiana, Anthropology, Vol. 36, No. 1, pp. 1-13, 1945b.

　Prehistoric Art of the Aleutian Islands. Fieldiana, Anthropology, Vol. 36, No. 4, pp. 77-92, Chicago, 1948.

　The Old Copper Culture and the Copper Eskimos, a Hypothesis. AINA, Technical Papers, No. 11, pp. 76-79, 1962.

Rainey, Froelich G. *Archaeology in Central Alaska.* AMNH-AP, Vol 36, Pt. 4, New York, 1939.

　Archaeological Investigations in Central Alaska. AA, Vol. 5, No. 4, pp. 299-308, 1940.

　Eskimo Prehistory: The Okvik Site on the Punuk Islands. AMNH-AP, Vol. 37, Pt. 4, New York, 1941.

　The Significance of Recent Archaeological Discoveries in Inland Alaska. Mem. 9 of the Society for American Archaeology, Vol. 31, No. 3, Pt. 2, pp. 43-46, 1953.

Rainey, Froelich G. and Elizabeth Ralph *Radiocarbon Dating in the Arctic.* AA, Vol. 24, No. 4, pp. 365-374, 1959.

Richter, S. *A Contribution to the Archaeology of Northeast Greenland.* Skrifter om Svalbard og Ishavet, No. 63, Oslo, 1934.

Rink, Henry *The Eskimo Tribes.* MoG, Vol. 11, Copenhagen and London, 1887.

Ritchie, William A. *Northeastern Crossties with the Arctic.* AINA, Technical Papers, No. 11, pp. 96-99, 1962.

Rowley, Graham *The Dorset Culture of the Eastern Arctic.* A Anthr, N.S., Vol. 42, pp. 490-499, 1940.

　An Unusual Archaeological Specimen from Foxe Basin. Arctic, Vol. 3, No. 1, 1950.

Rudenko, S. J. *The Ancient Culture of the Bering Sea and the Eskimo Problem.* AINA, Anthropology of the North: Translations from Russian Sources, No. 1, Toronto, 1961.

The Ust'-Kanskaia Paleolithic Cave Site, Siberia. AA, Vol. 27, No. 2, pp. 203-215, 1961.

The Culture of the Prehistoric Population of Kamchatka. AINA, Anthropology of the North: Translations from Russian Sources, No. 5, pp. 265-295, Toronto, 1964.

Schlesier K. *Die Bering-Landbrücke und die frühen amerikanischen Spitzen-Traditionen.* Saeculum, Vol. 15, No. 3, pp. 207-214, 1964.

Geschichte den Besiedelung Nordamerikas von den Anfängen bis zun Beginn der christlichen Zeitrechnung. Saeculum, Vol. 16, No. 1, pp. 29-41, 1965.

Skarland, Ivar and J. Louis Giddings *Flint Stations in Central Alaska.* AA, Vol. 14, No. 2, pp. 116-120, 1948.

Skarland, Ivar and Charles J. Keim *Archaeological Discoveries on the Denali Highway, Alaska.* APUA, Vol. 6, No. 2, pp. 79-88, 1958.

Solberg, O. *Beiträge zur Vorgeschichte der Osteskimo.* Christiania, Oslo, 1907.

Solecki, Ralph S. *New Data on the Inland Eskimo of Northern Alaska.* Journal of the Washington Academy of Sciences, Vol. 40, No. 5, pp. 137-157, 1950a.

A Preliminary Report of an Archaeological Reconnaissance of the Kukpowruk and Kokolik Rivers in Northwest Alaska. AA, Vol. 16, No. 1, pp. 66-69, 1950b.

Archaeology and Ecology of the Arctic Slope of Alaska. Sm R for 1950, pp. 469-495, Washington, 1951a.

Notes on Two Archaeological Discoveries in Northern Alaska, 1950. AA, Vol. 17, No. 1, pp. 55-57, 1951b.

Solecki, Ralph S. and R. Hackman *Additional Data on the Denbigh Flint Complex in Northern Alaska.* Journal of the Washington Academy of Sciences, Vol. 41, No. 3, pp. 85-88, 1951.

Sollas, William J. *Ancient Hunters and their Modern Representatives.* London, 1911.

Spaulding, Albert C. *Northeastern Archaeology and General Trends in the Northern Forest Zone.* IN: Man in Northeastern North America, Papers of the R. S. Peabody Foundation, Vol. 3, pp. 143-167, 1946.

Archaeological Investigations on Agattu, Aleutian Islands. Anthropological Papers, Museum of Anthropology, University of Michigan, No. 18, Ann Arbor, 1962.

Steensby, H. *An Anthropogeographical Study of the Origin of Eskimo Culture.* MoG, Vol. 53, Copenhagen, 1916.

Stefánsson, Vilhjálmur *The Stefánsson-Anderson Arctic Expedition of the American Museum of Natural History: Preliminary Ethnological Report.* AMNH-AP, Vol. 14, Pt. 1, 1914.

Sugihara, S. and M. Tozawa *Preceramic Age in Japan.* Acta Asiatica, Vol. 1, pp. 1-28, 1960.

Swadesh, Morris *Time Depths of American Linguistic Grouping.* A Anthr, Vol. 56, No. 3, pp. 361-377, 1954.

Linguistic Relations across Bering Strait. A Anthr, Vol. 64, No. 6, pp. 1262-1291, 1962.

Taylor, William E. *Archaeology in the Canadian Arctic.* Canadian Geographical Journal, Vol. 67, No. 3, pp. 92-95, 1958.

Review and Assessment of the Dorset Problem. Anthropologica, Vol. 1, pp. 24-46, Ottawa, 1959a.

Archaeological Work in Ungava and Mansel Island. Arctic Circular, Vol. 11, No. 4, pp. 66-68, 1959b.

A Description of Sadlermiut Houses Excavated at Native Point, Southampton Island, N.W.T. NMC, Bulletin 162, Contributions to Anthropology, 1957, pp. 53-100, Ottawa, 1960a.

Archaeological Work, Ivugivik and Mansel Island, 1959. Arctic Circular, Vol. 13, No. 1, pp. 1-4, 1960b.

Pre-Dorset Occupations at Ivugivik in Northwestern Ungava. AINA, Technical Papers, No. 11, pp. 80-91, 1962a.

Archaeological Collections from the Joy Bay Region, Ungava Peninsula. Arctic Circular, Vol. 15, No. 2, 1962b.

Comments on the Origin of the Dorset Culture. Problems of the Pleistocene and the Arctic, Publications of the McGill University Museum, Vol. 2, 1962c.

Hypotheses on the Origin of Canadian Thule Culture. AA, Vol. 28, No. 4, pp. 456-464, 1963a.

Implications of a Pre-Dorset Lance Head from the Eastern Canadian Arctic. Arctic, Vol. 16, No. 2, pp. 129-133, 1963b.

The Prehistory of the Quebec-Labrador Peninsula. Bibliothèque Arctique et Antarctique, Vol. 2, pp. 182-210, Paris, 1964a.

Interim Account of an Archaeological Survey in the Central Arctic. APUA, Vol. 12, No. 1, pp. 46-55, 1964b.

Archaeology of the McCormick Inlet Site, Melville Island, N.W.T. Arctic, Vol. 17, No. 2, pp. 126-129, 1964c.

The Fragments of Eskimo Prehistory. The Beaver, Spring, pp. 4-17, 1965.

Summary of Archaeological Field Work on Banks and Victoria Islands, Arctic Canada, 1965. ARAN, Vol. 4, No. 1, pp. 221-243, 1967a.

The Arnapik and Tyara Sites: A Contribution of Dorset Culture Origins. Soc. for Archaeology, Mem. 22, 1967b.

Taylor, William E. and George Swinton *Prehistoric Dorset Art.* The Beaver, Autumn, pp. 32-47, 1967.

Thalbitzer, William *Der ethnographische Zusammenhang der Eskimo Grönlands mit denen der Hudsonbai.* Baessler Archiv, Vol. 2, pp. 32-44, 1912.

Possible Early Contacts between Eskimo and Old World Languages. Proceedings of the 29th International Congress of Americanists, Vol. 3, pp. 50-54, 1952.

Thompson, Raymond M. *Notes on the Archaeology of the Utukok River, Northwestern Alaska.* AA, Vol. 14, No. 1, pp. 62-65, 1948.

Thomsen, Thomas *Implements and Artifacts of the Northeast Green-landers*. MoG, Vol. 44, No. 5, Copenhagen, 1917.

Thostrup, Christian Bendix *Ethnographic Description of the Eskimo Settlements and Stone Remains in Northeast Greenland*. MoG, Vol. 44, pp. 183-355, Copenhagen, 1911.

Turner, Charles G. *Two Carbon 14 Dates circa 8000 B.C. and Associated Core and Flake Industry from the Aleutian Islands*. (Manuscript).

Weyer, Edward M. *An Aleutian Burial*. AMNH-AP, Vol. 31, Pt. 1, New York, 1929.

    Archaeological Material from the Village Site at Hot Springs, Port Möller, Alaska. AMNH-AP, Vol. 31, Pt. 4, 1930.

    The Eskimos. Hamden, 1962.

Wintemberg, W. S. *Eskimo Sites of the Dorset Culture in Newfound-land, Parts 1, 2*. AA, Vol. 5, No. 2, pp. 83-102; Vol. 5, No. 4, pp. 309-333, 1939/40.

Wissler, Clark *Harpoons and Darts in the Stefánsson Collection*. AMNH-AP, Vol. 14, Pt. 2, 1916.

    Archaeology of the Polar Eskimo. Ibid, Vol. 22, Pt. 3, 1918.

Workman, William B. *Prehistory at Port Möller, Alaska Peninsula, in Light of Fieldwork in 1960*. ARAN, Vol. 3, No. 2, pp. 131-153, 1966a.

    Archaeological Reconnaissance on Chirikov Island, Kodiak Group: A Preliminary Report. ARAN, Vol. 3, No. 2, pp. 185-192, 1966b.

Wormington, H. Marie *Ancient Man in North America*. Popular Series, No. 4, 4th ed., Denver Museum of Natural History, 1957.

    The Paleo-Indian and Meso-Indian Stages of Alberta, Canada. APUA, Vol. 10, No. 2, pp. 107-114, 1963.

SUPPLEMENTS TO BIBLIOGRAPHY

Arutyunov, S. and D. Sergeyev *Two Millennia of Cultural Evolution of Bering Sea Hunters*. ARAN, Vol. 5, No. 1, pp. 72-75, 1968.

Bandi, Hans-Georg *Rapport préliminaire sur le "Projet de recherches archéologiques de l'Ile St-Lauren 1967" de l'Université de Berne (Suisse) et de l'Université d'Alaska*. Bulletin de la Société Suisse des Américanistes, No. 32, 1968 (In Press).

Dikov, N. N. *The Discovery of the Palaeolithic in Kamchatka and the Problem of the Initial Occupation of America*. ARAN, Vol. 5, No. 1, pp. 191-203, 1968.

Dumond, D. E. *On the Presumed Spread of Slate Grinding in Alaska*. ARAN, Vol. 5, No. 1, pp. 82-91, 1968.

Hadleigh-West, Frederick *New Evidence on the Time Placement of Affinities of the Denali Complex of Central Alaska*. (Manuscript).

Harp, Elmer *Five Prehistoric Burials from Port aux Choix, Newfound-land*. Polar Notes, No. VIII, pp. 1-47, 1968.

Hosley, Edward and Jeffrey Mauger *The Campus Site Excavations— 1966*. (Manuscript), 1967.

Knuth, Eigil *Archaeology of the Musk Ox Way*. Paris, 1967.

The numerals in *italics* refer to the figures and plates.